SEX LAWS AND CUSTOMS IN JUDAISM

BY

LOUIS M. EPSTEIN, L.H.D., D.D.

INTRODUCTION BY

ARI KIEV, M.D.

KTAV PUBLISHING HOUSE, INC.

NEW YORK

By Special Arrangement with American Academy of Jewish Research. First published 1948

Library of Congress Catalogue Card No. 67-22751

Manufactured in United States of America

To My Brother

DOCTOR JOSEPH W. EPSTEIN

INTRODUCTION

The study of customs and practices of other cultures at other times and places is most rewarding to anyone interested in finding old solutions to human problems and experiences. Jewish laws and customs are particularly interesting, as many of them are still practiced as they were in the ancient pastoral society in parts of the Middle East, and also, because they persist within the Jewish religious tradition, and are in varying degrees the foundation of Western morality and ethics.

The early foundations pertaining to the control of sex were related to the social situation of the ancient Hebrews. The Jews of the first commonwealth had a relatively simple view of sex matters and were not concerned about it as a problem in social conduct. A smooth and comfortable relationship between the sexes was seen as the basis of stable family life. Both men and women were seen as mutually interdependent and it was believed that a man discovers himself only through contact with a woman. By virtue of becoming one flesh and deriving from one flesh men and women were led to the building of the family, which was seen as the foundation of a humane society. The purpose of sexuality was thus to propagate the species through the creation of a family.

While the sexual morality outlined in the Bible was less complicated than later codes, it contained a number of interesting features, all geared to the stability of the family and the community.

Sexual intercourse was to be enjoyed at regular intervals and was a basic right of husband, wife and even concubine. There was no anti-sexual or ascetic tradition such as one finds later on in the Greek and Christian thought. As would be expected in a patriarchal society men had more rights, but women were acknowledged as people and their rights were considered at the same time. Hebrew society was fairly stable and sex was not a problem at all. Even polygamy, which was practiced in Israel throughout the Biblical period by rich or important men, was a crucial source of solidarity as it provided that every woman would have some kind of family structure to belong to.

While the right to divorce in this patriarchal society was invested in the husband, adultery was considered to be a major sin whether committed by husband or wife. Indeed the law condemned both the adulterer and the adulteress. There was no question of permitting the husband to mitigate or cancel the punishment, for adultery was not only a wrong against husband but a sin against God. Rape and other forcible sexual relationships were likewise seen as serious transgressions. Homosexuality was severely prohibited, and according to levitical law, could be punished by death.

Standards of sex morality radically changed during the period of the second commonwealth. The first trend to influence the family, Epstein notes, was urbanization and the development of a commercial society. After the Jews were exiled they had moved into city areas from rural areas and, consequently, commerce had to a large extent replaced agriculture. Life in this urban area was evidently a much more difficult one. There was more contact with other nations, commerce grew up in Judea and the Jewish people converted from an agricultural peasant community into a commercial city dwelling community. The city tended to become a center of immorality and turbulence and social codes were not commonly adhered to, a phenomenon noticeable today in some of the developing societies in the world where, with urbanization, there is increased alienation from tribal mores and moral boundaries, creating therefore a great need for institutions which will restrain and limit the activity of people. In this setting a new concept of man developed which held that man is weak and overwhelmed by impulses which frequently overcome him. This led to the notion of the evil within man, the sexual drive being seen as one manifestation of this.

Man was conceived as a weak helpless creature, heir to inborn evil tendencies, while women were seen as the sources of temptation. This new view of men and women was accompanied by an increasing emphasis on asceticism and a rather strict code of sexual conduct. Much of this had to do with the fact that the Jews were in exile, the destruction of the sanctuary in Jerusalem had occurred and there was great danger of assimilation and disintegration. One might, however, look at this radical change from a free, rather relaxed society to one with strict legalistic customs as the transition from a rural traditional society to an urban community, with the need for a stricter code to reduce anxiety. There were numerous restrictions relating to social contact between men and women; what the author calls the morbid teachings concerning the nature of the universe, the origin of evil, man's propensity toward sexual temptations and woman's part therein, which originated in the second commonwealth.

In the talmudic period the rabbis thought of women as less dangerous than they had been considered during the second commonwealth. They accordingly held that moderate discipline of women was proper, and that cloistering them and denying them social freedom was unreasonable and inhuman. There was a much more humanitarian outlook, opposed to asceticism, and the flesh was thought evil only through corruption. The rabbis taught that the evil drive which in part was seen as the sexual drive was the source of energy for properly sublimated activities, i.e. that man could control his passions. The goods of the physical world were to be enjoyed, but in moderation, and in accordance with the numerous laws promulgated during this period. Thus, in this setting, marriage was considered to be a very important institution, and the rabbis said the Jew who is unmarried lives without joy, without blessing, without good.

During the post-Talmudic period this moderate view of marriage was influenced by other cultures which introduced an ascetic strain into Jewish laws and customs. During the medieval period a duality of thinking developed among the moralists, who saw the body as evil and the soul as good. The medieval post-Talmudic moralistic view required, as Epstein points out, a life more disciplined than the law demanded. People were viewed as part animal and part divine. Sexual appetites were seen as the animal part of man's nature, the soul as the divine part and both these aspects, which sound familiarly like the Freudian concepts of the id and the superego, were seen to be in constant conflict. One part would not be satisfied except at the expense of the other. Human destiny demanded the viewpoint of the moralist, that the beast within man be subjected to wise rule and mastery of the soul. If such mastery was relinquished man would become a slave to his passions and would proceed to function in a way which was least satisfying and least beneficial to his happiness. By contrast, satisfaction of the soul and the higher ideals which countenanced modification and moderation led to a sense of elation, self realization, and the avoidance of remorse, rejection, confusion, loss of energy and poor health. For medieval Jewish philosophers, the immortal soul was reason seen as the essence of reality in the universe and the highest fulfillment of the human being. Immortality as Epstein notes "consists in the individual mind becoming part of the Universal Mind called the Active Intellect." This was accomplished through study and knowledge and rational abstract contemplation. Medieval Jewish philosophers, e.g. Maimonides, saw the exercise of the intellectual faculties as being the surest way to attain truth, the knowledge of universals and ultimates and the attributes of God and the highest destiny of man. It was recognized however that the needs of the body must be satisfied, and that by managing them in a satisfactory way, in moderation and never as an end in themselves, man would be able to concentrate his efforts in the exercise of his reason and thereby obtain divinity. Both the moralistic and the philosophical view generally tended to lead to ascetic doctrines, particularly because of their emphasis on spirituality and because of the duality noted between the body and the soul.

There also came into this period in the Middle Ages a cabalistic or mystical view of sexual activity, which held that there was something holy and divine about sexual relations. It was believed that when a man cleaves to his wife in holiness the Divine presence is manifested. The cabalistic view of spirituality was emotional rather than rational. The human body and its physical needs were seen as the manifestation of holiness. Man was seen as the expression of the universal union of the physical and the spiritual. Thus, as Epstein points out (page 22) "by virtue of his position as linked between the two worlds, man is a being of cosmic importance and every one of his acts contains cosmic significance." Cabalistic doctrine regarded physical needs as worthy and good and part of God's manifestation in the finite world. Thus to the cabalist the sexual impulse was not a passion to be suppressed but a holy urge, natural and noble, as expressed in loving union between man and wife. How akin to Freud's notion of the origin of neurosis is this view of the importance of sexual union in a loving relationship. Admittedly he did not see things as symbolically as did the cabalists, who felt that the union of the male and female was the mystical symbol of life and love. This same concept was held to later on by the Hasidim.

Thus through different periods there persisted a view of sexuality as noble and good. Despite differences it was taught in each period as related to the family, to love and mutuality. Inherent in the approach to sex was both a recognition of its biological or instinctive basis and a recognition that it must be socialized to fit in with the needs of society, i.e. a primarily ethical view of sexuality.

And so, while sexual behavior was acknowledged as at the foundation of married life, there was due recognition to the advisability of men and women avoiding situations in which they would be tempted and overwhelmed by their drives. Antinomian tendencies were to be combatted. Sexual life was regulated and governed by rules and restrictions, not left to sentiment or subjective feeling. If a person was weak and was overcome he was not to be stigmatized forever. There was always room for repentance and renewal.

While Jewish sex customs and laws were influenced by asceticism, legalism, liberalism and mysticism depending on historical circumstances certain fundamental themes persisted. With the exception of polygamy which had special meaning in the agricultural economy of Biblical days, these themes were in general essentially similar to contemporary ones. Adultery, rape, harlotry and homosexuality were severely condemned. Sexual activity was prohibited outside of marriage. A man was forbidden to pass by the house of a harlot within a distance of four ells. If a man was seen too often about the house of a woman of ill-repute disciplinary flogging was prescribed. Masturbation was looked upon as a form of coitus interruptus and was considered to be wasting the seed and was therefore prohibited. While homosexuality was endemic in the Roman Hellenistic civilization, it did not fufill for the Jews the religious prescription for true relations between sexual partners and was as such considered taboo. While many viewed it as a sickness, others suggested it stemmed from misdirection of energy, and that it would respond to religious counselling.

The interpretation of the First Commandment to be fruitful and multiply was considered a matter of life or death for the Jewish community. The Mishnah limited the command to be fruitful and multiply to the husband. However, later opinions ranged from those that considered the relevance of danger to life of the mother, to strict views which permitted no interference with the chances of conception. Views on abortion were similarly wide-ranging depending on the legal and theological status of the foetus, i.e. whether it was considered to be living or not living. Despite its feasibility in some situations, abortion was by and large considered morally wrong.

The code of Jewish sex morality is indeed remarkable when one considers how broad and extensive it is, and to what extent it takes into consideration certain aspects of the instinctual life of human beings and sets up restrictions, as well as a code of conduct, which minimizes the temptations and minimizes the risk of over-stimulation. Thus laws of separation between sexes, the chaperonage and the rigorous rules of separation of divorced or betrothed couples make sense in terms of what we know about human behavior today, and in terms of what we know about the prevention of psychiatric disorder. Most of the rules according to Epstein had the purpose of "keeping the passions down and the temptations out of the way, the eye out of sight of sexual stimulants and thus the mind is free from indecent thoughts." Thus a variety of rules for the dress and modesty of women help to keep the minds of women as well as men pure. Various provisions were made to reduce the likelihood of difficulties, temptations and psychological conflicts, such as the development of morbid jealousy and revenge following upon adultery.

In connection with these obvious mental hygiene implications, it is of interest to compare marriage in ancient times with marriage in the modern industrial world. Marriage took place at a much younger age and was more highly regulated and linked to other institutions than in the contemporary world, where people are much less in touch with the rules and regulations pertaining to proper conduct, and where there are fewer social sanctions to keep people in line. Marriage and the family in ancient times involved not only emotional ties but also mutually shared values, sentiments and activities, which undoubtedly contributed to far less strain than exists for the modern family, which is founded and persists on the basis of intense personal relationships unsupported by common activities and clearly defined goals.

With customs and prescribed patterns of behavior well outlined, individuals, in the ancient marriage, had fewer decisions to make than the modern individual, whose greater personal responsibility for his own destiny and decisions makes for greater psychological stress in interpersonal relationships. In earlier times, responsibility resided more in the community than in the family, and the greater visibility and clarity of norms and sanctions against improper behavior made it easier to keep within the prescribed boundaries pertaining to sexual behavior.

The extended family of earlier periods provided emotional support and opportunity for many secure personal relationships, thereby reducing the stress placed on the individual and the small family unit. Sexual relationships were less signicantly a barometer of interpersonal intrafamilial relationships than they are today; they were for procreation and the perpetuation of the community, which in turn had a great investment in the proper regulation of sexual habits and behavior.

Unlike his ancestors, modern man is in many ways rootless, knows no consistent set of roles for behavior, is considerably isolated from other people, and has an excessive amount of freedom which, with the burden this brings in terms of the need for responsibility and decision, often produces more stress than benefit. Although contemporary morality derives from these ancient laws and customs described in this book there are no consistent rules introduced to modern man regarding sexual behavior. Concepts of morality are introduced in vague and contradictory ways so that individuals often have no certainty regarding right and wrong, and no formula for traditional models or group sanctions to call upon to help decide how to act in different situations. In the absence of predetermined or internally programmed decisions, the individual must face more moral decision in daily life than was true in the past.

Thus our examination of ancient Jewish customs is of interest not only from the point of view of suggesting the range of human phenomena behavior and expectations, but also from the point of view of suggesting the kind of pattern which had become custom and law. It has psychological value, resolving everyday problems which the individual no longer has to contend with. Probably the crucial problem of modern man is that he has to work out an individual solution, in contrast to ancient man, whose solutions were instilled into his daily round of living with much greater clarity and force.

Modern man grows up in a permissive family and community situation with little knowledge of the do's and don'ts of behavior and little in the way of internal patterns of restraint built into his personality. This absence of an internal standard founded on an everpresent tradition, which in former times would be periodically reinforced by ritualistically and symbolically meaningful rites, is further perpetuated by the adolescent peer culture which takes on more significance than the family and the community as an arbiter of behavioral standards, and which compounds the individual's difficulties by offering an additional set of standards. While this may structure and define the world, thereby reducing anxiety, it does so in a way which not only may be in conflict with the larger society, but also acts to reduce individual self-reliance and responsibility, with all the consequences this has for problems of individual maturity and responsible behavior in the community.

Factors working against the development of maturity, independence, self-reliance and emotional health are also to be encountered later on, where one is exposed to the outer-directed pressures of contemporary society plus the sensual, provocative stimuli of the mass media, which sing the praises of a utopian, sensual, irresponsible playboy existence, and with electronic authority set new standards of behavior for the population.

In this kind of culture a number of problems are created. Where individuals have little self-control of their impulses one finds them forever seeking either external restraints, as in the case of delinquents looking for the controls of adults, anodynes in the form of sedatives, tranquilizers or alcohol to smother their drives, or new sources of thrills to escape the boredom that comes from too easy gratification of impulses.

The absence of a set of standards thus makes one prey not only to external stimuli and the demands of others, but also the prey of internal drives which must be subdued or acted upon. Where the individual attempts to control his inner demands and to disguise their presence from others he is likely to develop neurotic defenses which can only be partially successful in keeping drives in line, and which are likely to lead to neurotic symptoms. In addition, with no certainty as to how to behave he is likely to be dependent on sources outside himself to determine how to behave. These sources may be the mass media or they may be other individuals or the group. By becoming dependent on others he is likely to have to compromise his own self-interest and his own desire for expressiveness in the interest of maintaining quasi-relationships established with quasi-authority figures. The suppression or inhibition of responses can have nothing but deleterious effects and will prevent him from gaining a mastery over his own life, from which alone can he gain a real sense of freedom.

Indeed this is the curious paradox, that where the individual grows up and lives in a society without a set of internalized restraints and responsibilities, which on the surface appears to be an ideal state of freedom, he is in fact less free than where he has a built-in set of standards which help him to define himself, and so free him to act more decisively in the present. The modern individual accommodates himself to various situations rather than being able to accommodate situations to himself.

It is of interest that various psychological techniques for the emancipation of man from internal conflicts were developed in the Victorian era, in part as a reaction to a suppressive society unwilling to recognize the biological and instinctual side of man. Techniques were developed to enable the consciousness to expand, to recognize the naturalness of drives and to free them from the restraints of a too harsh sense of conscience, thereby rendering the individual better able to cope with everyday reality. Psychoanalysis, the most famous of these methods, was in this sense a cathartic technique. The needs of contemporary man are, by contrast, for a technique of control, a strategy which will strengthen his sense of mastery over inner needs and the demands of the environment. It is in this context that the Jewish customs and laws examined in this book make sense, having as they do sound psychological validity.

Firstly, they provide the individual with a set of formulas which reduce the number of decisions he must make as he encounters daily temptations. Secondly, there is a kind of gratification that comes from adhering to a set of rules. Thirdly, they make him less prey to inner drives, giving him more freedom to engage in areas of life other than the libidinal. Furthermore, they reduce his dependence on immediate stimuli, thereby freeing him to deal with more complicated concerns for the future and enabling him to act in his own best interest by reducing his susceptibility to momentary stimuli. It is thus of special interest to note the emphasis placed on methods of self-control which were meant to supplement the legislative and religious proscriptions on behavior, particularly as many of them make sound psychological sense.

Purity of mind was felt to be crucial in stimulating proper conduct and was seen as the goal and objective of proper conduct. Most of the rules were designed to keep sexual drives down; opportunities for sexual contact and for sexually stimulating activities were minimized so as to keep the individual from having indecent thoughts—this accounts for the rules of modesty in dress for women and indeed, in many other areas of their lives, which were designed to keep them from men so that men would not have lustful thoughts. We know today, however, that the continued presence of sexual stimulants, as defined in these traditional views, do not in and of themselves constitute sufficient stimulus to induce sexual drives in men or in women. Similarly, the prohibitions against song-making, drinking and dancing, mixing of the sexes, touching a woman, looking at her, walking behind her or listening to her voice, are likewise prohibitions which are based on assumptions about human behavior which are not valid for all times and places.

Undoubtedly with a view to the suggestibility of human beings it was felt that people must avoid the sight of copulation in man, beast or fowl, the exception being made for breeders of livestock. It was felt that all those things which might arouse sexual thoughts were to be avoided so as to enable individuals to practice and behave in accord with what was felt to be proper conduct. Thus it was felt that, as Epstein points out (page 149) "the heart and the eyes are the two agents for the promotion of sin. The eyes see and the heart lusts." Indeed, lustful thoughts were seen as sins, even if nothing had in fact occurred.

Another recommendation to keep people from being involved in the evils of unclean thoughts was early marriage. According to one Babylonian amora those who marry past the age of 20 remain burdened all their lives with unclean thoughts. One solution to keep man from evil thoughts and help him to control his mind was, according to the rabbis, to concentrate on Torah—an emphasis on study to preoccupy the mind with thoughts other than those having to do with the satisfaction of instinctual drives. This makes sense certainly as a defense against preoccupation with sexual thoughts.

Thus, in addition to the religious commands, a number of everyday practices were recommended in order to help people to lead the decent life. Many of these rules are certainly applicable today, although in many instances, particularly social regulations designed to minimize contact between the sexes, very difficult to follow.

For ancient times and for those who have adhered to these traditions these rules formulated early in life and tied in with daily life have considerable psychological and social significance: psychological in the sense of steering individuals towards healthier, more valued, more personally fulfilling gratifications of basic drives in more meaningful martital relationships, and social in the sense of discouraging those kinds of breaks with convention and custom which have socially disruptive effects. In the modern world where there are fewer opportunities for the community, religious or secular, to impose standards on individuals, the individuals and society are more susceptible to distress and disruption. It is doubly imperative, if we are to accept the general notion of satisfactory heterosexual relationships as the foundation of personal mental health and the health of society, that efforts be made to educate and train the young in proper ethical standards of sexual behavior, particularly as opportunities to impose restrictions and standards on them at a later date are much less successful.

There is a great argument then for increasing knowledge and understanding of drives, of the good life, and of the deleterious effects of psychologically harmful and socially undesirable practices which hold disadvantages not only for society but also for the individual. Therefore, as sexual education and direction no longer can be introduced to the same extent by religious rules of daily living, it is imperative that both religious education as well as secular education make every effort to educate the young in terms of the role and rules of proper conduct. Given the modern world situation, it is imperative that those rules and regulations which undoubtedly were effective in the past in steering people towards healthier and personally more rewarding lives should be explicitly introduced in both secular and religious education, making people more aware of the potential and the limitations of human beings, of the problems that come from excess in contrast to moderation, and of the problems that come from any other than normal heterosexual relations. Prepared for what they are likely to experience as they grow older, young people will be better able to cope with their feelings—their inner strivings and their sexual drives.

ARI KIEV, M.D.

PREFACE

The present study may be considered a companion to an earlier work, *Marriage Laws in the Bible and the Talmud*, Harvard University Press, 1942. While the first deals with sex morality within marriage, this volume endeavors to present the Jewish standard of sex conduct outside marriage.

Marriage regulations, as a form of sex morality, reveal the weight and wisdom of men learned in the law; in contrast, the code here presented is a people's code, law touching it only lightly in an effort to refine it, systematize it, and, in a few cases, provide for enforcement. The sources of the present study, therefore, are not primarily legal. The works of moralists, philosophers, cabalists, communal records, and ethical wills of simple, God-fearing people — all contribute to our knowledge and to the total picture of the standards of proper sex conduct among the Jews from antiquity to the present time.

Modern civilization, in which emancipated Jewry has shared to the full, has no doubt made Jewish life broader and richer in many ways. But it is questionable whether it has given the Jew a better code of sex morality than the one depicted here, which grew out of his native moral reactions and bore the stamp of religious authority. Many of the prohibitions and inhibitions in this code seem unreasonable, and yet perhaps not as much so as are the laxities of our modern standards of sex conduct. To find in a report of the sexual behavior of the American male an indication that the conduct of the orthodox Jew rates high according to accepted norms of chastity and purity is sufficient recommendation for our supposedly antiquated code with all its shortcomings.

Let it also be noticed that our code has few provisions for enforcement, and even these few have lost practical significance with the termination of Jewish self-government.

Its authority has been based entirely on its moral appeal, supported by public opinion, in contrast to the modern legal concept that a code is no code unless there be a police force behind it. Possibly a good teacher is sometimes more effective than a police officer.

These deliberations, however, must be left to the reader. The author has sought merely to present the historic facts without bias and without preachment.

L. M. E.

New York.

CONTENTS

CONTENTS

SEX LAWS AND CUSTOMS IN JUDAISM

CHAPTER I

MORAL FOUNDATIONS OF SEX CONTROL

THERE is rarely a race so primitive but it has a code of sex morality. Even where promiscuity prevails, there are rules and regulations determining permitted and prohibited sex conduct. Certainly in a society where marriage is properly established, a well formulated code of sex morality may be expected, for marriage is the ultimate attainment of regulated sex life among human beings. Reaching such a state of social development, we find a code normally consisting of primary rules, such as relate to incest, polygamy, perversion, and adultery, and secondary rules governing the conduct of the sexes where no carnal crime is involved, prohibiting the obscene, the indecent, or the immodest.

I. PRE-EXILIC SEX MORALITY

In the earliest sections of the Bible we already encounter such a code of sex morality. Yet it is a comparatively simple code in the legal sense. Prescribing marriage laws and prohibiting adultery, it has a few additional prohibitions and consequent penalties for acts not connected with marriage. Among them are rape and seduction, prostitution, buggery, wearing the attire of the opposite sex, a woman in quarrel attacking the genitals of her male opponent, copulation between male and male, and a father's (probably also mother's) nakedness in the presence of sons.[1]

[1] Harlotry is considered shameful — Gen. 34:31; Jer. 3:3 — but no prohibition or penalty is recorded in pre-exilic literature. When committed in defiance of paternal authority, it is penalized by death — Deut. 22:21 — under the rule of disobedience, not under the rule of sex morality. Sodomy is not prohibited in the pre-exilic section of Scripture — see Lev. 18:22; 20:13 — but the outraged feeling against the act is seen in Gen. 19:18; Judg. 19:24. There can be no doubt that the prohibition in Lev. is older than our text, but we have no record of an earlier injunction.

These prohibitions and condemnations represent no systematic program of sex morality nor are they based on any well defined theological principles. The people's aversion to certain forms of sex behavior seems to be the only basis for this earliest Hebrew moral code. There is a distinct lack of preaching on sex matters among the Hebrews of the pre-exilic period. Apparently sexual immorality had not yet risen to the level of a general national problem. Only one aspect may be said to have become national in scope and importance — namely, the sex orgies connected with the rites of heathen worship. Because of its special lure, preachment and denunciation were turned loose in full force against this particular evil; and the emphasis, it should be noted, was not so much on sexual immorality as on the idolatry involved. Ordinary infringement of the code of sex morality caused no special excitement; there were no axioms, no slogans, no generalizations. The Jew of the First Commonwealth was not morbid on sex matters. He did not treat sex offenses as though they belonged to a special department of human psychology. They were sins like every other sin.

It is interesting to note that the vocabulary of biblical Hebrew for sex morality is borrowed. Perhaps with the exception of the term *zimmah,* which we generally translate by wickedness, all words denoting sexual sin also denote other kinds of sin. Unfaithfulness (*zenut*), abomination (*to'ebah*), wantonness (*nebalah*), employed generally for sex crime, denote just as generally idolatry, violence, a disgusting act, or disgusting food.[2] Often the concept itself is hazy. Nakedness is shameful, immodest, and humiliating at the same time.[3] Rape is an act of immorality and at the same time a matter of physical or monetary injury.[4] All this indicates that the original code of sex morality emphasized less the term sex, and

[2] For *zimmah* cf. Judg. 20:6; Hos. 6:9. For *zaneh,* cf. Gen. 38:24; Hos. 9:1. For *tame',* cf. Gen. 34:5; Judg. 13:7. For *nebalah,* cf. Gen. 34:7; Is. 32:6. For *'alel,* cf. Judg. 19:25; Deut. 28:20. For *ta'eb,* cf. Deut. 13:15; 23:19. The word *tebel,* like *zimmah,* seems to apply to sex immorality only, but it is used in post-exilic sources alone. See Lev. 18:23; 20:12.

[3] See Gen. 2:25; 10:23; Hos. 2:5; Jer. 13:26.

[4] The legal aspect of rape is expressed in Deut. 22:29 as a matter involving property rights, while the moral aspect is suggested in Gen. 34:7, 31.

more the term morality; in other words, it bespeaks a lack of consciousness of sex as a special problem in the pattern of social conduct.

It is this naiveté that accounts for the comparative freedom of mingling between the sexes in early Hebrew society. The watering trough was an important meeting place for young people of both sexes in the pastoral community. The place of worship, whether tabernacle or temple, was a meeting place for men and women for common tasks and for observance of festivals and public assembly. In public celebrations women took a leading part in the performances as singers and dancers. Funerals and weddings were public functions at which large crowds of men and women mingled, the women leading the wailing at funerals and the dancing at weddings.[5]

The code of that period had no prescriptions as to women's dress, ornaments, or cosmetics. Women adorned themselves as lavishly as their station permitted, the richer women being quite extravagant with their fineries and costly ointments. However, there was some overdoing, especially in public places, with the intent of attracting undue attention from men. Such was the conduct of the immodest — "haughty, walking with stretched forth necks and wanton eyes, walking and mincing as they go and making a tinkling with their feet" . . . clothing themselves with crimson, decking themselves with ornaments of gold, enlarging their eyes with paint.[6] The woman of modesty reserved her charms for those within her legitimate social circle, made no coquettish display of them, and confined her ornamentation within sensible limits.

II. SOCIAL AND CULTURAL INFLUENCES IN THE POST-EXILIC ERA

The standards of sex morality were radically changed during the period of the Second Commonwealth. The naiveté and innocence which characterized the older period yielded to worldly suspicion. This worldliness was the result of the new setting in which the post-exilic Jew found himself, com-

[5] Jer. 9:16; 31:12, et passim.
[6] Is. 3:16f.; Jer. 4:30.

merce to a large extent replacing agriculture, city life succeeding narrow rural existence. The worldliness of the broader civilization quite naturally begot a sense of uncertainty, culminating in pessimism, and from pessimism there is but one step to asceticism. Uncertainty also has the opposite effect, that of tightening inner bonds, drawing in one's sails, so to speak, resulting in rigorous discipline and legalism. These four, worldliness, pessimism, asceticism, and legalism, had their combined bearing on the sex morality of the day.

Beginning with the seventh century before the Common Era there was a noticeable growth of commerce in Judea, accompanied by a trend toward city life. Political contacts with foreign nations during the reign of the later kings, foreign invasions thereafter, and finally deportations and captivity, converted the Jewish people from an agricultural, peasant community into a commercial, city-dwelling nation.[7] This economic change brought in its wake certain general cultural changes, including attitudes toward sex matters. Peasant life is naive, city life is sophisticated. Worldly wisdom is broadening, to be sure, but it begets certain moral laxities. Luxury and indulgence, the portion of the rich city-dweller, foster harlotry. "Take a harp, go about the city, thou harlot long forgotten, make sweet melody, sing many songs, that thou mayest be remembered," exclaims Isaiah with bitter irony.[8] Centuries later the talmudists prayed that God account Israel as a rural people, free from the vices of city dwellers,[9] and added that a young man living in the city and restraining himself against sexual sin displays a heroism worthy of God's own commendation.[10] It is a natural result of city life and the psychology thus engendered that among city people the woman holds an inferior position and her movements are more restricted, as is evident among orientals even today.[11]

[7] See J. P. Peters, *Religion of the Hebrews,* Boston and London, 1914, pp. 311–12. "Certain it is that with the captivity itself a change of far reaching importance was effected in the conversion of the Jews from an agricultural to a commercial people."

[8] Is. 23:16; Amos 7:17.

[9] 'Erub. 21b.

[10] Pes. 113a.

[11] See N. Slouschz, *Travels in North Africa,* Philadelphia, 1927, p. 204.

So also during the period of the Second Commonwealth the change from the agricultural to the commercial economy, from peasant to city life, adversely affected the social position of woman and restricted her movements to the point of making her a virtual prisoner in her own house.

The pessimism of the Jew of the Second Commonwealth does not in truth represent his dominant philosophy, but is sufficiently prominent to account for a certain morbidity in his attitude toward sex relations. It is evident in the early part of the period, when Koheleth wrote, "Vanity of vanities, all is vanity. What profit hath man of all his labor wherein he laboreth under the sun?" [12] At the end of the period we have a similar classical summary of human life: "The Shammaites and the Hillelites carried on a discussion for two and a half years, these saying it were better for man that he were not born, the others maintaining it better that he be born. A final vote was taken, and it was concluded that it were better that he be not born than that he be born." [13]

Man is conceived as a weak, helpless creature, heir to inborn evil tendencies from his original father, Adam, constantly tempted and irresistibly lured by evil, personified in Satan. Whatever self-mastery he may possess, he never can be entirely free from sin, "for there is not a righteous man upon earth who doeth good and sinneth not." His greatest weakness is the lure of sexual pleasures. Some people are greedy for power or wealth, others are given to comfort and bodily pleasures, but all people have the common lust for sexual satisfaction. This urge, so primitive, so rugged, so ferocious, more than any other passion seems to make man a helpless victim in the hands of Satan. The Patriarch Reuben says: "The seventh is the power of procreation and sexual intercourse, with which through love of pleasure sins enter in. Wherefore, it is the last in the order of creation and the first in that of youth . . . leading the youth as a blind man to a pit and as a beast to a precipice." [14]

[12] Eccl. 1:2–3.

[13] 'Erub. 13b.

[14] Gen. 4:7; 8:21; Prov. 20:9; Ps. 143:2; Eccl. 7:20; IV Ezra 3:21; 4:30; 7:118; Rom. 5:12f.; Jub. 1:20; Test. of Reub. 2:8–9. See G. F. Moore, *Judaism in the*

Satan takes advantage of this weakness in man and employs woman as his tool to entice and corrupt him. The Gloomy Preacher's idea of woman is typical of that period. "I find more bitter than death the woman, whose heart is snares and nets and her hands are bands; whoso pleaseth God shall escape from her." [15] But escape is not easy, for "She is tempestuous and rebellious, her feet abide not in her house. Now she is in the street, now in the broad places, and lieth in wait at every corner." [16] To refer again to Patriarch Reuben, he blames his own weakness on the wiles and guiles of women: "Women are overcome by the spirit of fornication more than men, and in their heart they plot against man." [17] Their beauty is a special snare; their ornaments are designed to capture souls.[18]

It is not difficult to see how so pessimistic a philosophy of life and such mistrust of human nature and condemnation of woman would lead to a morbid code of sex morality, in which every innocent social contact between men and women would be regarded with suspicion and condemned as immoral.

From pessimism to asceticism is a logical step, and the Jews of the Second Commonwealth took that step unhesitatingly. The prevalence of ascetic tendencies accounts for the popularity of the nazirite ideal in those days and the evident urge of the people to take on vows of self-mortification, or, in biblical language, "to bind oneself with a bond." The literature of that period deals with these tendencies in two ways; it sets down laws concerning naziritic and general vows, and again combats them by protest and denunciation.[19] A characteristic

---

First Century of the Christian Era, Cambridge, 1932, Vol. I, Part III, Ch. 3, pp. 474–96; Solomon Schechter, *Some Aspects of Rabbinic Theology,* New York, 1910, Ch. 15, pp. 242–63.

[15] Eccl. 7:26.

[16] Prov. 7:11. See Prov. 2:16; 5:3; 6:24; 7:5, 21.

[17] Eccl. 7:28; Test. of Reub. 5:3.

[18] Prov. 6:25; Sir. 42:12f.; Test. of Reub. 5:3, 5; Ahikar 2:2.

[19] Nazirism, of course, was known in pre-exilic times, but then it represented a lay priesthood; on the other hand, no law governing nazirism is found in the earlier portions of the Bible. In the later portions the laws are presented in detail, and nazirism became a form of vow for the average man in the street. Likewise, general vows were known before the exilic period, but the laws of vows belong to the post-exilic era, and vows became not an

story comes to us, connected with the name of Simon the Just. He tells that "Once a young man from the South came who had taken on naziritic vows, and I saw that he had beautiful eyes and was of comely appearance, and his locks were ordered in curls. Said I to him, 'My son, what made you destroy this beautiful hair?' He answered, 'I was a shepherd for my father in my town, and as I went to the well to draw water I saw myself in the reflection and my *Yeẓer* (evil inclination) leaped upon me, wanting to destroy me out of the world. Said I to him, "Thou wicked one, why dost thou pride thyself on a world that is not yours, on that which is destined to be vermin and worms? I swear that I will shave thee (the hair) off as an offering to Heaven." ' "[20] The account runs further that so pleased was Simon with this youth that he participated in his nazirite sacrifice, which he had never done in the case of others as a protest against nazirism.

Asceticism naturally condemns all legitimate sexual pleasures as sinful. The ascetic tendencies of the Second Commonwealth period, therefore, had a direct unsavory and unreasonable influence upon the contemporary code of sex morality. Pharisaic Judaism counteracted this influence by protests of the early teachers supplemented by sages of later date. But some of the peripheral sects carried on the tradition in their theology and in their moral code. Josephus reports of the Essenes that they "reject pleasures as an evil, but esteem continence and the conquest over passions to be virtue. They neglect wedlock . . . they do not absolutely deny the fitness of marriage, and the succession of mankind thereby continues; but they guard against the lascivious behavior of women and are persuaded that none of them preserve their fidelity to one

---

offering or promise to God or Temple but a declaration of self-restriction. See Numb. 6:1–21; Numb. 30. The protest against vows is expressed in Eccl. 5:4–5; and note the rabbinic comment, Ned. 9a–10a. Annulment of vows is an enactment probably also belonging to the Second Commonwealth period and meant as a protest and remedy against vows. The Mishnah confesses that it does not know the basis of such legislation. See M. Hag. 1, 8; I. H. Weiss, *Dor Dor ve-Doreshav,* Wilno, 1919, Vol. 1, p. 81. That the legislation of annulment of vows belongs to Temple days can be seen from M. Nazir 5, 3–4; Tos. Nazir 3, 19.

[20] Ned. 9b; Tos. Nazir 4, 7. See also Ned. 10a.

man."[21] That attitude is also reflected in the Wisdom of Solomon: "Happy is the barren that is undefiled, she who hath not conceived in transgression. She shall have fruit when God visiteth souls. And happy is the eunuch which hath wrought no lawless deed with his hands, nor imagined wicked things against the Lord."[22]

Christianity has perpetuated the old ascetic philosophy and brought it down to this very day. There is no legitimate pleasure altogether, and certainly no legitimate sexual pleasure. It is all of the flesh and as such a defiance of the kingdom of heaven. Celibacy is a virtue in Christian teaching, binding upon the priesthood and recommended to every faithful follower. "There be eunuchs who have made themselves eunuchs for the kingdom of heaven's sake."[23]

With legalism we complete our summary of the psychological features of the Jew of the Second Commonwealth bearing on his standards of sex conduct. Legalism was born when Torah, which in pre-exilic days meant "teaching," came to mean in post-exilic time "law," a discipline. Ezra and Nehemiah are properly credited with the establishment of legalism as a Jewish way of thinking, favored by the external as well as internal conditions of the time of the Restoration. Exile, new foreign contacts, intermarriage, the liquidation of the Sanctuary at Jerusalem and all its rites and ceremonies, the worldliness of the more prosperous elements — all these brought the Jews of the Captivity to a dangerous state of assimilation and disintegration. The pendulum had to swing back to extreme nationalism, to tightening the grip on old customs and traditions, to a discipline of law by which inner solidarity might be built up. Legalism was, then, the inner fortress of the people to insure its survival against the patent danger of disintegration.

Like the swing of the pendulum, the tendency toward legalism did not stop with the establishment and enforcement of existing laws and current traditions, but carried its momen-

[21] Josephus, *Wars,* II, 8, 2. See Kaufmann Kohler, "Essenes," in *The Jewish Encyclopedia.*

[22] Wisdom of Solomon 3:13–14.

[23] Mat. 19:12. See also Gal. 5:16–17; I Cor. 7:9.

tum into new restrictions of excessive rigor. One of the leading principles of the Men of the Great Synagogue, the religious teachers of the early part of that period, was "Make a fence about the law,"[24] so that by respecting the "fence" one would avoid transgressing the law itself. In the chain of tradition, as the Men of the Great Synagogue handed the law down to the Hasmonean court and they in turn to their pharisaic successors, a considerable number of restrictions beyond the requirement of the original law, called *taḳḳanot* and *gezerot,* were enacted and added to the law as "fences" or safeguards.

This process had a significant effect upon the code of sex morality. Nowhere is a fence needed so much as in the control of sex passions. This period, therefore, distinguished itself by unnumbered restrictions against social contact between men and women, against sitting alongside a woman at a festive table, against drinking a cup of wine with her at a social gathering, even against speaking to a woman or gazing upon her.[25] The separation of the sexes was thoroughgoing enough, but should an occasion arise when a man and a woman were thrown into each other's company, it was required that a chaperon be present.[26]

III. TALMUDIC FOUNDATIONS OF SEX MORALITY

Some of the morbid teachings concerning the nature of the universe, the origin of evil, man's propensities, sexual temptations and woman's part therein, which originated in the Second Commonwealth period, lingered on into talmudic times and found sympathetic followers among individual tannaim and amoraim. Rabbinic tradition as a whole was anything but cordial to these teachings. We should keep in mind that rabbinic opinion and rabbinic tradition are two separate

[24] Ab. 1, 1. See *Dor Dor ve-Doreshav* I, p. 40.

[25] Job 31:1; Prov. 6:25; Ahikar (Syr. Version) 2:5; Sir. 9:5–9; Test. of Reub. 6:3; Test. of Judah 14:3; 16:1–5; Mat. 5:28; Ab. 1, 5; 3, 13; M. Demai 2, 3. Additional restrictions in sex matters, come down to us from that period, are dealt with in M. Yeb. 2, 4; Yeb. 20a–21b; M. Nid. 4, 1; M. Sab. 1, 3; Tos. Sab. 1, 14; Sab. 17b; 64b; Ab. de R. Nat. Ch. 2. See L. M. Epstein, *Marriage Laws in the Bible and the Talmud,* Cambridge, 1942, pp. 257–8 and 326f.

[26] 'Ab. Zar. 36b; San. 21b.

things; there were impractical rabbis, ascetic rabbis, but the rabbinic tradition is neither impractical nor ascetic. Like a living organism, the chain of tradition digested and eliminated; that which it digested became the norm of Jewish life under rabbinic leadership, that which it eliminated remained relics, framed in the pages of sacred literature but excluded from life itself. On the whole, that rabbinic tradition which fashioned Jewish life for twenty centuries is the result of the common sense, the level-headedness, the close contact with life, and the practical piety of the talmudic sages. These qualities also characterized their approach to problems of sex morality.

The sophistication found in the Second Commonwealth continued through the talmudic era, because urban life and commercial economy continued. The rabbis of the Talmud, even if they wished it, could not go back to the naiveté of the peasant Jew of the First Commonwealth. When a sympathetic interpreter of rabbinic doctrine says, "It may be questioned whether the exponents of Jewish piety, like Christian saints, did not think more about the snares of women and the lusts of the flesh than was good for them," [27] he implies a wish that the rabbis were as naive in sex matters as the primitive Palestinian peasant or as indifferent to sexual sin as the modern sociologist — both, of course, impossible. As practical moral teachers they were conscious of the tendency to moral laxity inherent in the more worldly life of the city-dweller and sought to combat it by precept and preachment. They were not morbid, a few exceptions notwithstanding; they were not angry at the world; they did not give woman up to the devil.

To the pessimists of the earlier period who shouted, "Vanity of vanities; all is vain," they declared, in the words of the last verse of Ecclesiastes, "The end of the matter, all having been heard — fear God and keep His commandments, for this is the whole of man." [28] And likewise to the common decision of the Shammaites and Hillelites, that it is better for man that he be not born, they retorted, "But now that he is born let

[27] G. F. Moore, *Judaism,* Vol. II, p. 270.
[28] Eccl. 12:13.

him examine his conduct."[29] That is to say, life itself may not be worth while, but it has a purpose and the purpose is very much worth while; good conduct makes living a thrilling adventure, a great privilege, even if life be at its worst.

The rabbis ridiculed the fear of the "dangerous woman" which occupied the minds of teachers of the earlier period. They categorically denied that woman was a special tool in the hands of Satan as a temptress. Woman has her weakness as man has his, and the *yeẓer hara'* has no special preference for one sex above another. She can be good and she can be bad; when she is good she is very good, when she is bad she is very bad. They thought, therefore, that moderate disciplining of women was proper, but cloistering them out of sight of men and denying them a fair amount of social freedom was unreasonable and inhuman. They cite as a reprehensible example Popus b. Judah, who on leaving his house would lock his wife in her apartment in order to prevent her committing any wrong.[30]

They likewise ridiculed the fear of the *yeẓer hara'* of their predecessors, and presented their sentiments in the form of an ancient tale. The Men of the Great Synagogue, they tell, were much wrought up against the *yeẓer hara'* and the ruination thereby brought on. "Woe, woe," they exclaimed, "it is he who destroyed the sanctuary and burnt the Temple and slew the righteous and exiled Israel from their land, yet he is still dancing about among us. For what purpose has God given him to us, except that we may be rewarded? We want neither him nor the reward!" Whereupon in reply to their complaint, Heaven sent down a script with the word TRUTH upon it. They fasted thirty days and thirty nights, and the *yeẓer hara'* was surrendered to them, appearing like a fiery lion coming out of the holy of holies. They put him in prison for thirty days, and for that period of time not a single egg was to be found in all of Palestine. They could not kill him for fear of destroying the world, nor would Heaven grant a plea that he be reduced to half his power. So they blinded one of his eyes and let him go, affecting a minor reduction of

[29] 'Erub. 13b.
[30] Tos. Soṭ. 5, 9; Giṭ. 90a–b.

his power to the extent, at least, that one's sexual passions for close kin be considerably diminished.[31]

This story seems to indicate that too much persecution of the *yeẓer hara'* is futile and not even desirable. There is much good in him and we need him; just keep him under reasonable control. R. Simeon b. Elazar reflected the same sentiment when he said of the *yeẓer hara'*, "Hold him off with the left hand and draw him nigh with the right." [32] And R. Simeon b. Lakish remarked, "Come, let us be thankful to our parents, for if they had not sinned we would not have come into the world." [33] But R. Samuel b. Naḥman goes even further. The Bible speaks of Creation as good and sometimes as "very good." "Very good," says R. Samuel, refers to the coming into being of the *yeẓer hara'* — not only good but very good — for without him no man would build a house or get married or beget children or do business.[34]

The tenor of these remarks also indicates the rabbinic attitude to asceticism. They denied the belief that the flesh was essentially evil. The flesh is evil only through our corruption of it; uncorrupted, the flesh and its legitimate pleasures are essentially good. Characteristic is Hillel's statement, when he entered the bathhouse, that he was going to attend to the cleanliness of that which is the statuary representation of the King of kings. Any affliction of the body, any denial of legitimate enjoyment, making of vows, nazirism, fasting, even with the most pious of intentions, is sinful.[35] On the other hand, the rabbis pointed to a pair of jesters as the ones who were assured of eternal bliss in the hereafter, because they made people laugh.[36]

The most important corollary that follows from this teaching is the unequivocal opposition of the rabbis to celibacy. Marriage is a legitimate physical satisfaction; it furthers God's universal purpose in the perpetuation of the human species;

[31] Yoma 69b.
[32] Soṭah 47a.
[33] 'Ab. Zar. 5a.
[34] Gen. Rab. 9, 9.
[35] Lev. R. 34,3. Antagonism to vows and fasting is expressed in Ned. 20a; 22a; 77b. See also Ned. 10a; Ta'anit 11a; Yer. Ḳid. 66b.
[36] Ta'anit 22a.

it sustains the social unit, the family; and it helps us toward our personal salvation in that "it keeps us from sin." Hence the celibate is accounted by the rabbis as one who has "committed murder" or "detracted from the image of God." [37] The authoritative rabbinic law considers procreation a biblical command, from which no man is free, young or old.[38]

The legalism of the earlier day continued into the rabbinic period, and has in truth become part of the rabbinic mind. As pointed out above, it was born in the Second Commonwealth out of the need of counteracting disintegrating influences from without; that need was more pressing after the people lost their national home and independence and had practically nothing but the Law to hold them together. But law, and especially religious law, has a natural tendency to expand automatically into ever widening circles. If one does not want to displease God, the source of law, one will seek to keep at some distance from the exact line of demarcation between that which is prohibited and that which is permitted. He will thus be making "fences" around the law. The rabbis accepted this process of fence making as legitimate in legal progress. But at the same time they guarded against the danger of overbuilding the fence, of making the law unreasonable and impractical; they wanted the fence never to be considered equal in importance to the law itself; they warned against building fence around fence.[39] Their motto was: "Better a fence of one cubit that will stand up than a fence of a hundred cubits that will fall down." [40]

A goodly measure of emancipation came to woman under rabbinic teaching. She was no longer confined to her apartment as behind prison walls, as in former days, but had a reasonable amount of social freedom. She attended gatherings, visited the market, moved about freely in the streets, even did business on her own, sometimes supporting both herself and her husband by her earnings; often, too, she en-

[37] Yeb. 63b.

[38] M. Yeb. 6,6; Yeb. 62b.

[39] Beẓah 3a; Yeb. 21b; B. Ḳ. 79b; B. B. 60b. See an interesting article by Simon Federbush, *Lifnim mi-Shurat ha-Miẓwah*, in *Hado'ar*, Vol. XXIII, Nos. 10–13, New York, 1943.

[40] Ab. de R. Nat. Ch. 1; San. 29a; Gen. Rab. 19,4.

gaged in study either of the sacred literature of her own people or of the culture of other nations; she learned many domestic arts, she visited neighbors, she traveled abroad, she had a comparatively full and rich life. Levity, of course, was discouraged, and private meetings with men were prohibited under the law of chaperonage. Naturally their conception of levity was far different from ours; to the rabbis, exchange of greetings, or of glances, or touching one another physically, exposure of any hidden part of the body on the part of the woman, listening to a woman's voice or smelling her perfume on the part of the man, constituted levity and flirtation.[41] Clean and refined sexual conduct, such as they conceived it, was the fundamental objective of rabbinic teaching.

IV. POST-TALMUDIC DEVELOPMENT

The main current of rabbinic principles of sex morality runs through the halakah; a secondary current runs through the agadah. The two are not antagonistic; on the contrary, they supplement each other. Halakah puts down rules; agadah sets up ideals. Halakah teaches; agadah preaches. Halakah leads human life to uprightness; agadah leads it to saintliness.

The line of demarcation between the two was never clear nor was it meant to be too definite. It was therefore perfectly proper for post-talmudic teachers to blend the two together and out of the combination to formulate a code of sex morality. Naturally, a code of this kind must be severer than talmudic law, for one must go further to attain saintliness than to attain uprightness. Or as Maimonides puts it, there is a difference between the standard of permitted and prohibited and the standard of desirable and undesirable or noble and despicable, which standards are applied to saintliness as against legality.[42] The post-talmudic halakist, therefore, often introduced into the legal code of sex morality regulations which originally, in talmudic halakah or agadah,

[41] Ber. 24a; 61a–b; 'Erub. 18b; Sab. 33a; 64b; Ket. 17a; Ned. 20a; B. Ḳ. 16b; B. B. 55a; Gen. R. 60,13; Exod. R. 16,2; Der. Er. Ch. 1; Kallah, Ch. 1; Yer. Ḥal. 58c; Yer. Soṭah. 18c.

[42] *Mishnah Commentary,* San. 7,4; *Yad,* De'ot, 5,4–5; Issure Bi'ah (I.B.) 21,9.

were intended as rules of nobility rather than rules of legality.[43] That, of course, afforded him a generous extension of the code.

Again, the mediaeval halakist was not only a teacher but an administrator of his community, and as such the guardian of public morality. In that capacity he had the responsibility and the freedom to introduce new enactments governing sex conduct, regardless of the standard law, and to prescribe penalties for violation. Many such communal enactments, going far beyond the requirements of talmudic law, are recorded in post-talmudic rabbinic literature;[44] the penalties, of which there are very few in the Talmud, and which applied only to serious sex offenses, are extravagant and varied and often foreign to Jewish tradition, including the ban, flagellation, monetary fines, public disgrace, branding, shaving off the head, or cutting off the nose.

No new principles of sex morality can be ascribed to the mediaeval halakist, so far as he was only a halakist. He just continued the general views of the rabbis of the Talmud; he was no pessimist, no ascetic, was good-humored towards the evils in the world and the weaknesses in man; he was not fearful of the *yeẓer kara'* nor accounted woman especially dangerous; he was the practical, common-sense teacher, thinking life potentially good and capable of being good under proper control and regulation.

As the talmudic halakist had his agadist, so the post-talmudic halakist had his moralist. Often the same man was a combination of both, but as moralist he played a specific role and began with specific assumptions. He takes for granted, of course, all standards of legality established by the halakah, for obedience to law is the first requirement of moral conduct. From there on, his specific task is to develop saintliness. For that purpose he requires a life that is more disciplined than the law demands. Even that which is permitted by law is often not the best for a person's spiritual

[43] Yad, I.B. 21–22; *Eben Ha'ezer* (E.H.) 21–23; Isserles notes, E.H. 21,5, quoting Binyamin Ze'eb; *Ba'er Heṭeb,* note 3, ad E.H. 21,1.

[44] Yad, I.B. 21,2; E.H. 21,1; *Sha'are Ẓedeḳ* 13, p. 25a; *Asheri* 18,13; *Ba'er Heṭeb* l. c.

wellbeing.[45] In the domain of sex conduct he would counsel people to limit their approaches to their wives to the bare needs of procreation or to satisfy their marital obligations as recognized by the law.[46] There need be no unnecessary dealing with women altogether.[47] Music and song and laughter and love tales are all reprehensible.[48] Wicked is the woman who dresses to please men, and wicked is the man who dresses with an eye to finding favor with the women.[49] Women, married or unmarried, would do well to stay indoors altogether, take no walks in the park where they would of necessity mingle with men; even attending synagogue services is not desirable for them.[50] According to some, it would be best for men to find a secluded spot somewhere, away from their wives and families, where they could dedicate themselves to self-sanctification for the entire week, coming home only for the Sabbath to meet their marital obligation to their wives.[51]

His philosophy runs as follows. Man is partly animal, partly divine. By his appetites he is the former; by his soul he is the latter. The two natures in man are in constant conflict. One cannot be satisfied except at the expense of the other. The choice then is which side of our nature is to master the other, and our destiny as human beings demands that we subject the beast within us to the wise rule and mastery of our souls. Take away that mastery and we become helpless slaves to our passions, and there is no halt to our bondage, for the pit into which it drives us is bottomless. From one

[45] Baḥya, *Ḥobot ha-Lebabot,* Perishut, 5; Abraham b. David, *Sefer Ba'ale ha-Nefesh,* Ḳedushah (towards the end); *Orḥot Ẓaddiḳim,* Teshubah (Wilno ed., 1914, p. 49a); Baḥya b. Asher, *Kad ha-Ḳemaḥ,* Ḳedushah; E.H. 25,1.

[46] Saadya, *Emunot we-De'ot* 10,6–7.

[47] Testament of R. Eliezer of Mayence in Abraham's *Ethical Wills,* II, pp. 211, 216; *Sefer Ḥasidim* 57, 60.

[48] *Sefer Ḥasidim* 62; *Ḥobot ha-Lebabot,* Perishut, ed. Lemberg. 1837, section 2, p. 44; *Ḳobeẓ 'al Yad* XII, Jerusalem, 1936, p. 205; *Sefer ha-Yashar,* Koenigsberg, 1847, p. 27b.

[49] *Sefer Ḥasidim* 47; *Oraḥot Ẓaddiḳim,* Ga'awah.

[50] Testament of Eliezer of Mayence in Abraham's *Ethical Wills* II, p. 211; Letter of Elijah Wilno, ibid., pp. 315–16; *Ya'arot Debash* I, 12, at the end, cited by Israel Bettan, *Studies in Jewish Preaching,* Cincinnati, 1939, pp. 339–40.

[51] *Re'shit Ḥokmah,* Ḳedushah, 6 (ed. Warsau, 1868, p. 118b).

evil we go to another until we become despicable in our own eyes and dangerous to the world. And we pay for it in terms of health and happiness. When we satisfy our souls we experience elation, a sense of self-realization, and attain brilliance of countenance; but when we satisfy our baser passions we go through the whole complex of remorse, dejection, confusion of mind, pallor of face, dullness of eyes, and loss of energy. If carried to excess it impairs our eyesight, undermines our health, makes us old before our time, until finally our organism is totally disintegrated and we are brought down to our graves. Add to this the balance between virtue in which our Maker finds delight and rewards us with bliss eternal in the hereafter, and vice for which we suffer the punishment of Gehinna, and the argument is clear that it is worth sacrificing personal desire to every extent for the higher morality which leads to saintliness and ultimately to its reward here and hereafter.[52]

The dualism of the human personality, that of body and soul, posited by the moralists, was in reality the essence of the Jewish way of thinking in the Middle Ages, and no one had a greater share in formulating the concept than the philosopher. Characteristic of the mediaeval Jewish philosopher, however, is that to him the soul — the immortal soul — is Reason. Reason is the essence of reality in the universe and likewise the highest fulfillment of the human being. Immortality consists in the individual mind becoming part of the Universal Mind, called the Active Intellect, and that is accomplished by study and knowledge and pure, rational, abstract contemplation. In contrast to the halakist and the moralist, whose "spirituality" is clothed in the body of daily conduct and whose wisdom is rooted in mundane experiences, the "spirituality" of the philosopher is beyond and above any corporeal manifestation, although conduct of one kind encourages that spirituality just as conduct of another kind hinders it, and wisdom to him is not experience but

[52] *Emunot we-De'ot,* 10,6; *Hegion ha-Nefesh,* ed. Leipzig, 1890, p. 11; *Ḥobot ha-Lebabot,* II, pp. 22a, 30a; *Oraḥot Ẓaddiḳim,* pp. 13b, 21a, 62a; *Sefer ha-Yashar,* p. 25a; *Sha'are ha-Musar,* attributed to Maimonides, in Abraham's *Ethical Wills,* I, p. 113.

concepts and ideas. Were a man able to neglect his bodily appetites and faculties altogether, and yet survive, and draw into himself to exercise his reason, to attain truth, to reach the knowledge of universals and ultimates and the attributes of God, he would more easily achieve his highest destiny than under the burden of bodily functions. Since, however, he has a body and bodily needs, he must manage them in such a way as will be helpful to his rational development. His physical needs and his mundane desires, therefore, must never be ends in themselves, but must be employed as tools for the soul in the process of self-fulfillment. Even social virtues cannot be ultimate goods in themselves; they can only be helpful means of intellectual development, the only end-in-itself for man.

Halakic Judaism could not accept such a view, and what is more important, the philosopher of the Middle Ages could not teach doctrines contrary to the halakah. He had to yield and to compromise in respect to the practical problems of daily Jewish living, and three compromises are suggested, each one presenting a specific basis for sex morality. The first offers a grudging minimum to corporeal needs and interest. Seeing that we cannot forget our bodies, that the perpetuation of the species requires sexual functions, that the Law demands that we preserve our health and fulfill the duty of procreation, we should satisfy our bodily needs *only* to the extent which health and the normal functions of life require. Everything above that minimum is detrimental to the soul, both for the burden it puts upon the soul and for the temptations it encourages. "As one who drinks bitter medicine, drinking it with his mouth, not with his will, disliking the drinking for itself and avoiding as far as possible the bitter taste, except insofar as it is necessary to cure his illness, so should the needs of this world be in thine eyes." [53]

The second is more liberal toward the senses. It does not demand minimum but intelligent moderation. Under the control of reason, a fair amount of physical satisfaction is wholesome and even beneficial to the soul. "A saint is a

[53] Baḥya ibn Paḳuda is representative of this compromise program. See *Ḥobot ha-Lebabot,* at the end, p. 57a.

ruler. It is he who obtains obedience from his physical and spiritual senses and faculties . . . controlling appetites, not permitting them excess once they have obtained their due share . . . of moderate food and drink and cleansing . . . and employing his feet and hands and tongue toward useful ends . . . as well as his appetites and his imagination and his power of memory and his will . . . making them all active in the service of his reason, permitting none of these faculties more than specifically belongs to them while neglecting others." [54] This principle becomes very close to the rabbinic attitude to worldly pleasures, including sexual functions. It recognizes legitimate and illegitimate sex pleasures, denying no legitimate sex satisfaction so long as it does not destroy the balance and harmony of the human constitution as a whole nor threaten the loss of self-control. Since all human faculties are involved in the commonwealth governed by reason, the control involves not only the sexual act but also vision and speech and thoughts on sexual matters.

The third is akin to the second in content, accepting moderation as the proper compromise with the physical senses, but it proposes an Aristotelian formula for moderation which logically leads to a more cordial acceptance of corporeal needs. It is the principle of the Golden Mean. "Good deeds are balanced between two extremes, both of which are evil, one because of excess, the other because of defect. . . . Temperance is good . . . but indulgence at the one extreme and insensibility at the other are both bad. . . . The Torah has intended natural man just to follow the path of the mean, eat moderately of what he has, drink what he can in moderate amount, and enjoy legitimate sexual pleasure in moderate measure." [55] Of course, this is a concession to practicality and has in mind the Law which deals with the daily conduct of the average man. But self-fulfillment in the philosophical sense demands all the same that there shall be no sexual act or thought which aims at pleasure altogether; only that

[54] This form of compromise with the senses is offered by R. Judah Halevi in *Kuzari,* III, 3–5.

[55] Maimonides in *Moreh Nebukim,* III, 8; *Shemonah Peraḳim,* 4–5; *Mishnah Commentary,* San. 7,4; *Yad,* De'ot, 4–5; I.B. 21,9.

which aims at procreation and of that the very minimum.

The teachings of the moralist and the philosopher generally lead to ascetic doctrines, for two reasons, because of their emphasis on spirituality and because of the contrast they see between body and soul. Not so with the cabalist. He also demands spirituality, but his spirituality, as distinguished from that of the philosopher, is emotional rather than rational; and as distinguished from that of the moralist and the halakist, it is subjective rather than objective and calculated to lead to grace rather than to merit. The antithesis between the physical and the spiritual in the universe he conceives as a difference between God the Unlimited (*En Sof*) and God Contracted (*Ẓimẓum*) ; the physical world, therefore, and all its finite existences are in truth part of God. The human body and its physical needs, like everything else in the physical world, belong to that "Contracted" manifestation of God. But man has a preferred position in the mundane world; he is himself the best expression of the universal union of the physical and the spiritual, for he is himself that union, his body of the physical world, his soul of the spiritual. By virtue of his position as link between the two worlds, man is a being of cosmic importance and every one of his acts attains cosmic significance. But every act in itself has a body and a soul; it is partly physical movement and partly a state of mind. The mere physical act does not attain cosmic importance. It may be good or bad on the level of its occurrence, but does not attain cosmic significance until it is directed by mind, by motive or purpose. *Kawwanah* (intent) is the all important factor in determining the cosmic good or evil of human behavior.

Briefly then, four leading principles are contained in cabalist doctrine. The world is good; it is saturated with the very essence of God. Man's physical needs are in themselves worthy and good, part of God's manifestation in the finite world. Man's actions and general conduct, even in respect to things that appear trivial, have cosmic significance. And, in every act it is *kawwanah* that gives it cosmic value.[56] With

[56] See article "Cabala" by Dr. Louis Ginzberg, *Jewish Encyclopedia;* H. A. Wolfson, *The Philosophy of Spinoza,* Cambridge, 1934, I, pp. 394–5; II, p. 50.

these four principles the cabalist approaches the problems of sex morality and develops interesting views and tenets.

The sex impulse is to the cabalist not a passion to be ashamed of or suppressed. On the contrary, it is a holy urge, natural and noble, if expressed in loving union between man and wife. To some of the cabalists, the union of male and female is the mystical symbol of life and love in the realm of *sefirot.* Even as a mere human phenomenon it is a God-given impulse, and God gives us nothing that we are to be ashamed of. The sex organ should be considered no different from the hand or the foot or the nose. The hand is noble when it writes a Torah, ignoble when it steals; so the sex organ is noble when it expresses purity and love, ignoble when it is given to lust and sensuality. Nothing in the human body is ugly as a result of creation; it is by man's folly that ugliness is ascribed to things beautiful in themselves.[57] On the other hand, as cosmic benefits derive from loving and noble copulation, so are evil influences given dominance in the world by ugly and vulgar sex pleasures. Thought alone, i.e., *kawwanah,* is sufficient to make all this difference. A sexual connection for carnal pleasure alone opens the world to evil influences and to that extent dethrones God. Lascivious thoughts alone, without the sexual act, are efficacious enough to wrest power from God. In truth, the thought of sin is worse than sin itself, because thought is itself part of the spiritual world and its effect upon the *sefirot* is therefore more immediate. There are carnal contacts which the law prohibits, a woman in impurity, a harlot, a gentile woman, or a female slave; there are also vulgarities that come from the mind and pollute the soul, indecent talk, levity and song and wine, lascivious day dreaming, or gazing lustfully at women. Both kinds are in the service of Universal Evil (*Siṭra Aḥera*) and cause detraction from the power of God.[58]

Judaism, analytically, is the current of historic progress

[57] Naḥmanides, *Iggeret Haḳodesh,* at the beginning; Isaiah Hurwitz, *Shene Luḥot ha-Berit,* Otiyot, ed. Ostraha, 1806, p. 91b; *Re'shit Ḥokmah,* Ḳedushah, 16, p. 165b.

[58] *Re'shit Ḥokmah,* Ahabah, section 10, p. 74a; Ḳedushah, sections 16–17, also section 5, p. 116b, section 8, pp. 134b, 135b, section 11, p. 140b, and section 13, p. 152a. See also *Shene Luḥot ha-Berit,* Otiyot, pp. 86b–93a.

through the various trends and moods here enumerated, naiveté, morbidity, asceticism, pessimism, legalism, practical liberality, pietistic severity, rationalism, mysticism; synthetically, it is the combination of all these in proper and wholesome proportions. The resulting code of sex morality is at times a bit prudish, often severe, but always sound as an ideal of and a guide to sexual purity. There have, of course, always been deflections from the code; there have also been local deviations. But by and large, until the spirit of emancipation and modernity encroached upon inner Jewish life at the beginning of the last century, Jews lived by it and maintained an admirable record of purity and refinement in sexual conduct.

CHAPTER II

MODESTY IN DRESS

SEX morality is a discipline and an ideal which reaches out into the remotest avenues of social and personal conduct, regulating all acts that have the slightest bearing on sexual life. The most important aspect of this code of morality deals with the laws of marriage, to which the writer has dedicated a separate work.[1] But the code goes far beyond that. It has something to say as to the kind of person with whom one may associate, the kind of dress one may wear, the kind of language one may speak, the things one may touch or hear or see or smell. What the Freudians claim to have brought to light as to the importance of the sex interest in the complexities of the behavior of the individual, certainly seems to be true of group life. A person's conduct either as part of the group or in relation to the group is motivated, directed, or controlled to a surprising extent by the code of sex morality which the group establishes. There may be more jurisprudence on the subject of property rights, but more of our daily behavior is determined by the control that society imposes on our sexual self-expression. We may begin with the control of our manner of dress.

I. NUDITY

The attitude of the ancient Jew to nakedness of body is reflected in the early chapters of Genesis, where the author points to the curious fact that Adam and Eve in their primitive stage "were both naked . . . and were not ashamed." [2] The explanation for this lack of modesty is assumed to be that they had not yet tasted of "the tree of the knowledge of good and evil." When, in violation of God's command, they

[1] *Marriage Laws in the Bible and the Talmud,* Cambridge, 1942.
[2] Gen. 2:25.

did eat of the forbidden fruit, "the eyes of both of them were opened and they knew that they were naked." [3] Evidently, the revulsion to nudity among the early Hebrews was definite and deep-rooted. It would be superficial, however, to say that this revulsion was synonymous with sexual modesty. One gets the feeling rather that it was of the nature of shame and humiliation. It is more fair to say that to the ancients the fine distinction between that which is shameful and that which is obscene did not exist, and that in respect to nakedness the sense of shame was stronger among them than the sense of obscenity. In fact, throughout the Bible, nakedness is primarily conceived as shameful and only secondarily as immodest. This is even true of the Talmud in respect to the nakedness of the male body, while covering the female body is required more specifically as a matter of modesty.

It is in keeping with this sentiment that during the biblical period it was customary for the jealous husband, on discovering that his wife was unfaithful to him, to strip her naked "as on the day she was born" and turn her out to public gaze in vengeful humiliation.[4] The rabbinic tradition that all criminals executed by authority of the law were hung up naked to public view [5] is probably a correct account of the ancient Hebrew usage, intended to heap humiliation upon the corpse; and it is probably in the interest of moderation that the Bible sets a limit by prescribing that the body be removed before sundown.[6] There were other situations where humiliation was intended, sometimes for a slave or a war captive, sometimes self-humiliation by mourners in their grief; but there they went only so far as exposing parts of their bodies, never appearing altogether nude.[7]

In biblical times, it seems, the Hebrews did not come in contact with tribes that were not sensitive to the shame of nakedness. This unfortunate experience came in their con-

[3] Gen. 3:7.

[4] Hosea 2:5; 11:12; Is. 3:17; 47:3; Jer. 13:26; Ez. 23:26.

[5] Sifre Deut. 21:22, ed. Friedmann, p. 114b.

[6] Deut. 21:22.

[7] Is. 47:2–3; II Sam. 3:31; 15:30. However, the rabbis believed that nakedness was sometimes the lot of war captives in ancient times. See Pesikta Rabbati, ed. Friedmann, Vienna, 1880, ch. 28, p. 135a.

tact with the Hellenic world, and unfortunate it was because it developed into a point of conflict between Hellenism and Hebrew tradition, with grave dangers to the latter. At the time of the Maccabean revolt, the Hellenist party among the Jews, enamoured of the Greek way of life, of their glorification of physical form and prowess, encouraged the building of a gymnasium in Jerusalem, where games were held with male athletes in the nude. The loyal Jews resented this exceedingly, considering it an affront to the conscience of the Jewish people, for nudity was to them both barbaric and indecent.[8] We are not told whether these games were visited by women also, but it is likely that women Hellenists did not hesitate to flock to the show, like their Greek sisters. Philo, a century and a half later in the city of Alexandria, apparently had absorbed enough of the Hellenic way of thinking to have made peace with the gymnasium and nude athletes, so long as only males were admitted, but he could not bear the thought of women visiting these places. He says: "It is fitting to praise those who have been . . . the managers of the gymnastic games, who have kept women from the spectacle in order that they might not be thrown among naked men and so mar the approved coinage of their modesty. . . . For neither is it right for men to mix with women when they have laid aside their garments, but each of the sexes ought to avoid the sight of the other when they are naked."[9]

But even according to Hellenic standards, nakedness was a vulgarity that had its place in the gymnasium but was offensive in an atmosphere of decency and holiness. To enter into a temple naked was considered an outrage by the heathen Romans, which Rabban Gamaliel II believed no heathen would perpetrate "for any amount of money."[10] It goes without saying, therefore, that to the Jews nakedness was a bar to the performance of any religious duty even in private, not to speak of entering holy places. Thus one cannot read the *Shema'* or recite his daily prayers or pronounce any bene-

[8] I Mac. 1:15; Jos. *Antiq.* XII, 5, 1.
[9] Philo, *de special. leg.* III, 31, 176, ed. Cohn, Vol. II, p. 237.
[10] M. 'Ab. Zar. 3,4.

diction or meditate on the words of the Torah while he is naked or in the presence of a naked person.[11] This ruling created difficulty for the proselyte who had to undergo ritual immersion in connection with his conversion, and for the woman who required a ritual bath to be cleansed of her monthly impurity. In both cases a prayer had to be recited at the time of the immersion. Hence the law recommends letting the water cover the body up to the neck and stirring the water around with the feet so that the body beneath the surface will not be clearly visible.[12]

In secular context, however, and so long as they were in private surroundings, it seems that the Jews of the talmudic period permitted themselves to be wholly stripped when doing their work or when relaxing indoors, both men and women.[13] But the rabbis considered it a vulgar habit, and accounted it contrary to the dignity of man as God had intended it.[14] They considered it immodest, especially for a person to stand naked before a candlelight.[15] This talmudic sentiment is followed by R. Judah he-Ḥasid, a saint of the twelfth century, in application to an immodesty current in his own time. He says: "Even when there are no people about, a man shall not stand naked, nor shall he appear naked (from the waist up) in the presence of people, as do the laborers who wear only trousers."[16]

Nakedness in public for men is barbarity of the most abhorrent kind; nothing is so hateful and abominable to the Almighty as one who goes about nude in the street. This rabbinic sentiment does not refer to any tribe they knew among the neighbors of Palestine, but to inhabitants of far-off lands — Berbers, Mauritanians, and Tunisians. It is of tribes like these that the Bible (Deut. 32:21) says: "And I will rouse them to jealousy with a no-people; I will provoke

[11] M. Ber. 3,5; Ber. 25b; M. Ḥal. 2,3; M. Dem. 1,4; Tos. Ber. 2,15, 23; Suk. 10b; M. Ter. 1,6; B.M. 114b.

[12] Yoreh De'ah (Y.D.) 200,1.

[13] Tos. Ber. 2,15; Yer. Ber. 13c; M. Ḥal. 2,3.

[14] Tos. ibid. Josephus, *Wars,* II, 9, 13, refers to the Essenes, both men and women, as avoiding nakedness at stool or in bath.

[15] Pes. 112b.

[16] *Sefer Ḥasidim,* 1060.

them with a vile nation."[17] The Mishnah rules that causing shame to a naked person constitutes injury, and the offender must pay for the mental anguish thus caused his victim. The amoraim, however, ask: How can a naked person suffer mental anguish because of shame? They answer, it is possible only when a person has become naked through an accident, as for instance when a tornado has torn off his garments.[18] In other words, a person who is naked by his own choice, according to the amoraim, is incapable of suffering shame or insult.

So much for the aspect of shamefulness implied in nakedness; but there is also the implication of sexual immodesty. This latter consideration, though overshadowed by the former, attains emphasis occasionally when women are involved in the situation.[19] We have seen how Philo felt about the immodesty of men naked in the gymnasium in the presence of women. The rabbis, of course, felt the same way. To some extent the rabbis of tannaitic times had not yet altogether lived down the memory and social influence of the Roman bath, where men and women bathed together in the nude. Their contemporaries among the early Church Fathers waged a lively battle against the practice of nude bathing by men and women, or that of male slaves in the nude attending their mistresses in the bath.[20] However slight and unusual, it

[17] Sifre Deut. 32.21 (p. 137a); Midr. Tannaim, ed. Hoffmann, Berlin, 1909, p. 196; Yeb. 63b. See *Talmudische Archäologie,* Krauss, Leipzig, 1910, Vol. III, pp. 516–17 and notes 1, 2.

[18] B.Ḳ. 86b.

[19] An interesting suggestion concerning some ancient conceptions about sex morality should be noted here. The male slave and the female slave had no sex personalities in the eyes of the ancients. They were considered as having no shame and incapable of causing the sense of shame in others. Rebecca was unveiled in the presence of Eliezer but veiled herself when she beheld Isaac. See Gen. 24:66, and *Miḳra ki-Peshuto* thereto and to Is. 47:2. M. Soṭah 1,6 excludes slaves from the sight of the ordeal of bitter water, because the woman would feel support rather than shame in their presence. Mohammed also permitted women to appear unveiled before male slaves (Koran, Sura XXXIII, 55). In the middle ages it was the custom to employ female slaves as attendants for males in the bath house, and Jewish law permitted it. E.H. 21,5. However, levity with slaves or privacy that might lead to carnal contacts were rigorously avoided. See Ber. 45b; 'Erak. 3a; Pes. 91a.

[20] See citation by Havelock Ellis, *Studies in the Psychology of Sex,* Vol. I, Part I, pp. 25–27.

seems that infractions of morality of that nature did sometimes occur even in Palestine, for the tannaim teach that a man is duty bound to divorce his wife if she bathes together with men. The amoraim no longer could conceive the possibility of a woman bathing together with men, and they believed that the tannaim warned against women bathing in the same place where men bathe, when the latter, of course, were no longer there.[21] There is nothing in the Talmud, so far as known, concerning the practice of males being attended at the bath by female slaves or women being attended by male slaves. One gets the impression that certainly women were not permitted to be handled naked by male slaves,[22] but we have nothing to guide us as to the rule concerning men being washed by their female slaves. Strange enough, this practice among non-Jews continued in European lands till fairly recent times, and some Jewish teachers considered it proper even according to the Jewish code of morality.[23] Most rabbinic authorities, particularly those of Sephardic origin, denounce such practice as vulgar and immodest.[24]

Laxities in the bath-house, to the extent to which they did exist, in no way reflected an indifference to nakedness in other contexts. The Mishnah prescribes, in execution of a male criminal, that his privates be covered with a loin cloth for the sake of modesty. There is a view, probably the older one, that such partial covering is enough for execution of a woman criminal, but the dominant ruling is that she must be covered with a robe reaching over her entire body.[25] The severity of the rabbis where a woman's nakedness is involved is illustrated by the following case. A man was overcome by an uncontrollable, irrational passion for a certain woman, and the physicians declared he would die unless his passion

[21] Giṭ. 90b; Tos. Soṭah 5,9.

[22] Since women were not even to eat at table with male slaves in privacy — M. Pes. 8,7; Ber. 45b.

[23] See note of Isserles, E.H. 21,5, quoting Mordecai. The lack of shame in the presence of slaves, as observed in note 19, is partly responsible for this ruling.

[24] Yad, I.B. 21,5; Ṭur E.H. 21; *Bet Yoseph* and *Bet Ḥadash* thereto.

[25] Sifre Deut. 21:22, p. 114b; M. San. 6,3; Tos. San. 9,6; San. 45a; Yad, San. 15,1.

were gratified. The court positively refused to allow this; let him die! The physicians thought he might survive if he were permitted to see the woman naked and have his passion spent harmlessly. The court refused to permit this; let him die, but let no Jewish woman appear naked to the gaze of a man! [26]

II. EXPOSURE

In our code of sex morality, exposure constitutes a violation equal in quality if not in degree to nakedness, for exposure is part nakedness. As with nakedness, therefore, the revulsion is born, in the first place, out of the sense of shame. Hence in biblical times slaves and war captives were humiliated by exposure of parts of their bodies, baring the head, showing the naked leg and thigh, and even uncovering the private parts. Women and men were thus humiliated.[27] Also mourners in self-humiliation would uncover their chests by tearing open their garments, would bare their heads by removing the head covering, and would go barefoot. [28] Likewise the woman charged by her husband with unfaithfulness and brought to the priest for the "ordeal of the bitter water" had her head uncovered as a humiliating introduction to the ceremonial.[29] According to rabbinic tradition, the priest tore down her blouse, thereby baring her chest, while men and women assembled in crowds around her so as to render the disgrace the more hurtful.[30] It should be mentioned also that the priests who ministered in the Temple, and especially the high priest, were exceedingly cautious not to uncover any part of their bodies. For that purpose trousers and a cap were worn, and the removal of either in the Temple constituted a capital sin.[31] Even the layman, according to later

[26] San. 75a; Yer. Sab. 14d.

[27] Is. 47:2–3.

[28] II Sam. 3:31; 15:30.

[29] Numb. 5:18.

[30] M. Soṭah 1,5; Sifre Numb. Naso, 12, ed. Horovitz, Leipzig, 1917, p. 17; Soṭah 8a.

[31] Lev. 10:6; 21:10; cf. Exod. 20:26. According to rabbinic interpretation, the word *Pera'* in this connection means causing hair to be overgrown. Yet the rabbis admit that bareheadedness for the priest at the time of his ministration is a capital offense. See Sifra ad Lev. 10:6; San. 83a; Yad, Kele ha-

halakah, committed a grievous transgression if he came into the sanctuary with garments torn in such a manner that his chest was uncovered.[32]

In tannaitic times, a headgear for men was not deemed necessary, but a woman with uncovered head was considered partly naked, as we shall see in a later section of this chapter. Such exposure meant dishonor to the woman, as I Corinthians (11:5f) has it: "But every woman . . . with head uncovered dishonoreth her head, for that is even as if she were shaven." And with this New Testament citation comes to mind the case in which R. Akiba fined the offender four hundred *zuzim* for uncovering the head of a woman in public.[33] A similar fine would have been imposed if he had uncovered her leg or thigh, for it is all a matter of humiliation. Privacy was required in olden days for women doing their laundering at the brook, because they had to uncover their legs during the washing. This need for privacy, says the Talmud, supersedes certain property rights of neighbors, "because Jewish women cannot humiliate themselves at the laundering brook." [34] Out of a similar consideration an exception is made for women regarding the law which requires mourners to tear their garments at the death of a parent or close relative, in that they are not required to bare their chests, but may either rend the outer garment only or tear the inner garment first and cover it up, permitting the outer garments thereafter to be torn without exposing the naked flesh.[35]

While the sense of shamefulness in exposure is definite enough, the implications of sexual immodesty are by no means to be overlooked. All incestuous relations are denounced in the Bible as "uncovering the nakedness," and

---

Miḳdash 1.5, and *Kesef Mishneh* thereto. See S. Zeitlin, First Canonization of Hebrew Liturgy, *Jewish Quarterly Review*, Vol. 38 (1947–8) pp. 298 f. on the subject of covering the head at worship both among Jews and non-Jews during the Second Commonwealth period.

[32] See Yad, ibid. 1,17. Talmudic law rules that any slight exposure of a woman's body or hair makes the reading of the *Shema'* impossible. Ber. 24a.

[33] M. B. Ḳ. 8,6.

[34] B.B. 57b.

[35] Semaḥot 9,7, ed. Higger, N. Y., 1931, p. 171.

the "nakedness" here means the naked genitals. One sometimes wonders whether the Bible was not quite literal in this expression, that is to say, that the mere exposure of the genitals between the male and the female of close kin was in itself incest to almost the same degree as sexual intercourse.[36] Our suspicion is strengthened by the incident of Noah, whom Ham his son found in a state of drunkenness with his genitals exposed. Ham is recorded as guilty of seeing his father's nakedness in terms that resemble a charge of incest, and for the offense Noah cursed him and his descendants with eternal slavery.[37]

The sense of carnality about seeing the nakedness of a father is primitive and has worn off since, but the sense of privacy and shame which does not permit exposure of the body in the presence of a father or other kin of the same category has continued in the Hebrew tradition. To this we owe the law forbidding a man to go to the bath house with his father, father-in-law, or brother-in-law, that is, sister's husband. By local custom even two brothers may not bathe together. The law was further extended to prohibit a pupil and his teacher to bathe naked in each other's presence.[38] This law, however, was softened and modified in post-talmudic time, apparently because the people did not take it seriously. Alexander Süslin, a talmudic scholar of the fourteenth century, records the fact that in his day people disregarded the restriction and for very good reason, because it was the custom to wear a cloth around the loins in the bath house. R. Moses Isserles gives full authority to this statement of his predecessor, and rules that where the custom is to wear tights in the bath house, thus having the genitals covered, there is no objection to father and son or teacher and pupil bathing together.[39]

The exposure of parts of the body on the part of the male,

[36] The Talmud considers the contact of the genitals alone, without actual intercourse, as incest in the fullest sense. See M. Yeb. 6,2; Yeb. 55b. Notice the expression in Lev. 20:17: "and he will see her nakedness and she will see his nakedness."

[37] Gen. 9:21–27.

[38] Pes. 51a; Semaḥot 12,12, p. 199.

[39] *Sefer ha-Agudah,* Cracow, 1571, p. 163b; Y.D. 242, 16; E.H. 23,6.

except in the context here mentioned, was never taken seriously as a breach of sex morality. The concepts of modesty and decency were applied mainly to the social requirement that a woman's body be not exposed. One gets this feeling both from the Bible and from the Talmud. One or two talmudic laws will make the point clear. Female nurses may attend male patients suffering from intestinal disorders, even though seeing the patients' privates is involved; but a male nurse may not attend a female patient with such an ailment. Likewise a woman may prepare a man for burial by putting shrouds on him and binding him up, although it means viewing the corpse in the nude; but a man cannot function in that capacity for a woman.[40] It was also out of regard for the immodesty of exposure of a woman's body that R. Judah, a tanna of the second century, maintained that in the ordeal of bitter water exposing the woman's chest should be omitted, and his contemporary R. Johanan b. Baroḳah advised having a screen set in front of the woman when her chest was uncovered.[41]

By social standards, necessarily reflected in the law, a woman's exposure of parts of her body was a sure token of her easy virtue. The Assyrian Code regards the professional harlot who covers her head as hiding her harlotry behind a mask of respectability, for only respectable women cover their heads.[42] It is an old trick of loose women to lure their victims by uncovering sexually suggestive parts of their body. This was the experience of Joseph, according to the apocryphal report, with the strategy of his master's wife: "She was wont to bare her arms and breasts and legs that I might lie with her." [43] No wonder that the social mind was trained to look upon a woman's exposure of her body as both immodest and suspicious. Hence in talmudic law a husband can prefer charges against his wife for misconduct, if she has bared her hip or leg or arm or shoulder or chest, or if she has done her weaving in public — implying a certain looseness of gar-

[40] Semaḥot 12,10, p. 198.
[41] M. Soṭah 1,5; Soṭah 8a; Sifre Numb. Naso, 11, p. 17.
[42] Assyrian Code I, 40.
[43] Testament of Joseph 9:5.

ment — or bathed in a place not private enough.[44] More than this, any display of the naked flesh on the part of a woman is accounted an indecent sight, provocative of unclean thought and dangerous to social morality.[45]

Legend records special scrupulousness of certain families on this particular point. A family quarrel is depicted in the Midrash between King David and his wife Michal, the daughter of Saul. David, the Bible records,[46] led his people in jubilant celebration on the occasion of the return of the ark of the Lord to the city of David, leaping and dancing with all his might. That displeased Michal, and the Midrash undertakes to explain why. David had uncovered his legs as he rolled up his long robes in order to facilitate dancing. Said Michal to him: "See the difference between you and my father's household, who were people of modesty and holiness . . . they never bared heel or toe." [47] Similar piety is reported of Ḳimḥit, who was the mother of seven high priests. She ascribed that special honor to the fact that the walls of her house never beheld the hair of her head nor the hem of her undergarments.[48]

This rigorous standard of modesty was naturally modified by the influence of non-Jewish standards. In oriental countries, where non-Jewish women were held to similar rules of modesty, the rigor of the older law continued. Even in the various countries in Europe, under the segregation of the ghetto or the discipline of Jewish self-government, the Jewish standard of feminine modesty in the post-talmudic period closely approximated the talmudic prescriptions. Bemoaning the ravages of non-Jewish fashion upon the moral conduct of Jewish women, R. Jonathan Eybeschuetz in one of his sermons says: "In our sinful generation they (the women) have learned from the gentile manner of dress to bare their necks. . . . I warn you, cease this evil thing, for the woman whose neck is uncovered is destined eventually to be drawn

[44] Ber. 24a; Tos. Soṭah 5,9; Giṭ. 90a–b; Ket. 72a–b; Yer. Soṭah 16b; Numb. R. 9,8.

[45] Ber. 24a.

[46] II Sam. 6:14, 16.

[47] Numb. R. 4,21, p. 25b.

[48] Yer. Meg. 72a; Numb. R. end of ch. 2; Yoma 47a.

unto the slaughter by the angel of death . . . for she is wicked and causes sin to others." [49] A younger contemporary of his appeals for the modesty of having the arms covered. "I plead with my brothers of the house of Israel not to conduct themselves according to the latest fashion wherein the daughters of Israel go about with bare arms, because the blouse and the shirt are made without sleeves long enough to cover the arms up to the wrist, but only so short as to cover the shoulder and a little below, the rest being visible to everybody. . . . And I command all my descendants . . . that they go about only with arms covered up to the wrist." [50]

With emancipation of Jewry in European countries at the beginning of the last century, the practice of Jews has taken a turn from the rigor of the traditional rabbinic standards toward the fashion of the day, for better or for worse. Jewish women have been covering as much of their bodies as the gentile women. There has been rumbling about this dereliction in the circles of the pious. The fashion of décolleté has offended the sensibilities of many a good Jew; evening dress with bare arms and back has made even a poorer impression. Such attire in the synagogue at a marriage ceremony has aroused numerous public protests in pulpit and press. The modern bathing suit has certainly exposed too much of the woman's body, and given old-fashioned moralists plenty of concern. But fashion seems to be mightier than tradition, good style more appealing than good taste.[51]

III. THE VEIL

The tradition that women veil themselves when they go out in public is very old in the Orient. Probably the first reference is to be found in the Assyrian Code, where it is ruled that wives, daughters, widows, when going out in public, must be veiled, but unmarried sacred prostitutes, harlots, and maidservants must not be veiled, under threat of pen-

[49] *Ya'arot Debash* I, 12, ed. Warsau, 1889, p. 30a.

[50] Meshulam Solomon Kohn, *Naḥelat Abot,* Fürth, 1811, p. 19b.

[51] The law recognizes that immodesty consists in "uncovering that which is customarily covered"—Oraḥ Ḥayyim (O.Ḥ.) 75,1—and probably accepts these uncoverings as standard for women's wear, even though it does not approve of it.

alty.[52] The impression one obtains from this document is that the veil served to set the woman of quality on a level of dignity and aloofness. It suggested that the woman was unapproachable, not quite in the distinctly sexual sense, but rather in the sense in which holy objects are held at a respectable distance. There is much in common between the veiling of the ancient Assyrian woman and biblical instruction that the sacred objects of the tabernacle shall be veiled before taken up to be carried by the Levites; and one can hardly miss the same sentiment implied in the veiling of Moses' countenance.[53]

We also find the veil in use among Jewish women in biblical times. It is designated in the Bible by a number of terms, such as *redid, ẓammah, re'alah, ẓa'if, miṭpaḥat,* but the specific character of each or the difference between one and another is not known to us.[54] As in the Assyrian document, there is no suggestion in the Bible that these garments were worn by women out of a sense of modesty. The suggestion is rather clear that they represented garments of distinction and luxury. Isaiah refers to them as *tif'eret,* objects of "splendor." [55] In fact there is no trace of a rule in the Bible, as in the Assyrian Code, that women of any class must be veiled when they go out in public. The likelihood is that women were generally not veiled except when they dressed for an occasion.[56]

Two specific cases are mentioned in the Bible of women veiling themselves in the presence of men. One is that of Tamar covering her face when met by Judah,[57] the other is

[52] Assyrian Code I, 40.

[53] Exod. 34:35; 3:6; Numb. 4:20.

[54] Is. 3:19, 22, 23; 47:2; Gen. 24:65; 38:14; Song 4:1; 5:7; 6:1; Ruth 3:15. See Benzinger, *Hebräische Archäologie,* Tübingen, 1907, pp. 78–79.

[55] Is. 3:18.

[56] Krauss, *Talmudische Archäologie,* I, p. 189 and note 797. It is interesting to note that the Mishnah (Ket. 6,7) speaks of the indecency of bareheadedness for women as a violation of "Jewish usage" in contrast to "Mosaic law." Nevertheless, we agree with the statement made by most writers on the subject that the headdress was accepted as a standard item in women's wear in early biblical times. See A. Büchler, Die Schneiden des Haares als Straffe der Ehebrecher, WZKM, XIX, p. 91ff; I. Benzinger, *Hebr. Archäologie,* p. 78; H. Ewald, *Die Alterthümer des Volkes Israel,* Göttingen, 1866, p. 269.

[57] Gen. 38:15.

that of Rebecca veiling herself when she was about to be met by Isaac.[58] The first case seems to have little significance, for the veil had only the purpose of hiding the identity of Tamar. The second does suggest that the bride was veiled at her first meeting with her bridegroom. It seems to be the standard marriage ceremonial of ancient times, which has continued throughout the ages either as a legal requirement or as a social formality, to have the bride veiled at her marriage. The Assyrian Code declares that the veiling ceremonial establishes the status of legitimacy for a wife.[59] Also the Bible uses the veiling of the bride as a symbol of marriage,[60] and rabbinic terminology follows in the same tradition.[61] In post-talmudic times the legal significance of veiling the bride was lost sight of, but the ceremonial has persisted to this very day, as a prominent social formality in Jewish marriages.

The meaning of this unbroken tradition of veiling the bride is variously interpreted. Anthropologists would have us believe that it was intended to protect the bride against the evil eye or the envy of demons.[62] It is not impossible that such superstitions have grown up about the ceremonial, but our early sources do not indicate that they played any significant part in its origin and development. The same may be said of some of the ethical or legal motives assumed by later authors.[63] It is natural that the motive of sexual modesty should be read into it, and no doubt at a time when women were expected to hide themselves from the gaze of men the veiling of the bride was partly motivated by the sense of modesty.[64] But sex morality is not at the root; at best it is only a secondary and indirect implication. The direct mean-

58 Gen. 24:65.

59 Assyrian Code I, 41.

60 Ez. 16:8; Ruth 3:9; The same is implied in Deut. 23:1; 27:20.

61 Mekilta, Mishpaṭim, ad Exod. 21:8, ed. Friedmann, Vienna, 1870. p. 78b. Targum Onḳelos and Targum Jonathan thereto; Ḳid. 18b.

62 Westermarck, *History of Human Marriage,* II, pp. 527–8; Z. Lauterbach, *Hebrew Union College Annual,* II, p. 356.

63 Ibn Yarḥi, *Ha-Manhig,* Berlin, 1855, pp. 91b–92a, gives the reason that it shall not appear as a "betrothal in the public market," which the law prohibits. The Karaites cover the bride to impress upon her the virtue of humility — Jacob Mann, *Texts and Studies,* II, p. 1133.

64 See Ḳimḥi commentary ad Gen. 24:64; A. Hirschowitz, *Oẓar Kol Minhage Yeshurun,* Lewow, 1930, p. 30.

ing is the symbolical significance of ownership or mastery. By covering up the bride the thought is expressed that she is taken possession of, perhaps also that, as a result, she is taken out of circulation as a free woman.

We have seen above that the veil for women in general suggested the dignity and unapproachability of the woman in the sense of a holy object. The veiling of the bride, which suggests being owned and set aside, is in reality of the same cloth. Dignity of position in the social sense is synonymous with being owned or "belonging" in the legal sense; unapproachability in social terminology corresponds to the married status in the legal way of thinking. It is interesting to note that even in talmudic times it was understood that "possession" and "sanctification" are terms interchangeably applied to marriage, because through the husband's ownership of his wife she becomes prohibited to everyone else, like an object of holiness.[65]

In the post-exilic period the veil probably became a standard requirement for decent women. That it should become standard was only natural, because style and fashion have a way of turning socially authoritative, so to speak, and binding as a social requirement. That it should become a token of modesty was partly due to the same natural development, and more so to the morbidness of the post-exilic Jew on matters of sex morality. In a society where looking at a woman is sinful and where women are expected to be secluded within their homes, any requirement of dress for women would naturally be fraught with the sanctimony of a moral injunction. Therefore in the ordeal of a woman suspected of unfaithfulness, as described in Numbers (5:18), the woman's hair was uncovered with the intent of depriving her of her modesty.[66] Likewise when Susanna was brought to court on

[65] Ḳid. 2b; Tosafot ibid. s. v. *De-assar.*

[66] The word *U-para'* may be translated "dishevel" or "uncover" and both translations are given in the sources. See Solomon Stern, Das Abschneiden des Haupthaares, in Geiger's *Wissenschaftliche Zeitschrift für jüdische Theologie,* 1837, pp. 354 f., and Geiger's additions thereto, p. 365; Büchler, o. c., WZKM, XIX, p. 93, note 1. Geiger and Büchler suggest that "uncovering" and "disheveling" are really one process, i.e., by removing the head cover the hair falls down loose. I put much store by the fact that the early sources prefer the translation of "uncover"—Septuagint a.l.; Philo, *de special. leg.*

charges of adultery, the judges caused her to remove her veil.[67] Probably the talmudic teachers are right in inferring that even in biblical times it was already recognized as a principle of modesty for women to have their heads covered;[68] yet this can not be proclaimed as certain, because we have only one instance to go by and this may represent special standards of reserve observed at court trials or at similar public appearances.[69]

It is certain, however, that in the early rabbinic period, even during Temple days, the woman was required by the current code of sex morality to be veiled, else her decency was questionable.[70] In a few instances the rabbis imply that this was a distinctively "Jewish usage" but was not observed by non-Jews.[71] This may mean only that there was greater laxity among non-Jews, but the fact is that even non-Jews in the Orient maintained the same standard of modesty.[72] In the west that rule of modesty was not recognized, and Saint Paul was much displeased over the fact. In his Epistle

---

III, ed. Cohn, II, p. 200; Jos. *Antiq.* III, 11,6. This tradition is carried over into rabbinic literature — Sifre Numb. a.l.; Tos. Soṭah 3,3; Ket. 72a; Numb. R. 9,13; 23, 42. On the other hand some rabbinic texts speak of disheveling her hair — M. Soṭah 1,5; Tos. Soṭah 1,7; Sifre Numb. ibid.; Numb. R. 23. 42. In all these texts it seems evident that the translation "uncover" is admitted, except that the addition of "disheveling" is understood to be implied. That *u-para'* means "uncover" is referred to as "the literal meaning," *ke-mashema'o,* Sifre Numb. 6,5, p. 31. The rabbis conceived the ceremony of soṭah to consist first of uncovering the woman's hair and then disheveling it, which second step was not known to the earlier sources. But Krauss, *Talmudische Archäologie,* I, pp. 194–6 and notes 874–9, differs with this view.

67 Sus. 32.

68 Sifre Numb. a. l.; Ket. 72a.

69 Jos. *Antiq.* XIV, 9, 4, indicates that it was the standard court procedure to have the defendant appear "in a submissive manner . . . with his hair disheveled and in black and mourning garment."

70 Definitely stated by Philo, ibid. "which (veil) all women are accustomed to wear who are completely blameless."

71 M. Ket. 7,6; Numb. R. 9, 13; Midr. Bereshit in Ginzberg's *Ginze Schechter,* N. Y., 1928, Vol. I, p. 4; Tertullian, *de Cor.* ch. 4, *de virg. vel.,* 17.

72 See Lagarde, *Materialien,* II, p. 31, recording the veil as in use among Syrians, and Wellhausen, *Arabische Heidenthum,* p. 196, claiming the veil to be a pre-Mohammedan Arabian custom. See Tertullian, *de virg. vel.* l. c. M. Ned. 3,8, according to the amoraic and apparently correct interpretation (Ned. 30b), indicates that all women had their heads covered. San. 58b takes it as an accepted practice even among Noahides.

to his followers in Corinth he demands that women have their heads covered, but tactfully stresses less the implication of sexual immorality and more the thought that bareheadedness for a woman is shameful — as though she were shaven — and in addition is a defiance of the husband's authority over her.[73] Contemporary rabbinic law unequivocally stressed the immorality of a woman's appearance in public with uncovered head. To the Shammaites who recognized no cause for divorce other than adultery, the wife's going out in public places with head uncovered constituted legitimate cause for divorce, as though it were synonymous with unfaithfulness.[74] When divorced on charges of bareheadedness, the wife is fined by the law to the extent of losing all her ketubah rights.[75] We have mentioned above that R. Akiba fined a man four hundred zuzim for uncovering a woman's head; the humiliation was considered in the category of exposing a sexual organ.[76] So general was the use of the head cover by women that, according to the ruling of the Mishnah,[77] if a man in making a vow referred to the color of hair, women were not included in his vow, because women's hair was never exposed. Homiletically, the rabbis explain why women cover their heads "like one who commits a crime and is abashed by it in the presence of people." [78] In another characterization of women, they describe her as "one who is veiled like a mourner and banished from people." [79]

These two descriptions make sufficiently clear the original and basic ground for the social disapproval of a woman's appearance in public bare-headed. Altogether a woman's place was in her home; gadding about in public places was unbecoming. If she did go out at all, she was expected to avoid brazen-facedness in her manner. Bare-headedness suggested haughtiness and arrogance. The veil was her retreat, and

[73] I Cor. 11:5–7.

[74] Yer. Soṭah 16b.

[75] Ket. 72a; Tos. Soṭah 5,9; Giṭ. 90a; Numb. R. 9,8. See Epstein, *The Jewish Marriage Contract,* pp. 212–13.

[76] M.B.Ḳ. 8,6.

[77] M. Ned. 3,8 and talmudic commentary thereto, Ned. 30b.

[78] Gen. R. 17,13. They refer to the fact that woman was the first sinner in the Garden of Eden story.

[79] 'Erub. 100b.

under it she could draw into herself with a sense of privacy and modesty becoming a daughter of Israel.

IV. FACE

How much did the veil cover? Was it merely a headgear, perhaps hanging down over the shoulders as well, or did it also hide the woman's face from view? In answer, we are inclined to believe that as a standard of conduct sanctioned by Jewish law, women were never required to cover their faces. Some women may have been over-scrupulous and drawn their veils over their faces when in the presence of strange men, especially when they were in a situation of embarrassment. In some localities Jewish women veiled their faces in accordance with the non-Jewish standards of their neighbors.[80] True, the rabbis always had a word of praise for modesty beyond the requirement of the law, and in that spirit they sometimes offered praise to the woman who covered her face, but never ventured to demand such conduct as a matter of legal standard. Any danger to public morality resulting from the woman's exposure of her face the rabbis had to accept, and the best they could do was to minimize the danger by teaching women to keep away from public places and men to avoid gazing at a woman's beauty.

Obviously, in the early biblical period, when head covering was merely a matter of style, there was no legal requirement for women to cover their faces. Besides the absence of any such suggestion, there are references to women of honorable conduct whose beauty of countenance was admired by men. The same may be said of the period of the Second Commonwealth, when, even though a rigorous code of sex morality prevailed, not the slightest suggestion is made to compel women to veil their faces before strangers, and likewise, the beauty of women's faces was admired by men without implication of guilt.[81] In fact, the one moral teaching ascribed to the period of the Second Commonwealth, that men avoid looking at women, would be meaningless if women had been required to cover their faces. Josephus records as a peculiar

[80] See M. Sab. 6,6, and Rashi Sab. 65a s.v. *Yoẓe'ot.*
[81] Judith 10:7.

law among the Persians that they forbade their wives to be seen by strangers.[82] For the rabbinic period, in addition to positive evidence,[83] there is sufficient proof that women were not required to cover their faces in the significant fact that no such law or legal opinion is recorded in all of talmudic literature. The Talmud being the basis of all rabbinic halakah, it becomes evident that to the post-talmudic teachers, too, a woman's exposing her face was never considered a breach of authoritative law, even where local custom required her to be completely veiled, but a mere infringement upon local usage.

Nevertheless, the sense of modesty of the Jewish woman in the ancient Orient tended to be more rigorous than the law, and once a veil over the head was in common use, the woman of dignity drew it down over her face as well. This was particularly true when the woman was put in a conspicuous position with the eyes of the public upon her, as when she appeared in court to face criminal charges. The solemnity of the court, as a matter of fact, required the judges also to be veiled;[84] could a woman facing serious charges, impressed with the dignity of the court, not draw her veil lower down? This may explain the account in the apocryphal book Susanna: "The lawless pair (the judges) ordered that she be unveiled that they might sate themselves with the beauty of her allure."[85] The implication would be that she appeared in court totally veiled, and that in unveiling she also uncovered her face. Assuming this to be correct and

[82] *Antiq.* XI, 6, 1.

[83] M. Ta'anit 4,8, girls inviting men to look at them; Sab. 80a (with Rashi commentary, s.v. *be-'Iraniyot*), and especially Yer. Sab. 11b in the same connection, where the implication is evident that women showed their faces in public and employed cosmetics for that purpose. See 'Ab. Zar. 20b; 'Erub. 18; Ber. 61a, where the implication is that free gazing at women's faces was possible.

[84] See e.g. Yer. 'Ab. Zar. 40a at the bottom and Büchler referred to in note 87 further.

[85] Susanna, verse 32, dating back to the first century B.C.E. The quotation follows the LXX version in Charles' edition. The reading in the Theodocian version gives the same impression. The unveiling itself was in accordance with biblical prescription for the woman suspected of adultery, but the significant suggestion here is that her face was veiled when she came to the court so that the judges could not see her beauty. See note 69 above.

that it was not the general practice among Jewish women, we can understand the special modesty of Susanna in this situation, in terms explained by Tertullian: "She had come an accused woman blushing for the dishonor cast upon her (and) with good cause hiding her beauty." [86]

Like Tertullian, the rabbis felt that covering the face was good for the soul of woman, that it represented laudable modesty. Even as applied to men, they spoke of open-facedness in the sense of impudence, arrogance, forwardness.[87] Certainly for the sake of refinement, if not as a legal standard, the rabbis deemed it proper to proclaim the veil over the woman's face a token of feminine virtue. They thought Tamar showed good taste in covering her face when she met Judah, and Rebecca acted likewise in veiling herself on the approach of Isaac. [88] Tertullian tells us that Arabian usage in his day required that women have their faces veiled.[89] Since this is contemporary with the tannaitic period, it would not be surprising to find Jewish standards of modesty gradually influenced, if not legally, at least in a practical way, by those of their neighbors. In the time of the amoraim, therefore, the practice of veiling the face became more general among Jewish women in Palestine.

Rab Dimi no doubt reflected Palestinian conditions when he described woman as "veiled like a mourner and banished from people," [90] keeping in mind that mourners were required to cover their faces.[91] Another Palestinian amora

[86] Tertullian, *de Cor.*, ch. 4 in the translation of C. Dodgson, Oxford, 1854.

[87] See Büchler, WZKM, XIX, p. 132–4, in his analysis of the term *gilui panim.*

[88] Gen. R. 85,9. Rebecca and Tamar are recorded as equally deserving of praise in Gen. R. 60,14 and 85,8, where veiling alone is referred to and where covering the face is implied but not specifically mentioned. It is interesting to note that the rabbis teach (Gen. R. 85,9) in that connection that it is improper to veil her face in the presence of those who are of incestuous kinship to her, a teaching which we find also in Mohammedan law — (Koran, Sura XXXIII, 55) Westermarck, *History of Human Marriage,* I, p. 310, quoting Lane.

[89] Tertullian, *de Virg. Vel.* 17. See also Wellhausen, *Arab. Heidenthum,* p. 196. The same is true for Syrian women, Lagarde, *Materialien,* II, p. 31. See note on the subject by Dr. Saul Lieberman in *Ginzberg Jubilee Volume,* Hebrew, p. 267.

[90] 'Erub. 100b; Pir. deR. E. ch. 14.

[91] Mo'ed Ḳaṭ. 24a.

urges students to employ both reserve and forwardness in their conduct, each on the correct occasion, "like the bride who while in her father's house keeps herself in retirement so that no one knows her, but when she is about to enter nuptials she uncovers her face, as to say, if any one can testify aught against me let him do so." [92] If this be the original reading of this text, and we are inclined to believe it is, then it certainly implies that women, even unmarried virgins, had their faces covered. Another midrash, probably of Palestinian origin, reports a complaint of Hadrian, Emperor of Rome: "The (Jewish) women go out with their faces covered and our women go out with their faces exposed; is not such modesty rather becoming to us (Romans) whose kings rule the world!" [93]

The Palestinian tradition of having Jewish women cover their faces continued through the Middle Ages. An Italian traveler in Palestine of the sixteenth century records that the Jewesses there had their faces veiled, so that they could not be seen by men.[94] Modern travelers in Yemen, North Africa, and the Caucasus report that this is not a usage peculiar to Palestine but to the entire Orient.[95] It must be assumed that ideas of modesty among orientals largely influenced Jewish standards in the countries of the East.

On the other hand, the custom of women veiling their faces did not find a kindly reception among the Jews of Babylonia. A Babylonian text quoting the bride simile mentioned above does not refer to uncovering her face, but to her first public appearance, evidently because their women seldom, if ever, had their faces covered.[96] In respect to the prohibition against reading the *Shema'* in the presence of a

[92] Ex. R. 41,6; Tanḥuma Ki-Tissa, p. 112; Yalḳut, Song 4,9. In all these texts the reading is *he megalah panim,* while in D. E. ed. Higger, p. 122, the substitute phrase is *he mefarsemet 'aẓmah,* probably because in Babylonia maidens had their faces uncovered even before their bridal day.

[93] *Ginze Schechter,* Vol. I, p. 4. Its closeness to *Pirḳe de-Rabbenu ha-Ḳadosh* suggests that the Midrash is Palestinian.

[94] Ḳobeẓ 'al Yad IV, pp. 27–8; so also reported by R. David b. Zimra (16th century) for Egypt, quoted in *Ba'er Heṭeb,* E. H. 21,2.

[95] Cf. Slouschz, *Travels in North Africa,* p. 204; *Eben Sapir,* I, p. 10b; Charney, *Sefer ha-Masa'ot,* p. 58.

[96] See note 92 above.

woman indecently exposed, Hai Gaon rules that "exposure of the face or any part of the body that is not usually covered" does not constitute indecent exposure.[97] Babylonian halakah, of course, moulded Jewish life in Europe, and Rab Hai's ruling was accepted by the leading teachers of the West, by such men as R. Abraham b. David of Posquieres, R. Solomon ibn Adret of Barcelona, R. Aaron ha-Kohen of Lunel (12th to 14th centuries), and others, who likewise speak of exposure of the woman's face as usual.[98] The extensive literature on ethics and the numerous ethical wills produced by mediaeval Jewry offer not the slightest suggestion that women were expected to cover their faces. The same Italian traveler records that in Italy of his day women did not have their faces covered. What was true of Italy then has been true of all European lands since then; in accordance with the Babylonian tradition, Jewish women have not been expected to veil their faces.[99]

V. HAIR

In amoraic and post-talmudic halakah it is considered that the main purpose of the veil was to cover the woman's hair. That was not the original intent. Exposure of the head was the main objection to the ancients; it suggested licentiousness.[100] In truth, the hair was helpful to a woman's modesty, for it served as something of a cover over her head. Thus reasons Saint Paul: "Doth not nature itself teach you that if a man have long hair it is a shame to him; but if a woman have long hair it is a glory to her, for her hair is given her as a covering." [101] Likewise R. Johanan b. Zakkai recounts how in the years of distress at the time of the fall of Jerusalem hunger so ravaged the population that once a young woman in utter starvation came to him begging for a bit of food. She

[97] Lewin, *Oẓar ha-Ge'onim,* Vol. I, section 2, p. 30.

[98] *Orḥot Ḥayyim,* Ḳeri'at Shema', 36, p. 13c; Adret, Novellae, Ber. 24a; *Bet Yoseph* ad *Ṭur* O. H. 75.

[99] Abrahams, *Jewish Life,* pp. 92 and 282, cites a communal decree of Metz of the year 1697 which seems to imply that women were required to veil their faces when appearing in the synagogue. See note 132, further.

[100] The same sentiment is expressed in the Talmud (Sab. 156b) about men, that covering of the head is conducive to fear of Heaven.

[101] I Cor. 11:14–15.

had no veil but in her modesty had wrapped herself in her own hair. She identified herself as the daughter of Naḳdimon b. Gorion, one of the wealthiest Jews of Jerusalem.[102] In general it may be said that there is no indication in the earlier sources that the head gear worn by women was intended to hide the woman's hair from view.[103]

In due course, however, display of hair by a woman was in itself considered a breach of modesty. The hair on her head was "her glory," as Saint Paul puts it; it was one of the means by which she attracted attention. She grew it long, anointed it with scented oil, added switches to make it longer and fuller, and wove it through with pearls and precious stones.[104] Women then, like those today, counted on their hair to give them feminine charm and draw the attention of men. In an age, therefore, when moral rigor required that men avoid looking at a woman's beauty, it was natural that the display of woman's hair to masculine gaze should be considered dangerous to public morality. A righteous woman, such as Ḳimḥit, mother of seven high priests, boasted that she had never uncovered her hair, even in her own house.[105] Among tannaim of the second century there is a view recorded in the name of R. Judah that, despite the fact that the Bible requires uncovering the head of the woman charged with adultery at the ordeal of "bitter water," this should not be done if the woman has beautiful hair, because it might undermine the morals of the young priests.[106] In the prudishness thus expressed in tannaitic times lay the germ which grew into a law in amoraic days — that the *Shema'* cannot be recited in the presence of a woman with uncovered hair, because this comprises indecent exposure.[107]

This amoraic law and the older usage of women covering their heads when going out in public are not synonymous. Here we deal not with the propriety of a woman showing her

102 Ket. 66b.

103 See Krauss, *Archäologie,* I, pp. 185–198.

104 Krauss, ibid.; Büchler, WZKM, XIX, pp. 91 ff.; Stern, Das sorgsame Bedecken des Haupthaares, *Zeitschrift für jüdische Theologie,* 1837, pp. 354 f.

105 Yoma 47a; Yer. Meg. 72a; Numb. R. end of ch. 2; Lev. R. 20,7.

106 M. Soṭah 1,5; Soṭah 8a.

107 Ber. 24a.

hair in public, for the law applies to recitation of the *Shema'* in private, where a woman is permitted to go about with uncovered head. Furthermore, it also applies to any unseemly exposure by a man, even to himself, when reading the *Shema'*. The intent of this law is therefore not one of sex morality, but of proper atmosphere and surroundings for the reading of the *Shema'*. The conclusion to be drawn is not that display of a woman's hair is immoral but that a woman, even in the privacy of her home, would not consider herself properly dressed if her hair was open to view, and would probably not receive company in that condition. Yet even according to this interpretation the inference may still be justly drawn that she certainly would not go out into the street with uncovered hair.[108] Post-talmudic authorities, however, think of this amoraic law in terms of sexual modesty. It is to them either a rule in the code of sex morality, having nothing to do with the proper atmosphere for the *Shema'* or, at the least, it is a prescription for the reading of the *Shema'* derived from the sex code.[109] In either case they see in this talmudic teaching a clearly formulated law that a woman may not show her hair in public.[110]

VI. EXCEPTION FOR VIRGINS

Our basic sources would seem to indicate that this rule of modesty — having head and hair covered in public — applied to married and unmarried women alike. The law in the Assyrian code, mentioned above, requires veiling for daughters as well as for wives.[111] The two biblical instances of women veiling themselves in the presence of men concern

[108] This means that any manner of dress improper for indoors in respect to the reading of the *Shema'* is also improper in public, but the reverse does not follow. Hence the view of *Ṭur* and *Shulḥan 'Aruk* — O. H. 75,2 — that the *Shema'* may be recited in the presence of a virgin with uncovered hair, does not contradict their ruling — E.H. 21,2 — that even a virgin may not go out in public with hair uncovered. See the discussion of the subject in *Magen Abraham* ad O. H. 75,2.

[109] Maimonides apparently considers this amoraic law as one of sex morality and having nothing to do with the reading of *Shema'*. See *Kesef Mishneh* ad Yad, Ḳeri'at Shema', 3,16. But *Ṭur* and *Shulḥan 'Aruk* (O. H. ibid.) recognize that the law deals with the reading of *Shema'*, but in a derivative way consider the exposure of hair inappropriate because it is immoral.

[110] E.H. 21,2; O.H. 75,2; see *Zohar*, Naso, ed. Wilno, 1911, p. 250.

[111] See p. 37 above and note 52.

a virgin and a widow.[112] Two motives may be ascribed to the usage of covered head and hair, as indicated in the literature, to keep from sight any display of sex charm that might arouse passion in men,[113] and to impress upon woman her subjection to the male.[114] Both these motives apply to the maiden in practically the same degree as to the married woman. Tertullian takes his example from the orientals in pleading that virgins be veiled as soon as they attain sexual consciousness.[115] The rabbis of the Talmud speak of "the proper usage for Jewish women to be veiled," [116] nowhere indicating that it was the usage only among married women. In one place only they relate that virgin brides had their heads uncovered during the wedding procession; no deduction, however, should be made that virgins went about in public with uncovered heads until the time of their marriage. In fact, referring to this marriage ceremonial of uncovering the bride's head, another rabbinic text calls it a first public appearance for the maiden.[117] In the light of these citations, it should appear that the amoraic law prohibiting exposure of a woman's hair would apply equally to married and unmarried women.

On the other hand, though not reflected in the law, the social standards during the talmudic period probably did put greater emphasis upon covering the head and hair of married women than of the unmarried. From the fact that Tertullian pleaded that virgins be restricted to covered heads like married women, it is evident that people acted and felt otherwise about the matter. We can understand their attitude. In the first place married women were more active socially than young girls, who were kept confined within the household.[118] Second, veiling the woman as a symbol of her

[112] See notes 52 and 53 above.

[113] As for example the citation in note 106 above.

[114] Such as given in I Cor. 11:7–10.

[115] *De Virg. Vel.*, 17.

[116] Gen. R. 17,13; 'Erub. 100b; Num. R. 9,13; Sifre Numb. 54; M. Ned. 3,8; Ned. 30b.

[117] Exod. R. 41,6; Tanḥ. Ki Tissa, p. 112; Yalḳuṭ, Song 4,9; D.E. 6,2, ed. Higger, p. 122.

[118] Philo, ed. Cohn, II, p. 235; II Mac. 3:19; Exod. R. 41,6, where the expression *maẓne'et et 'aẓmah* should be taken literally, that she kept indoors. This subject will receive fuller treatment later.

accepting mastery had more immediate application to the woman with a husband than to the maiden who could think only in general terms of the mastery of the male sex over the female. Third, a married woman had to take into consideration the jealousy of her husband should her appearance in public attract the attention of other men.[119] Fourth, it is admitted, at least from amoraic records, that young children did not cover their heads, neither male nor female.[120] A girl is considered sexually a child in the halakah until at least eleven years old.[121] This is about the time she becomes betrothed or married, according to ancient oriental standards. Therefore the unmarried maiden may have been excused from covering her head on the ground that she was only a child. Last, veiling the bride as part of the marriage ceremonial was a custom of great antiquity. It naturally enough turned gradually from a marriage rite into a symbol of the married state, so that "common-law marriage" among the Noahides, according to the Talmud, is considered dissolved when the husband removes the covering from his wife's head.[122]

But evidently the legal ruling of the Talmud, to have women cover their heads in public, made no exception for the unmarried girl. Maimonides, among post-talmudic teachers of the Orient, maintains the same traditional standard of modesty, prohibiting exposure of head or hair both for the married and the unmarried woman.[123] The early post-talmudic teachers in the West, among them R. Jacob Tam and R. Eliezer b. Joel Halevy, however, report that in their surroundings it was customary for unmarried girls to expose their hair. Accordingly they rule that the *Shema'* may be recited in the presence of a virgin with hair exposed.[124] To infer from this that they permitted virgins to go about in public with uncovered hair would not be justified. Probably

[119] See Westermarck, *History of Human Marriage,* I, p. 310–11.
[120] Ned. 30b.
[121] Ber. 21a; Yad, Ḳeri'at Shema' 3, 19.
[122] San. 58b.
[123] Yad, I.B. 21,17.
[124] See *Orḥot Ḥayyim,* I, Ḳeri'at Shema', 36, p. 13c; REBJH, Ber. ed. Aptovitzer, 76, p. 52. See also Asheri and Mordecai ad Ber. 24a.

that was contrary to social standards, as it was considered contrary to Jewish law. The leniency they proposed in respect to virgins concerned only the reading of the *Shema'*, and was based on the fact that *in home surroundings* girls customarily had their hair exposed and thus appeared before male members of the household as well as occasional visitors. At least the matter was so understood by the codifiers, who set down the rule that married and unmarried women may not expose their hair in public, but the *Shema'* may be recited in the presence of a virgin with uncovered head.[125]

However, this rule contained an admission of a psychological nature, that when people become accustomed to exposure of part of a woman's body, it loses its sexual suggestiveness and ceases to be considered indecent. Thus exposure of hands, feet, face, or of locks of hair where style required it, was ruled permissible.[126] If this be admitted, it renders the law easily adaptable to fashion. Until recently the law did not yield to fashion to the point of permitting married women to appear in public with uncovered head, since this prohibition was established in tannaitic times and was regarded as a biblical injunction,[127] but it did yield steadily in permitting exposure of head and hair of unmarried girls where because of general usage this was no longer considered immodest.

The leniency of the law in respect to the unmarried, as may well be expected, did not start in the oriental countries, where the veil is in common use for virgins as well as for married women. Reports from these lands, including Palestine[128] and North Africa,[129] indicate that Jewish maidens were heavily veiled when in public and most often were kept indoors. The practice of having unmarried girls appear in public unveiled belongs to the western countries.

[125] *Ṭur* and *Shulḥan 'Aruk* O. H. 75,2 and E.H. 21,2; *Lebush ha-Buz* 21,2 and *Lebush ha-Tekelet* 75,2. See note 108 above.

[126] R. Hai Gaon in *Oẓar ha-Ge'onim*, ed. Lewin, Vol. 1, sec. 2, p. 30; *Orḥot Ḥayyim*, I, p. 13c; Adret, *Novellae*, Ber. 24a; Responsa Moses Alshakar, 35; Isserles, notes, O.H. 75,2.

[127] Ket. 72a.

[128] *Ḳobeẓ 'al Yad*, IV, Berlin, 1888, p. 27.

[129] Responsa *Mayim Rabbim*, Meldola, Amsterdam, 1737, III, #28. See also Slouschz, *Travels in North Africa*, p. 204.

We have seventeenth century records of this practice in Italy, also in Constantinople, where there seemed to be some western influence. A short time later the Amsterdam rabbis faced the same social condition.[130] Laxity in the matter of veiling in general and of unmarried girls in particular also prevailed in Lorraine in the same historic period.[131] During that time we discover permission for maidens to go unveiled by East European scholars such as Joel Sirkes, Moses Lima, Samuel Phoebus, Isaac Halevy, Abraham Abele Gombiner, and others,[132] all authorities of the first rank in the halakah. Since those days the practice in the West has been general, of unmarried women wearing no head covers in public, and its legality has been generally recognized.

According to the strictest interpretation of this law only a virgin not yet betrothed is permitted to expose her hair in public. A widow or divorcee is not.[133] The betrothed maiden is a subject of controversy among the authorities, some permitting, others prohibiting, exposure of her hair.[134] The controversy extends further to the case of the girl who has had premarital relations with men; according to some she should be treated as though married, according to others she would enjoy the leniencies of the virgin.[135] However, where a girl's honor was involved, the teachers were inclined to apply the leniencies rather than the severities of the law.

VII. PERUQUE

In the sixteenth century European Jewish women discovered a substitute for the veil, the *peruque, sheitel* or wig.

130 Respons. *Mayim Rabbim,* ibid.; Abrahams, *Jewish Life,* p. 92.

131 Abrahams, ibid., p. 282. The exact meaning of the Metz enactment cited there is not clear to me. Does it mean without head cover or with exposed face? Does it imply that no veils were needed outside the synagogue, or that no veils were used by maidens even when attending synagogue services? See note 99 above.

132 Sirkes, Notes on *Ṭur* E.H. 21,2; Lima, *Ḥelkat Meḥokek,* ad E. H. ibid.; Isaac Halevy, Responsa, Neuwit, 1736, I, 9, p. 7d; Gombiner, *Magen Abraham,* ad O. H. 75,2.

133 See *Ba'er Heṭeb,* E.H. 75,2.

134 See *Mayim Rabbim,* 28, 29, 30; Responsa *Ḥavvot Ya'ir,* 196; Responsa *Shebut Ya'aḳob,* I, 103; Responsa Isaac Halevy, 9.

135 *Ḥavvot Ya'ir,* ibid.; Responsa *Panim Me'irot,* I, 35; *Piṭhe Teshubah,* E. H. 21,2.

This itself was not new to the Jews; it was the substitution for the head cover that was novel. The "switch" of false hair was known in tannaitic times and used by women to fill out their pompadours.[136] In amoraic days the technique was developed to the point of providing women with a wig of artificial hair in case their own locks were lost or shaven.[137] Various questions of law [138] are raised in connection with the wig or switch, but whether it may serve as a head-covering for women in place of the veil is not touched upon by the Talmud. It was not thought of in that light at all; it was merely one of the toilet accessories of the women of that day. The wig appeared again as an artificial, luxurious covering of the natural hair in France during the early part of the sixteenth century — a refinement of dress for men and women of the court and nobility. Fashion has a weakness for court manners, and that custom was adopted as the general style of headdress for the woman of distinction. Jewish women would not yield to their gentile sisters in the matter of distinctiveness in dress, and they too donned the wig.

For the Jewish woman, wearing a wig was a problem of Jewish law and standards of modesty. Many there were, of course, who were not troubled about the law, but law-abiding women who had formerly had their heads covered in the fashion of the nuns met this innovation of the wig with uncertainty. Some felt that the wig itself was a satisfactory head cover, others wore the wig and put a veil or shawl over it.[139] Rabbi Joshua Boaz Baruch, a European rabbi of that period, in his notes to Alfasi ruled, on the basis of talmudic sources, that the wig itself was legally satisfactory as a covering of the hair.[140] Isserles followed that ruling and included it in his notes to the Shulḥan 'Aruk.[141] However, some teachers of the period took issue. They argued that the talmudic prohibition against display of woman's hair was based on the fact that this

136 M. Sab. 6,5: *Pe'ah Nakrit.*

137 Naz. 28b.

138 Sab. 64b; San. 112a; 'Erak. 7b.

139 Notes of Isserles, O. H. 75,2.

140 *Shilṭe ha-Gibborim,* ad Alfasi, Sab. 64b; *'Ein Mishpaṭ,* glosses on Talmud, Naz. 28b.

141 Notes of Isserles, l. c.

special feminine attraction offers a lure to men or at least stimulates unholy thoughts in them. The wig, then, which simulates the woman's tresses, in no way diminishes but rather emphasizes the feminine attractiveness of the hair. Rabbi Samuel Judah Katzenellenbogen of that period sermonizes as follows: "Women must not uncover their hair nor should they ornament themselves with wigs, for it is indecent to display woman's hair, and to the eye it appears as though it were their native hair." He refers to the fact that a certain headband woven of silk and simulating human hair, called "bindi," had once come under discussion, and "our fathers and fathers' fathers of ancient days protested in their respective generations in all German communities against wearing it on the head, because its color is that of human hair." [142] An ethical teacher of a later date, summarily dismissing the pilpulistic arguments of his predecessors who permitted use of the wig, objects, among other reasons, because it is a manner of ornamentation in the style of the daughters of the gentiles, and commands his descendants never to countenance it among the women in their families.[143] Other rabbis, as late as the eighteenth century, mustered an array of halakic arguments to substantiate its prohibition.[144] Ultimately, through the ruling of Isserles, whose authority was supreme among European Jews, but more so through the pressure exerted by the women, whose legitimate claim to the right of making themselves as beautiful as possible the law always recognized, the general decision favored the wig, requiring no shawl over it.

In due time the fashion of the wig among non-Jews came to an end. Among the Jews, however, it continued not as a matter of style but as a religious necessity. Jewish women were not prepared to resume the head-cover of the nuns, yet they could not with conscience go about in public with their hair exposed. Between the shawl and the wig they chose the latter. True, it was outmoded, it was archaic; it certainly was no

[142] *Derashot,* ed. Venice, p. 8a.

[143] Meshulam Solomon Kohen, *Naḥelat Abot,* Fürth, 1811, p. 19b.

[144] Jacob Emden, *She'elat Ya'abeẓ,* I, 9; II, 7–8; *Be'er Sheba',* 17; *Keneset ha-Gedolah,* O. H. 75,3.

ornament. But it was a head covering which the law required. As mentioned, unmarried maidens were not duty-bound to cover their hair. Hence the sheitel was donned by the bride at her marriage and worn throughout her married life. But headgear contrary to fashion could not for long remain popular with the ladies. There was silent dissatisfaction and gradually open revolt. Only the extremely pious women submitted; the others defied the law and went bareheaded in public, to the dismay of the halakists.[145] Oriental Jewry had nothing to do with the problem, because they never accepted the sheitel and never rejected it — the law-abiding among them using the veil as in olden times. To European Jewry, for whom the emancipation of a century before undermined many a well-rooted religious tradition, the revolt against the wig was too much to cope with. Even among orthodox rabbis there has arisen agreement with the revolt of the women, arguing that it is contrary to the Jewish sense of fairness to impose the ugliness of the sheitel upon women of good repute, and thus deprive them of the charm of beautiful hair which God and nature have given them.[146] While the sheitel is still in use by women of excessive piety, it has generally been discarded by the Jewish women of western countries. Full and free display of a woman's hair in public is still an offense in the law, but it is accepted as normal and even proper among the Jews of western background, in Europe as well as in America and Palestine.

VIII. CUTTING THE HAIR

As though veiling the head or donning a sheitel were not enough to insure that woman's hair be hidden from view, European Jews in the last century or two demanded that married women have their hair cut or shaven. Accordingly, a special ceremony was arranged, either immediately before the nuptials or soon after,[147] of cutting the bride's hair, and ap-

[145] See *'Aruk ha-Shulḥan*, O. H. 75,7.

[146] A daring treatise on the subject in defense of the women's revolt is to be found in a commentary on *Sefer ha-Mizwot*, entitled *Yad Halevi*, by Rabbi J. B. Hurwitz, late of Hartford, Conn., published in Jerusalem, 1925, pp. 143a–b.

[147] Resp. *Ḥatam Sofer*, Y. D. 195.

propriate celebrations were held in connection therewith. This idea and ceremonial are rooted in traditions of great antiquity, partly Jewish but mainly non-Jewish, but their development as tokens of modesty as conceived by European Jewry is extremely confusing.

Among various ethnic groups in antiquity it was a common practice to cut the hair both of men and of women as a token of subjection. Such was often the treatment of the captive and the slave. It was also employed as a means of humiliation; in that spirit was the faithless wife humbled by her outraged husband. Mourners also cut their hair to dramatize their grief. Cutting of the hair was also the practice of some monastic orders, to express renunciation of the world and consecration to the Deity. By this practice, then, the ancients indicated humility, subjection, self-abasement, consecration, and self-denial. With evident logic, therefore, it was customary among various ancient groups to cut the bride's hair at marriage to express her subjection to her husband, her humility before him, her abandonment of worldly pleasures, and her consecration to the marriage bond.[148]

The Jews of antiquity originally indulged in that practice like their non-Jewish neighbors. It was employed to subject the slave and the captive, to humble the faithless wife, to give evidence of grief in time of mourning, and to express self-consecration in connection with a naziritic vow. Professor Büchler [149] offers the suggestion that this practice ran counter to the taste of the ancient Hebrews, and in many instances they substituted dishevelment of the hair in the place of cutting. This we find in connection with the unfaithful wife [150] and in the treatment of slaves and captives.[151] Remnants of the old practice are still evident in the Bible. There are records of mourners cutting their hair,[152] of the nazirite shaving his head at the end of the naziritic period,[153] and of the captive

[148] See Westermarck, *History of Human Marriage,* I, p. 509, note 3.

[149] A. Büchler, Die Schneiden des Haares, WZKM, XIX, pp. 91 f.

[150] Numb. 5:18.

[151] Is. 47:2.

[152] Job 1:20; Lev. 21:5.

[153] Numb. 6:13. Tos. Naz. 4,7 indicates that cutting the hair was part of the pious motives of the nazirites.

wife being shaved before marriage to her captor.[154] In the last case we do not know whether she was shaved as a captive, as a mourner for her father and mother, or as a bride.

In the talmudic period even that remnant of the old practice was lost. Disheveling the hair, instead of cutting it, was the accepted manner of expressing grief.[155] The captive wife ceased to exist in talmudic times; theoretically the rabbis justified cutting her hair — evidently it needed justification — as a means of alienating the captor's affection for the foreign woman.[156] The naziritic vow continued in rabbinic days, but the sacrificial rite connected therewith, and also the ceremonial of cutting the hair, ceased after destruction of the Temple.[157] Furthermore, the rabbis opposed the naziritic institution altogether,[158] and offered special opposition to naziritic vows of women, just because they would have to cut their hair.[159]

So definite and deeprooted was the social compulsion in talmudic times for women to wear long hair that St. Paul considered it a law of nature, saying: "Doth not even nature itself teach you that if a man have long hair it is a shame unto him; but if a woman have long hair it is a glory unto her?"[160] To depict the abject poverty that prevailed in the city at the time of the fall of Jerusalem, a contemporary relates: "A beggar came to the door of my father's house . . . and it was a woman who had lost her hair, and one could not tell whether she was male or female, and all she asked was one fig."[161] The great sacrifice made by the wife of Rabbi Akiba to enable him to study Torah is demonstrated in the rabbinic tale by the fact that she sold the locks of her hair to raise the needed funds.[162] These evidences would seem definite enough to prove that the average Jewish woman in talmudic times, except under extreme stress, preserved her hair and never cut

154 Deut. 21:12.
155 M. Ḳ. 24a; Yeb. 116b; Pesiḳ. Rab. ed. Friedmann, Wien, 1880, p. 131b.
156 See Sifre ad Deut. 21:10–14; Yeb. 48a–b.
157 Yad, Nezirut 2,20–22.
158 Ned. 10a.
159 Naz. 28a–b.
160 I Cor. 11:5, 14–15.
161 Lam. R. 4,11.
162 Yer. Sab. 7d.

it. It was no different in post-talmudic days. Maimonides rules that it is prohibited for a woman to cut her hair, because she thereby disguises herself as a man; and this ruling has been followed by the great codifiers.[163]

With this consistent opposition by the teachers of Judaism to a woman's shearing her tresses, it does not seem likely that the Jews ever practiced the custom of having the bride cut her hair at marriage. There is no mention of this either in the Bible or in the Talmud. The one case in the Bible, that of the captive wife, where cutting the hair of the woman is required, seems to prove that taking a free woman in marriage did not require that ceremonial. It is strange that the Jews should have adopted the practice altogether, but when they did, it meant assumption of a distinctly foreign custom. The first reference in rabbinic literature is found in the Zohar, generally dated as of Spain in the thirteenth century.[164] A century later Rabbi Samson Duran refers to a standard Jewish ceremonial of "cutting the locks, as is the custom among the (Jewish) daughters."[165] He probably refers not to Mohammedan Algeria but to Christian Spain, for we have no record of such a custom in Mohammedan lands either before or after him. Thus his testimony and that of the Zohar converge to the same country and approximately the same period.

When the custom did appear among the Jews it must have been restricted to limited territories. In the Orient apparently it was not known, as may be judged from the Maimonidean rule that a woman may not cut her hair, and from the various regulations in the code of Karo on treatment of the hair for a woman taking her ritual bath.[166] A commentator on Maimonides' code, of unknown date and origin but probably oriental, reports "hearing" that "there are some women who shave their heads," and concludes that while there is no biblical prohibition against the act, it is a violation of rabbinical law.[167] Likewise an oriental rabbi of the last century

[163] Yad, 'Akum 12,9; Y. D. 182,5.

[164] Zohar, Naso, ed. Wilno, 1911, p. 127a.

[165] Resp. TSBZ, III, 299.

[166] Y. D. 198,2, 6, 40.

[167] *Yad ha-Ḳeṭanah,* 'Akum, 56,1, quoted in *Sede Ḥemed,* letter Lamed, section 16.

reports not knowing of such a custom among the Jews of Palestine, but hearing of it while in the Crimea, and reading of it in the writings of contemporary rabbis.[168] We get the same report from travelers in Yemen, North Africa, Crimea, and the Caucasus, where we are told the custom of cutting women's hair is not known at the present time.[169]

Even in Europe this custom did not take root and seems to have been limited to specific localities. A Polish talmudist of the sixteenth century reports that in his day the majority of Jewish women did not remove their hair.[170] Leon di Modena, at the beginning of the seventeenth century, implies in his code that the custom was not known in Italy.[171] Apparently it was limited to Central and Eastern Europe, and while in the sixteenth century, as the Polish talmudist tells us, it was practiced only by a minority of the women, it seems to have grown in popularity in the course of time.

No doubt it began as a marriage ceremonial taken from foreign sources, as already mentioned. But in its development in Europe it took on the character of a standard of modesty for married women.[172] Its acceptance was favored by the fact that Jewish law prohibited married women to show their hair. The veil covered the shaven head and no one knew the difference. The introduction of the sheitel made the hair-cut even more acceptable to the women, for therewith they provided a substitute for their own hair. The law did not readily subscribe to this practice at first, but could not fail to see in it a commendable sense of modesty. Furthermore it sensed in the shorn head certain legal advantages in respect to the ritual bathing demanded of married women. The law requires that every part of the woman's body, including her hair, be immersed in the water of the ritual bath, and in order that the water may reach every part the hair may not be tied up. Thus,

[168] *Sede Ḥemed,* ibid.

[169] Jacob Sapir, *Eben Sapir,* Lyck, 1866; Joseph Tcharney, *Sefer ha-Masa'ot,* St. Petersburg, 1884; Ephraim Deinard, *Masa' Ḳrim,* Warsau, 1878; Slouschz, *Travels in North Africa,* Philadelphia, 1927.

[170] *Bet Ḥadash, Ṭur* Y. D. 184.

[171] *Shulḥan 'Aruk,* ed. Robin, Vienna, 1867, p. 93 and note.

[172] *Ḥatam Sofer,* Y. D. 195, reports that in his day it was a custom among women to cut their hair after the wedding, not before.

with long, loose hair, it was almost unavoidable that some ends would float on the surface and spoil the efficacy of the bath. Short hair was the logical solution to the problem from a legal point of view.[173] But this was not the only solution, and therefore the law, while commending the practice as a token of piety and modesty, did not make it obligatory.[174] But the super-piety of the Jewish communities in Eastern and Central Europe prior to the enlightenment was such that they went beyond the law and established the cutting of the hair as a fundamental requirement of modesty for married women. At the beginning of the nineteenth century the custom was so general that a woman who defied it was severely condemned as immodest. A German rabbi of that period writes as follows: "Since my earliest childhood I have heard, from conversations of women among themselves as well as from exhortations of rabbis in the synagogues, expressions of fervent condemnation of women who do not cut their hair at their marriage. The anathema pronounced by the rabbis at first frightened me also." [175]

The emancipation has changed it all. Very few if any women today cut their hair. If they belong to that group that still clings to the rule against showing their hair in public, they satisfy themselves with the sheitel, which is itself being borne to oblivion by the current of modern life.

IX. ORNAMENTS AND COSMETICS

The proper use of ornaments and cosmetics by women has always been a subject of concern to public morality. Early in history women had already acquired great skill in the use of artificial beautifying methods. A list of these things in Isaiah,[176] a more elaborate list in the Mishnah,[177] are testimony to the excellence of that early art. It seems that of all human interests, that of beauty for women was the foremost in the minds of ancient society, for the progress in that field out-

173 *Sede Ḥemed,* l. c.; Schneerson, *Ẓemaḥ Ẓedeḳ,* E. H. I, 139.

174 *Ẓemaḥ Ẓedeḳ,* ibid.

175 Solomon Stern, *Wissenschaft. Zeitschrift f. jüd. Theologie,* 1837, p. 354.

176 Is. 3:18–24.

177 M. Sab. 6, 1, 3, 5, 6; M. Kelim 11, 8. See Tos. Sab. 5; Tos. Kelim, subdivision B. M. 2, 3, 4, 5; Yer. Sab. 7c, 7d, 8b; M. Ḳ. 9b; Lam. R. 4, 19.

distanced any other field of human endeavor. From the point of view of social morality, it may be looked upon as an innocent matter, if the age be not one suspicious of woman or morbid on sex matters. In that case ornaments and cosmetics are accepted as proper for women of honor, so long as they be used with a sense of refinement and in moderation. When too extravagant they take on the character of coquetry and vulgarity and suggest an attitude of seeking to attract the attention of men in the manner of harlots. There may be another point of view, fostered by an age morbid on sex matters. This view is that ornaments have no other purpose but to display woman's beauty; the display of woman's beauty has no other purpose but to arouse the passions of men. Therefore ornaments are snares set by women to capture their male victims. Whether much or little, in good taste or in bad taste, ornaments or cosmetics used by women in the presence of men other than their husbands are the fulfillment of the evil designs of Satan.

The pre-exilic period maintained the earlier attitude to the artificial beautification of women. It accepted the normal amount of ornamentation as thoroughly innocent and proper. Only carried to excess does it become vulgar and offensive. Popular revulsion is conveyed in one of the prophecies of Isaiah, wherein the prophet enumerates a long list of ornaments, and that alone constitutes their condemnation. He suggests there is something sexually indecent in them, but his main objection is their implied haughtiness and display of splendor.[178] The sarcasm of Jeremiah[179] helps to emphasize the sexual aspect, but he too deals with extravagances such as employed by the harlot. There still remains room for moderate and innocent ornamentation for the pre-exilic Jewess.

Post-exilic Jewry became suspicious of such beautifying agents. The art of making metal ornaments is ascribed to Azazel, the wicked angel, who thus corrupted man.[180] That situation is analyzed in the Testament of Reuben: "Women are overcome by the spirit of fornication more than men, and

[178] See Is. 3:16–24.
[179] Jer. 4:30.
[180] I Ahikar 8:1–4.

in their heart they plot against men; and by means of their adornments they deceive first their minds, and by the glance of the eye they instill the poison, and then through the accomplished act they take them captive." [181] The early Pharisees prohibited a woman's use of ornaments or cosmetics even before her own husband during the period of her impurity, because of their power to arouse passion.[182] Later Pharisees changed this ordinance and took a more liberal attitude, but the New Testament carried on the spirit of suspicion. In his Epistle to Timothy, St. Paul urges "that women adorn themselves in modest apparel with shamefacedness and sobriety, not with braided hair or gold or pearls or costly array." [183]

The rabbis of the Talmud took a practical and realistic attitude, which placed them in a position midway between the teachers of the First Commonwealth and those of the Second. Ornamentation, they agree, is intended for display of a woman's beauty; but display of beauty is not in itself evil. It has its place in the proper relations between the sexes. It is evil only when it is employed out of place. "The sages taught: every person must give his family something of delight for the festivals . . . for the males wine, for the females colorful garments." [184] A woman gives her husband proper cause for divorce if she has taken a vow not to wear colorful garments or ornaments.[185] A fine principle of ethics in household economics is expressed by the rabbis who teach that one should live within his means, but for clothing for his family should go beyond his means.[186] An example in point is that of R. Akiba, who purchased his wife an expensive gold ornament with an engraving of Jerusalem upon it. Some women complained of the extravagance, others delighted in her reward for the years of privation suffered for her husband's sake.[187] In order that the unmarried maiden lose no chance of attracting a good marriage prospect, the law permits her to em-

[181] Test. Reuben 5:3.
[182] Sab. 64b; Yer. Giṭ. at the end.
[183] I Tim. 2. See I Pet. 3:3.
[184] Pes. 109a.
[185] Ket. 71a; Yer. Ket. 31c. See also M. Ket. 7,3.
[186] Ḥul. 84b.
[187] Ab. d. R. Nat. ch. 6; Sab. 59b; Ned. 50a.

ploy ornaments and cosmetics even in time of mourning.[188]

Yet the principle must never be lost sight of, that "ornaments are given to woman in order that she may beautify herself within her home only." [189] Therefore, "the woman who has a husband and does not ornament herself (for him) invokes a curse upon herself. . . . On the other hand, the woman who has no husband . . . and ornaments herself (to attract the attention of strange men) invokes a curse upon herself." [190] Ornaments, then, like a woman's own beauty, say the rabbis, are to be freely displayed before the male whose love the woman has a right to claim or to cultivate, but may not be displayed to gain illegitimate love. This seemed reasonable during the talmudic period, when it was considered sinful to look at a woman or even at her clothes, when the woman's standard of modesty was to remain as much as possible within her apartment. The woman's world was then her home, and there she was permitted to wear all the ornaments she possessed.

Loud ornaments and cosmetics were offensive to the sense of modesty, as they were indicative of lack of refinement. A talmudic saint, we are told, tore a flashy ornament from a woman's head, thinking it was a Jewish woman, but it turned out that she was non-Jewish and he was fined four hundred zuzim for the insult.[191] Display of expensive ornaments became offensive for another reason. It created envy in the hearts of the gentiles, who were stirred to plunder and persecution. In the Middle Ages a series of sumptuary laws were enacted by the Jewish courts and communities, restricting women and also men to utter simplicity in dress and ornamentation.[192] The pietists demanded observance of the rule on several grounds, some new, some old. It was more than

188 Ta'anit 13b; Ket. 4a.

189 Tanḥ. Va-Yishlaḥ, 5.

190 Tos. Ḳid. 1,11.

191 Ber. 20a. The geonic interpretation of the case is that it involved *sha'aṭnez* (Lewin, *Oẓar ha-Ge'onim,* Ber. ibid.) but *'Aruk* takes it to be a case of a breach of modesty because of the loudness of the ornament. See Resp. Joseph Kolon, 88.

192 Finkelstein, *Jewish Self-Government,* pp. 285, 373; Abrahams, *Jewish Life,* pp. 181, 295; Neuman, *The Jews in Spain,* Philadelphia, 1942, II, pp. 183, 207; Dubnow, *Pinḳas Medinat Liṭau,* p. 39, etc.

immodesty to them for humans to be loudly ornamented; it was corruption of the soul, yielding to the passion for possessions and to pride. It was also a stumbling block for others, who were thereby tempted to envy. It made one vain. In addition, the culprit was guilty of squandering wealth that could be employed to useful purposes, and in the case of a married woman, of spending her husband's money and impoverishing him.[193]

X. GARMENTS OF THE OPPOSITE SEX

Among the many regulations about dress included in the Jewish code of sex morality is the biblical injunction: "A woman shall not wear that which pertaineth to a man, neither shall a man put on a woman's garment; for all that do so are an abomination unto the Lord thy God."[194] The obvious meaning is a prohibition against the practice of homosexuality in any form, with which is generally associated wearing the garments of the opposite sex. Perhaps the biblical author knew of the psychosis of males desiring and imagining themselves to be females, and of females delighting in imagining themselves males, and creating the illusion by donning the garments of the opposite sex; except that he treated it not as pathology but as moral depravity. The likelihood, however, is that the abandonment of the heathens to corruption and unnatural lust, such as sodomy and the like, created a class of depraved males and females who actually played the part of the opposite sex sexually, and the biblical author condemned the practice and warned his people against it.

Philo and Josephus[195] believe that this biblical injunction particularly condemns sex disguise as a method of warfare. Women have no place in battle altogether, and for them to wear armor or to carry weapons is a vulgar disfigurement of nature's design of tenderness and beauty in the female form. For men in battle to employ disguise to appear as women is sneaky and cowardly, and degrading to the male form in-

193 Meldola, *Ḥuppat Ḥatanim,* Ẓeni'ut, Lublin, 1872, pp. 38–9. See *Orḥot Ẓaddiḳim,* Ga'avah; *Sefer Ḥasidim,* 1794.

194 Deut. 22:5.

195 Philo, *On Courage,* ed. Cohn, II, p. 324, emphasizes the virtue of courage and manliness; Josephus, *Wars,* IV, 9, 10.

tended for strength and bravery. Josephus describes this criminal military strategy adopted by the band of John of Gischala: "They . . . indulged themselves in feminine wantonness till they were satisfied therewith; while they decked their hair and put on women's garments and were besmeared with ointments; and that they might appear very comely, they had paints under their eyes and imitated not only the ornaments but also the lusts of women, and were guilty of such intolerable uncleanness that they invented unlawful pleasures of that sort. And thus did they roll themselves up and down the city as in a brothel-house and defiled it entirely with their impure actions; nay, while their faces looked like the faces of women, they killed with their right hand; and when their gait was effeminate, they presently attacked men and became warriors, and drew their swords from under their finely dyed cloaks and pierced through everybody whom they lighted on."

Maimonides believes that the Bible had in mind an ancient heathen practice of a strictly religious nature, in which masquerading in the garments of the opposite sex was required in the ritual of worship and in the orgies connected therewith. The injunction, therefore, condemns the practices on the basis of sexual immorality and with greater emphasis on the basis of idolatry.[196] The halakah has no argument with any of these interpretations, but believes that basically the Bible means to safeguard the demarcations between the sexes, that otherwise the door is opened for unnatural lusts, for illicit relations between the sexes, for lascivious imaginations, and for like immoralities. The halakah, then, not only brings this biblical law into play in the normal routine of life as against the abnormalities of homosexuality or war or idolatry, but extends its application still further. At first blush the prohibition should apply only to full disguise of man for woman or woman for man, but not to wearing an article of dress or ornament belonging to the other sex. According to the halakic interpretation, if this injunction is to preserve the distinction in dress between male and female, even minor changes of dress of one sex for the other's is prohibited.

[196] *Moreh Nebukim,* III, 37; *Sefer ha-Miẓwot,* neg. command 40. For this reason Maimonides places this law in his code in the section on idolatry.

The primary prohibition is, naturally, complete disguise, a man dressing as a woman and a woman as a man.[197] The extension of the prohibition applies as follows. Women are prohibited to bear arms in battle or even to don military equipment, such as helmet, breastplate, or sword.[198] The turban or cap is recognized as a headgear for males; it is therefore prohibited to women.[199] Women have long hair, but men short; hence it is an infringement of the law for a woman to clip her hair short.[200] Correspondingly, men may not use cosmetics, may not wear bright-colored garments nor jewelry nor ornaments, such as usually worn by women.[201] They may not shave the hair on the hidden parts of their bodies, usually a practice of women; they are prohibited the vanity of dyeing gray hairs to make them black, nor even to pluck out the gray hairs so that only the black remain.[202] Dressing in front of a mirror is also part of woman's vanity; men may not do so.[203] Just looking in a mirror is prohibited for men, except for shaving, which involves the danger of cutting oneself.[204] It is said of a famous post-talmudic authority that when he had an inflamed eye and had to glance into the mirror in order to apply medicine, he covered his entire face, leaving only an opening for the eye.[205]

Observance of these laws is supposed to be enforced by flagellation, as for most biblical laws.[206] Yet in certain respects this law is more forgiving than the others; it yields to fashion and takes into account the motive of the violation. It bends to fashion in the sense that where the mode changes the style

197 Sifre Deut. 22:5, p. 115b; Nazir 59a.

198 The view of R. Eliezer b. Jacob, Sifre and Nazir, ibid.; Josephus, *Antiq.* IV, 6, 3; Yad, 'Akum 12,10; Targum Onḳelos, Deut. 22:5.

199 Yad, ibid.

200 See note 163 above.

201 Sifre, l. c.; Targ. Jonathan, Deut. 22:5; Midrash Tannaim, Deut. 22:5, p. 143.

202 Nazir 59a; Targum Onkelos, l. c. Maimonides (Yad, l. c.) rules that the prohibition of shaving the private parts of a male body is only rabbinical. See also Sab. 94b prohibiting men to pluck grey hairs and Yad, ibid., concerning the prohibition of men dyeing their hair.

203 *Shulḥan 'Aruk,* Y. D. 182,6.

204 *TSBZ* (Samson b. Zadok), Warsau, 1902, 542–3.

205 Ibid.

206 Yad, 'Akum, 12,10.

of apparel for men and women the law changes with it. In no instance is it as true as in this case, that "custom supercedes law." What may be prohibited in one generation or in one country, may therefore be permitted in another. In a few significant instances it takes into account the motive. In the twelfth century, Jewish women on the road fearing attack from gentiles would resort to disguising themselves as men, and the leading personality of that day, R. Judah he-Ḥasid, granted permission for that infringement of the law.[207] It was also the custom in mediaeval Jewish communities to celebrate the feast of Purim by a kind of masquerade in which men would dress up as women. In a similar manner wedding feasts were celebrated with men dressing as women and women donning men's clothes. The more rigorous teachers objected [208] because the hilarity, they thought, was unwholesome from the point of view of public morality. But leading scholars permitted the practice, since the motive was entirely innocent.[209]

[207] *Sefer Ḥasidim,* 206–7.

[208] *Sefer Yere'im,* end of section on idolatry; *Sefer Ḥaredim,* neg. command 69; *Ṭore Zahab,* ad Y. D. 182,5; *Bet Ḥadash,* ad *Tur* Y. D. 182; *Ba'er Heṭeb,* O. H. 696, 13; *Be'er ha-Golah,* Y. D. 182,5.

[209] Notes of Isserles, O. H. 696,8.

CHAPTER III

SEX SEGREGATION IN PUBLIC PLACES

Most impressive in any sex code are the regulations governing social mingling of the sexes. These seem to run in a curve. In a more primitive society, where people are more natural and less sophisticated, the restrictions are generally fewer; as life becomes more complex and infringements on accepted standards of morality become more common, restrictions are added. They vary, however, with the position of woman. The more dependent she is on her father or husband or guardian, the greater the limits set on her freedom of movement and the more likely she is to be excluded from the company of men; conversely, the more independence she gains the greater is her freedom to mingle with men in innocent social contact. Since the course of human civilization has tended toward granting more independence to woman, it follows that the old restrictions against innocent social mingling with men have been gradually whittled down to a minimum. Thus the curve is formed; under primitive conditions the woman has a fair amount of freedom, then restrictions multiply with the development of more complex forms of life, then these restrictions are reduced with cultural progress wherein she attains a greater measure of independence. At the peak of the curve women may be completely secluded from the world — the male world — and kept imprisoned in their apartments; at the beginning and at the end of the curve they may enjoy complete freedom to mingle with men so long as this is innocent and arouses no suspicion. Jewish teaching on the subject of mingling of the sexes has followed the same curve, albeit without striking bottom at either end.

I. SECLUSION

Keeping women confined indoors, apart from public life, was not the ideal of the Jews of the First Commonwealth.

Many aspects of life were shared by men and women together. Under pastoral conditions they tended flocks together with the men shepherds and met with them at the watering trough, a popular assemblage place where more than one romance had its beginning.[1] In an agricultural economy they gathered the sheaves behind the reapers and sat alongside them at meal time.[2] In the building of the sanctuary the women shared the labors with the men, and joined them there for worship, for observance of festivals, and for public proclamations.[3] They sometimes were included in the political organization of the nation or tribe and sat at councils with the male leaders.[4] They participated in public celebrations as dancers and singers,[5] hailed military heroes with loud acclaim,[6] and in exceptional cases went to war together with the men.[7] At meals they sat with the men; [8] at weddings they stood out among the wedding guests with their singing and dancing; at funerals they led the procession as professional wailers.[9]

While separate apartments were maintained for the women,[10] this was not meant to segregate the sexes for moral purposes, but rather as a practical device for giving women the comfort necessary for their service in the household, to care for their minor children and to receive their husbands in privacy. Sometimes, under conditions of polygamy, it was necessary to organize the household on the basis of separate apartments for the several wives, more to be apart from one another than from the men. The institution of the harem, wherein many "secondary" wives were kept together under the guard of eunuchs, and male strangers were not readily admitted, was known to pre-exilic Jews only in limited form, as a luxury and indulgence of the rulers or nobility, a corollary of concubinage, and an obvious imitation of the splendor

[1] Gen. 29:7; 24:15; Ex. 2:16.
[2] Ruth 2:3, 7, 9, 14.
[3] Ex. 35:22; Deut. 31:12; Josh. 8:35.
[4] Judg. 4:4–8, 18; II Sam. 14:2–4; I Kings 19:2; 21:8.
[5] Ex. 15:20; Judg. 16:27; 21:21; Jer. 31:12.
[6] Judg. 11:34; I Sam. 18:6.
[7] Judg. 4:8, 18; 9:53.
[8] II Sam. 6:19.
[9] Jer. 9:16.
[10] Gen. 24:67; 31:33.

of the heathen monarchs.[11] Non-Jewish in its origin, adopted only by the ruling class, the rules of the harem certainly did not reflect the standard of sex morality of the average Jew of that period. Generally men made innocent visits to the women's apartments without restriction and without apology.[12]

In the period of the Second Commonwealth woman came to be considered a "temptress" and association with her was accounted perilous. To prevent danger to public morality, the code of that day required women to remain indoors and away from public places. The woman of easy virtue is thus described in post-exilic sections of the Bible: "Her feet abide not in her house, now she is in the streets, now in the broad places." [13] To this day the technical term among Jews for the harlot is the old Aramaic expression *nafḳat bra',* or, in abbreviated form, *nafḳah,* which means she who goes outside. In contrast, the virtuous woman is designated: "All glorious is the king's daughter (confined) within the palace." [14] In fact the distrust of woman was so great, especially of virgins, that out of sheer fear of disgrace parents or guardians would keep them imprisoned in their apartments. Sirach describes the state of mind of a father concerning his daughter: "Worry about her gives him no sleep at night; when she is young lest she be seduced, when she attains puberty lest she commit harlotry, when she attains maturity lest she remain unmarried. . . ." [15] Married women probably had more freedom, because their household duties required them sometimes to go out of their apartments, either into the market or to the temple for sacrificial rites. Young maidens had no business outside the confines of the household at all; marriageable girls, too, could afford to stay indoors, while parents sought desirable matches. Yet on special matchmaking occasions at public festivals, such as held in Jerusalem on the fifteenth of

[11] See Epstein, *Marriage Laws,* pp. 9–10, 39.

[12] Judg. 4:17. Contra W. Nowack, *Lehrbuch der hebräischen Archäologie,* I, Leipzig, 1894, p. 137; A. S. Herschberg, *Ha-Halbashah ha-'Ibrit ha-Ḳedumah,* Warsau, 1911, pp. 144–5.

[13] Prov. 7:11–12.

[14] Ps. 45:14.

[15] San. 100b; Sirach, 42:10.

'Ab and on Yom Kippur,[16] the marriageable daughter was permitted to go out, the parents being assured that proper supervision would be maintained by the authorities. Philo records the standard of seclusion for women in his day. "But taking care of the house and remaining at home are the proper duties of women; the virgins having their apartments in the center of the house within the innermost doors and the full-grown women not going beyond the vestibule and the outer courts. . . . Therefore let no woman busy herself with those things which are beyond the province of the home, but let her cultivate solitude and not be seen to be going about like a woman who walks the streets in the sight of men; except when necessary to go to the Temple . . . let her not go at noon . . . but after the people have returned home." [17]

The author of II Maccabees, describing a scene in Jerusalem of mourning and supplication under threat of the ransacking of the Temple, records the women as "girt with sackcloth under their breasts, thronging the streets," but of the young girls he says, "The virgins that were kept in ward ran together, some to the gates, others to the walls, and some looked out through the windows." [18] The seclusion of the virgin girls and the comparative seclusion of the adult women, except under stress, accounts for an enactment recorded in the Talmud and ascribed to Ezra, that "pedlars shall make their (regular) rounds in the cities in order that ornaments may be made available for the daughters of Israel." [19] That enactment was made necessary because the moral standards of the day did not permit the women to go to market themselves to buy their fineries.

In talmudic times social conditions were little different basically from those of the Second Commonwealth. People still thought it dangerous for women to be out in public. Male children were considered an unmitigated blessing; fe-

[16] M. Ta'anit 4,8; Ta'anit 31a.

[17] Philo, *de special. leg.* ed. Cohn, II, p. 235.

[18] II Mac. 3:19. See also III Mac. 1:18–19.

[19] B. B. 22a; B. Ḳ. 82a–b. The custom of pedlars visiting women's apartments later became the cause of indecencies — see Yeb. 24b at bottom. Because more seclusion of women was prevalent in the city, since the city was considered more dangerous to morals, therefore the enactment refers to the cities.

male children a blessing requiring a watchful eye.[20] A woman who went into the street unprotected invited the hazards of attack, proved by the case of Dinah, daughter of Jacob.[21] Separate quarters were maintained in the household for the women; the rabbis speak of "the house of women" [22] in the inner confines of which the virgins were kept.[23] Strangers could not visit the women's quarters; even the master had to knock on the door or otherwise make known his request for permission to enter.[24] Within their quarters the women relaxed their dignity and reserve, threw off their veils and head covers, bared their arms for washing and for spinning, and even stripped themselves naked if they wished.[25] If they desired to see the outdoor traffic they would look from their windows or from the rooftops of their apartments.[26] Much of the burden of marketing for the house fell upon the husband,[27] and most of woman's work was indoors, such as spinning, weaving, washing, cooking, baking, and grinding flour.[28] Probably when male visitors entered the house the women fled for hiding to their own apartments, a rule of etiquette observed by some oriental Jewish groups even today.[29] It was therefore said of woman in rabbinic times that "she is banished from people and confined in prison." [30]

Nevertheless, though social conditions continued on an almost even level, the rabbis of the Talmud raised the cultural level of their generation and thus softened the restrictions against a woman leaving her cloistered apartment. There was nothing wrong in her going out to attend to her needs or her duties, which increased with cultural progress, which in turn enhanced her freedom. She sometimes had to support

20 Numb. R. 11, 13. See Midrash Esther, 1. 3.

21 Gen. R. 8,14. Cf. Gen. R. 65, 3.

22 Tos. Neg. 6, 3; 'Erub. 68a.

23 Tanḥ. ed. Buber, p. 112; Ex. R. 41,6; D. E. Zuṭa 7.

24 Nid. 16b; Lev. R. 21,7. See also B. B. 99b on top.

25 B. Ḳ. 48a; Yer. Ber. 12a. Cf. Yoma 47a.

26 Gen. R. 98,23; Numb. R. 4,25.

27 Sab. 119a, etc.

28 M. Ket. 5,5.

29 *Eben Sapir,* I, ch. 27; Deinard, *Masa' Ḳrim,* p. 28. See also Slouschz, *Travels in North Africa,* p. 104.

30 'Erub. 100b. See Gen. R. 65,3.

herself by her own earnings; occasionally she even supported her husband.[31] She farmed the products of the field, dealt in realty, or traded in commodities.[32] She attended public lectures,[33] visited the house of study,[34] joined the men in public assemblies,[35] and participated in synagogue services.[36] She had her social life, attended weddings and funerals, made close friends among her neighbors, and visited her relatives; and it was not given to the husband to restrict her in these diversions unless he could show reasonable grounds. A husband who interfered with this legitimate social freedom of his wife was guilty of cruelty for which the wife could demand a divorce.[37]

The reasonable position of the rabbis on seclusion of women is recorded by the Talmud in an observation of R. Me'ir: "As there are different tastes in respect to food, so there are different attitudes to a woman. Some people, when a fly falls into their cup of wine, discard the cup and do not drink it; corresponding to this temperament is that of Papus b. Judah, who used to lock up his wife when he went out. Another man discards the fly but drinks his cup; that represents the attitude of the average man, who permits his wife to speak to her brothers and her relatives. Still another squeezes the fly out into the cup and then drinks it down. This is the way of the wicked man, who permits his wife to go about with uncovered head and exposed shoulders, knitting in the market place and bathing in the company of men."[38] The method of Papus b. Judah is considered reprehensible. A husband or society has a right to expect modest, blameless conduct from a wife, but cannot interfere with her legitimate social interests.

In practical terms this means that woman, according to rabbinic teaching, is free to go about her business unre-

31 Tos. Ket. 4, 6; Ket. 58b; Pes. 50b.
32 M. Ket. 8,1; 9,4. See Krauss, *Archäologie,* II, p. 46.
33 Lev. R. 9, 9.
34 'Erub. 53b–54a; Ab. de R. N. ch. 2.
35 Ḥag. 3a.
36 Soṭah 22a.
37 M. Ket. 7,5; Ket. 72a.
38 Tos. Soṭah 5,9; Giṭ. 90a–b.

stricted, insofar as it is legitimate business within the program of a woman's needs and interests. Going about, however, for no reasonable need, but to see or to be seen or to amuse herself or to meddle in public affairs, in other words, to be just a gadabout, is immodest and unwholesome and leads to immoralities against which the woman who remains at home is fully sheltered. The rabbis subscribe, therefore, to the principle that under normal circumstances staying home is the best policy for women. If God had meant woman to rove, He would have created her out of Adam's foot instead of from his rib.[39]

The interest of the talmudic rabbis in keeping woman at home has remained on the agadic level, as an ethical ideal, but has not been formulated into law. No precept of that nature is found in the codes. Moralists, however, have made much of it and have given it undue emphasis, because they felt if that ideal could be attained all sexual license troubling their respective generations could be eliminated. R. Eliezer of Mainz in 1357 wrote one of the famous ethical wills of mediaeval days in which he begs his daughters to "keep within their homes and not be gadabouts; neither shall they stand in the doorway to watch what is going on." [40] A more recent scholar, R. Elijah Gaon of Wilna (18th century) bequeaths the same thought to the female members of his family: "They shall not leave the house except for a very pressing need or for the sake of carrying out a holy meritorious mission. Even visits to the synagogue shall be short; it is better (for women) to pray at home. . . . It is likewise preferable for your daughter that she do not go to the synagogue, for there she sees embroidered garments and the like and is aroused to envy . . . but 'all glorious is the king's daughter within.' " [41]

One can think up special reasons for keeping women indoors — as does a mediaeval moralist: "Modesty for women in all matters (requires) that she be reserved and shall stay in her house and not leave it except under great stress. Neither is she to stand in the doorway of her house . . . for as she

[39] Gen. R. 18,2; Tanḥ. Va-yesheb, 6.
[40] Abrahams, *Ethical Wills,* II, p. 211.
[41] Ibid. II, pp. 315–16.

stands in the doorway she may possibly remind herself of something (humorous) between her and her husband and may smile. At the same time a young man may pass by, and people seeing this will say there is an immoral relation between this woman and that young man, for she waited for him in the doorway and when he passed she greeted him with a smile. If the woman has a definite need for going out of her house, she shall not go through main thoroughfares where there are crowds of people, but through the by-paths where men are not likely to walk." [42]

In some distant oriental communities the seclusion of the Jewish woman is practiced almost entirely according to this standard of the moralists,[42a] not so much in compliance with what they think to be the accepted Jewish norm but more in imitation of their non-Jewish neighbors. In the Occident the seclusion of women never had great support among the Jews, and Jewish emancipation at the beginning of the nineteenth century killed whatever chance therefor may have been left. Jewish law did not require it and the voice of the moralist was drowned in the call of modern life. The modern Jew lives in a wide-open world, together with his wife and his sister and his daughter, for all it has to offer of economic opportunity, cultural attainment, public service, entertainment, and recreation. Neither law nor ethics raises a voice of protest; the Jew is at peace with himself under the modern concept of the equality of the sexes.

II. SEGREGATION

Seclusion was never so successfully carried out as to prevent all possibility of immorality. During the greater part of Jew-

[42] *Reshit Ḥokmah,* section on Derek Ereẓ, p. 224b; *Menorat ha-Ma'or,* ed. Enelow, N. Y. 1932, IV, pp. 447–8.

[42a] See *Sefer ha-Taḳḳanot,* Eliashar, Jerusalem 1883, section 55, p. 45, citing an enactment in Jerusalem of 1757 that no Jewish woman may go in the street without a wrap called *lisar;* nor may she deal in liquor; nor — if she is younger than 50 — may she go to the (communal) bake-oven to take bread there; nor — if she is below 40 — may she go to the synagogue for afternoon or evening prayers, neither in week-days nor on the Sabbath or holidays, except on New Year and the Day of Atonement; however, on *Simḥat Torah* and certainly on *Simḥat bet ha-She'ebah* no woman may be there at all; also a woman below the age of 60 may not enter the house of a gentile for business or service whatsoever.

ish history seclusion was not even deemed desirable as a discipline. It seemed to be the wiser course to institute restrictions upon free mingling of the sexes in order to reduce to a minimum any possible moral laxity.

The first attempt at segregation of the sexes is found during the Second Commonwealth period. Sirach has a lengthy preachment on the proper conduct toward women: "With a married woman sit not at table and mingle not wine in her company lest thou incline thine heart toward her." [43] The Patriarch Reuben, penitent over his own transgression, likewise commands his children: "Do not associate with another man's wife, nor meddle with affairs of womankind." He applies the same injunction to the women, who should "not associate with men that they be pure in mind, for constant meetings, even though the ungodly deed be not wrought, are to them an irremediable disease." [44]

In talmudic times, as already mentioned, there was a generous mingling of men and women in the daily routine of life. Nevertheless when such commingling opened up avenues of immoral relations or gave ground for unbecoming suspicions, the law stepped in. Certainly giving a coin of charity to a poor woman is in itself a worthy act, yet if done privately and in an air of secrecy it is accounted an immoral act, because it casts suspicion upon the relations of donor and donee.[45] A lofty biblical law is known to us (Deut. 24:13), that a pledge taken from a poor man as security for a loan must be returned to him before nightfall. Even greater consideration is given the widow, from whom a pledge may not be accepted at all (Deut. 24:17). According to rabbinic interpretation, the greater consideration for a widow is due to the fact that the lender would be required to return the pledge at nightfall and would thus render his relations with the widow suspect. From a rich widow, therefore, a pledge may be taken, not to be returned at nightfall; and from a poor widow no pledge may be taken at all, so that there be no need to return at night. In either case, too frequent meetings

[43] Sirach 9:9; San. 100b.
[44] Test. Reuben 3:10; 6:2–3.
[45] Ḥag. 4a; Lam. R. at the end.

of the male lender and the widow are avoided out of consideration for public morality.[46] In the ordinary routine of business, a man whose vocation brought him too often in contact with women customers was looked down upon as a vulgarian, and it was believed he had an innate streak of commonness in his make up. No high public office was entrusted to him. Hence the rabbis taught it improper for a father to teach his son a trade of this kind, such as jeweler or pedlar.[47]

In mediaeval Europe, where the non-Jewish standards of morality permitted much free mingling of the sexes, the moralists made it their special task to train their people in the traditional habit of keeping the sexes apart at all times and on all occasions.[48] They gave special attention to the need of separation in public places and at public events. Even in talmudic times the priestly woman was not permitted to come to the field to fetch her share of the heave-offering, because, according to certain amoraim, it meant close hobnobbing with men, which might lead to levity. Raba, a leading Babylonian amora, attended to cases involving the presence of women ahead of the others, considering it improper for women to crowd among men in the courtroom.[49] Consonant with this talmudic sentiment, mediaeval teachers added legislation of their own to keep men and women apart in public places. Maimonides rules that court authorities must send their constables to public parks and the seashore on holidays to watch the conduct of the men and women there, and keep them from immoral relations.[50] Rabbi Joseph ibn Leb, a Turkish rabbi of the sixteenth century, reports that an oriental community had enacted a ruling that women be prohibited to walk in the park on the intermediate days of a festival for fear of moral laxity but, finding the rule too flagrantly violated, was now anxious to rescind it and was

[46] Sifre Deut. 24:17; M.B.M. 9,13; Tos. B.M. 10,10; B.M. 115a.

[47] Ḳid. 82a.

[48] *Sefer ha-Yashar,* R. Jacob Tam, Koenigsberg, 1847, p. 27b; Testament of R. Eliezer of Mainz in Abrahams, *Ethical Wills,* II, p. 211; *Sefer Ḥasidim,* 57 and 60.

[49] Tos. Pe'ah 4,4; Yeb. 99b–100a.

[50] Yad, Yom-ṭob 6,21; O. H. 529,4.

asking the rabbi's permission to do so.[51] R. Jonathan Eybeschuetz in the eighteenth century makes a special point of urging women to keep away from the parks and the river banks at such time when men promenaded there. He also set aside special days for women to visit the cemetery when men were not present in large numbers, leaving the other days for men only.[52]

Under the principle of segregation, the law and its administrators had to deal with the problem of separation of the sexes at specific community functions, either of a strictly religious or of a semi-religious nature or even of a purely social character, in which the women participated as members of the community. These problems arose in connection with the synagogue, the school, weddings, funerals, public celebrations, socials, musicals, dances, and the like.

III. SEGREGATION IN THE SYNAGOGUE OR TEMPLE

There was apparently no separation of the sexes at worship in the First Temple and no portion is recorded as set aside for women especially. There was one in the design of the Second Temple known as *Ezrat Nashim,* the women's court. It is difficult to say whether this enclosure was in the original design of the Second Temple or was added later — perhaps by Herod — and, if it did form part of the original structure, when it acquired the name *Ezrat Nashim.* Certain, however, it is that toward the latter part of the Second Commonwealth there was an outer court on the eastern side of the Temple, inferior in sanctity to the more western sections, which was the assembly place for women designated as the "women's court." Nevertheless, it is equally certain that neither in practice nor in theory was this meant as a means of segregating the men from the women. In the first place, it was used for general public worship for both men and women. Second, it was many times as large as the section designated for male Israelites and could not possibly have been reserved for women only. Third, a number of "chambers" for temple

[51] Responsa of R. Joseph b. Leb, IV, 4.

[52] *Ya'arot Debash,* ed. Warsau, 1889, I, 12, p. 64a, and I, 14, p. 68d. See Bettan, *Studies in Jewish Preaching,* Cincinnati, 1939, pp. 339–40. This ruling finds its parallel in *Pinkas Medinat Liṭau,* 1023, p. 272.

functionaries opened out to this court, and the most popular entrance for males to the section reserved for Israelites and Levites was by way of the eastern gate leading through the women's court.

The fact of the matter is that this designation of "women's court" was not legal in character and was probably not adopted by any authoritative legal body, but was the appellation the general public gave the outer court or the court of general assembly in the Temple. This came about by the simple fact that women, maintaining a certain reserve, did not intrude into the innermost parts of the sanctuary but remained to the rear, in the large public court. The male Israelites remained there too, except when participating in some sacrificial rite. When it was necessary for a woman to take part in such a ceremonial — a rare event — she advanced to the inner part of the Temple.[53] By no stretch of the imagination could this arrangement in the Temple at Jerusalem be considered an attempt at segregating women from men at public worship.[54]

For ordinary worship and sacrificial rites the teachers were satisfied that mingling of the sexes would cause no immorality. But they were disturbed by the levity of men and women crowding in the Temple to witness the festal celebration of drawing water on the Succot holiday. The festival was joyous to the point of hilarity and, in the minds of the teachers, created temptations for sexual improprieties among less scrupulous men and women. Here for the first time we have a definite, deliberate attempt at separating men from women in the Temple on grounds of morality. At first, we are told, the men were outside and the women inside the women's court; then the order was changed, men inside and women outside. But still there was levity. Thereupon a balcony was built in the court, and the women were sent there to watch the men at the celebration.[55]

[53] M. Kelim 1,8. See Tosafot, Ḳid. 52b, s. v. *ve-ki.*

[54] In due time, of course, less opportunity was given to women to penetrate the inner part of the sanctuary. They were thus exempted from resting their hands on the sacrifice, and those who continued the older usage of having women also perform this rite, would carry the animal into the women's court so as not to make it necessary for them to go up to the altar. See Ḥag. 16b.

[55] Tos. Sukkah 4,1; Suk. 51b.

During this period, the closing days of the Second Commonwealth, we hear of no further extension of the separation of men and women at worship except in sectarian practice. Philo gives a description of the routine of life among the Therapeutae, a Jewish sect of his day that settled in the neighborhood of Alexandria. This sect comprised both men and women, and worship was the foremost rite engaging their attention; the women, therefore, were of necessity part of the daily prayer assemblies. Because of this situation, Philo reports, their assembly house was constructed in a "twofold circuit, being separated partly into the apartment for the men, and partly into a chamber for the women. . . . And the wall which is between the houses rises from the ground three or four cubits upward, like a battlement." [56] For a time, it appears also, the Christian Church in the Orient adopted the practice of separating men from women at worship by a structural partition, and this is so recorded by Chrysostomus.[57] But neither the Therapeutae nor the Christians adopted this practice from Judaism. Though the separation of the sexes at the festival of the drawing of water may have served as an example, it could not have meant to them a general segregation at worship.

Something fundamental about the position of woman in the ritualist aspect of Judaism must be grasped in connection with this problem. The Jewish woman belonged to the Jewish community, her life was governed by Jewish law, she was present as often as she wished at public religious functions, she prayed if she so desired or studied Torah if so inclined. But she was not part of the cult either as functionary or administrator or as member of the cult fellowship. Setting aside a special place for her at ritual service implies at the least giving her part in the ritual as a member of the fellowship. That was possible for the Therapeutae or Christians; it was not possible for Jews. The Temple had a woman's court in the sense that it had a public place for those who had no

[56] Philo, *On a Contemplative Life,* ed. Yonge, London, 1855, IV, p. 8. See J. E. "Therapeutae."

[57] Quoted by Leopold Löw in MGWJ, 1884, p. 459. See also S. Zeitlin, First Canonization of Hebrew Liturgy, *Jewish Quarterly Review,* Vol. 38 (1947–8), p. 307.

share in the ritual, where women assembled as part of the public. The synagogue in those days had no women's compartment, like many oriental synagogues today, simply because no woman was there as one of the religious fellowship but as a visitor, as a guest, who came irregularly. There was no need to provide a special place for her. She remained in the entrance hall or sat silently and reservedly in the rear, following the prayers or listening to the discourse of the teacher. There was no demand for a wall of separation between her and the male congregation, except when the synagogue, as was the case in the Temple, became the locus of a general public assembly where women came as of right and in large numbers.

This pattern was followed through the entire talmudic and probably also geonic periods. No distinct section in the synagogue for women is mentioned in the literature of that era, but again and again evidences are found of women coming to the synagogue at will without restriction. They brought their young children there,[58] stayed for prayer,[59] lingered for the teacher's lecture,[60] and, were it not for the implied reflection on the ignorance of the male congregation, they might even ascend the pulpit and read the scriptural portion before the worshipers.[61] Apparently women came and went in and out of the synagogue undisturbed, without any policy of segregation being suggested. However, holiday seasons, when the synagogues were crowded and the mood of levity was felt among the people, gave the Babylonian amoraim some concern.[62] Here too, as in all public gatherings, the amoraim, out of regard for public morality, instituted marks of separation between the sexes. Abaye set up rows of pottery, Raba rows of sticks, to keep both sections fenced off.[63] Even so there was no permanent wall between the sexes, nor were lines of demarcation used except when the service took on the character of a general public assembly.

A separate section for women came into use in post-geonic time. This indicated two facts — that women had become

[58] Ber. 17a.
[59] Soṭah 22a.
[60] Lev. R. 9,9.
[61] Meg. 23a.
[62] Ḳid. 81a.
[63] Ḳid. ibid.

more regular in attendance at services, and that they were being reckoned with as part of the religious community. At first, as indicated by Rabbi Solomon b. Adret at the end of the thirteenth century in Spain, a certain part of the synagogue was set aside for women, and men were not allowed there except when the women were away. He wrote that he was not acquainted with the practice from his own experience.[64] In his time the second stage had already been attained, when a women's section was built in the synagogue, reserved for women worshipers although used by men on special occasions when the women were not there.[65] Both in the men's section and in the women's seats were deeded to and owned by the male and female occupants respectively for life, and inherited by their children after them.

In Germany too the earlier custom was to have no special section for women in the synagogue, but when larger gatherings assembled to hear the Sabbath discourse by the rabbi a curtain was stretched across to divide the men from the women.[66] This practice comes to us from records of the beginning of the thirteenth century. At the end of the century we already find references to sections designated as "the women's synagogue." [67] Its exact structure and the manner in which it was separated from the men's section are not always clear, and probably were not uniform in all lands adopting the practice, but the principle of segregation seems to have spread from that time on to all European lands, and to have been adopted also by the larger synagogues in the Orient. The women's gallery is an architectural convenience for carrying out the principle of segregation, and a special sense of modesty which regards looking at a woman as improper is responsible for the curtains stretched across the railing of the gallery, to hide women worshipers from the view of the men.

People are generally most tenacious of traditions connected with public ceremonials, and in particular with such as are connected with the synagogue. Hence, though originally the

[64] Adret, Responsa, II, 182.

[65] Adret, Responsa, VI, 7. See Neuman, *The Jews in Spain,* II, p. 149.

[66] *Mordecai,* Sab. 311; *Mahril,* ed. Warsau, 1878, p. 30a.

[67] *Hagahot Maimuniyot* ad Yad, Shebitat 'Assor, at the end; *Mahril,* p. 46b. See Löw, MGWJ, 1884, pp. 462–4.

synagogue afforded more freedom for the mingling of the sexes than was permitted in secular assemblies, in our century. on the contrary, the synagogue retains the restrictions against the free mingling of men and women, while all other restrictions have broken down in Jewish social life. For the most part Jews today do not challenge the validity of separating men from the women in the synagogue. Even the moderate Reformers of Central Europe to this day retain the women's gallery in their temples. The extremists among Reform Jews were the first to break down the wall of separation. The conservatives in America tend to follow that policy. The orthodox in other countries are at peace with the old tradition, but in America they find preservation of the women's gallery a most difficult task, because it seems to run counter to the taste of the women and to the trend in American Jewry.

IV. SEGREGATION IN SCHOOLS

Segregation of males and females in the schools has approximately the same history as their separation in the synagogue. Indeed, house of worship and house of study are so nearly identical in Judaism that one may take for granted that the story of one institution suffices for the other. Yet this is not quite correct. Religious education was more than attendance at the synagogue and listening to Torah readings and rabbinic discourses. Always close to the synagogue, still it was an independent activity either of the household or the community, and as such it had to maintain its own policy in respect to the mingling of the sexes.

It should be kept in mind that formal instruction in schools and academies was a later device. Education was originally carried on by two methods, home instruction with parent as teacher and child as pupil, and public instruction by means of readings and exhortations at public assemblies. In home instruction, it would seem, there never was a problem of segregation of the sexes. Surely brothers and sisters under the supervision of their parents did not have to be kept apart on moral grounds. If they were separated it was because the subject matter and the level of instruction were not the same for boys and for girls.

Home instruction continued as an educational method throughout the ages. For boys it represented the preliminary stage of education until — as in its later development — they were enrolled in schools. For girls, until a much later date, education began and ended at home under the training of parents. Furthermore, while the duty of parents to teach their sons Torah is of primary importance, the halakah decides that parents have no obligation to teach their daughters.[68] It is even a matter of controversy among tannaim whether it is at all desirable to teach a daughter Torah,[69] and the final halakah renders a compromise decision that it is profitable for women to know Scripture but it is ill advised to teach them the Oral Law.[70] These rules indicate that even the home instruction the girl received was not on the highest level. Probably it consisted of practical guidance in religious observance and transmission of the beliefs and loyalties that Jewish women were expected to maintain. The level of culture among women in general in antiquity was not very high. The Jewish woman was probably no outstanding exception. A tradition has it that education had at one time attained so high a level that from Dan to Beer-sheba there was no man or woman who was not versed in the laws of purity.[71] Perhaps the kind of home instruction the girl received was sufficient to train her in the purity laws, but it may be doubted whether she knew much more than that. Of course, we have exceptions, such as Beruriah the wife of R. Me'ir,[72] or Yalta the wife of R. Naḥman.[73] Among the exceptional women were also those capable of reading the scriptural lesson in the synagogue[74] or of being employed as teachers for children.[75] Probably like Beruriah and Yalta, they were blessed with fathers who were scholars of the first magnitude and who took the education of their daughters seriously.

68 Ḳid. 30a.
69 M. Soṭah 3,4.
70 Yad, Talmud Torah 1,13.
71 San. 94b.
72 'Erub. 53b; Pes. 62b; Tos. Kelim 1,6.
73 Ber. 51b.
74 Meg. 23a.
75 M. Ḳid. 4,13; Ḥag. 4b.

Supplementing home instruction and probably more broadening in effect was the second method, that of public assemblies for reading and discourse. There the problem of segregation had more meaning. However, until the fourth century C.E. there seems to have been no interference with the women's attendance at these assemblies together with the men. Possibly the visits people made on Sabbaths and New Moons to the prophets were for the purpose of instruction, and women freely joined the throng.[76] One feels inclined also to think of the women prophets as lecturing and exhorting before public assemblies. The Bible commands that in the sabbatical year at the festival of Succot a general public assembly be held for the reading of the Torah, to include both men and women.[77] In fact the Babylonian Talmud records a tradition that these public readings were held in the women's court in the Temple,[78] a tradition that is not illogical, since that was the only public court in the Temple.

The liberal attitude toward the mingling of men and women at public gatherings for instruction in Temple days, continued after the destruction in respect to houses of study. In rabbinic literature we find numerous examples of visits by women to the house of study, in a matter-of-fact manner. A few may be mentioned. The mother of R. Joshua, in the early part of the second century, carried her babe and crib about in the houses of study so as to saturate him in infancy with the atmosphere of Torah.[79] A certain woman was so absorbed in R. Me'ir's discourses on Friday evenings that one evening she remained in the house of study too late to please her husband.[80] It would seem that the above-mentioned Beruriah, R. Me'ir's wife, had a hand in the management of the academy, for she scolded a pupil for not singing out his lesson, maintaining that a chant was helpful to the memory.[81] Of a certain widow who mourned the premature

[76] II Kings 4:23.
[77] Deut. 31:12.
[78] M. Soṭah 7,8; Soṭah 41b; Yer. Soṭah 22a.
[79] Yer. Yeb. 3a.
[80] Lev. R. 9,9.
[81] 'Erub. 53b.

death of her husband it is told that she carried her complaint against God from one house of study to another. The scholars had no answer, but Elijah revealed the fact that though the man was reputed to be a saint, he had been guilty of one sin which justified his death.[82] Of another widow it is told that she came every morning to the house of study presided over by R. Johanan, and was rewarded not only for her regular attendance but also for the distance she had to cover to reach the academy.[83] In a text of the early geonic period we are told it was a widespread custom among Jews to have young girls in attendance at public gatherings for religious discourses.[84]

In all these cases there is not the slightest suggestion that there was segregation of the sexes in the house of study. Yet it is logical to assume that the lines of demarcation set up by the Babylonian amoraim between men and women at crowded public gatherings, as mentioned above, were also employed at public lectures when there was congestion in the lecture hall.[85] These, however, were set up as safeguards only in unusual cases; in the normal situation no separation of any kind was used, because women did not come to the house of study in large numbers and those who did come made themselves at home in the rear or in a corner of the academy, without interfering with the students or being interfered with. The problem of segregation in the house of study did not arise until girls became regular pupils in the schools, or until their position as teachers was contemplated as a possibility. This happened under the third system of education, that of formal schooling, which we must now consider.

Formal schooling in academies or in elementary schools among the Jews has a long history. Discipleship existed even in the time of Moses and the academies of advanced studies thus developed. From a remark by the Men of the Great Synagogue, "Raise up many disciples," [86] it may be judged that in the early days of the Second Commonwealth the

[82] Ab. de R. N. ch. 2; Sab. 13a.
[83] Soṭah 22a.
[84] Soferim 18,8, ed. Higger, p. 320.
[85] Ḳid. 81a. See Rashi, s. v. *gulfe*.
[86] Abot 1,1.

academy was already in existence. Elementary educational institutions were established by Ezra, according to a talmudic text; but the authenticity of the text is doubtful.[87] More reliable is an amoraic tradition that Joshua b. Gamala (65 C.E.) is the father of the Jewish public school system.[88] However, scholars are inclined to believe that it is not Joshua b. Gamala but Joshua b. Peraḥya (130 B.C.E.) who should be recorded as organizer of the Jewish elementary school system.[89] Concerning this formal type of religious education either in school or academy, we have reason to believe that it was meant exclusively for male pupils and no girls were enrolled. The problem of coeducation as a concern of public morality did not arise, therefore, during the entire talmudic period.[90] Even the problem of male teachers for girls' classes is not raised in the Talmud, because there were no girls' classes. Only the question of female teachers for boys is dealt with. Some women, through the system of home instruction, attained sufficient knowledge to teach in elementary religious schools and sought to make teaching their profession. The tannaim did not permit this, because they thought it contrary to public morality.[91] The amoraim apparently did not see any objection to the mingling of sexes as between teacher and pupil, and explained the tannaitic prohibition on the ground that the woman teacher might find herself in a situation of unchaperoned companionship with a pupil's father.[92]

In the time of Maimonides we already discover formal schooling for Jewish girls in private schools. One of his responsa tells of a blind male teacher for girls, before whom the little pupils did not hesitate to remove their veils. Blindness, of course, proved an advantage, but there is no implication that it would otherwise be prohibited for him to teach girls. We also learn that there were women teachers for girls, but men were preferred because of their superior

[87] B. B. 21b. See Tosafot B. B. 22a on top.
[88] B. B. 21a.
[89] See Krauss, *Archäologie,* III, p. 210 and note 10.
[90] Krauss, ibid. p. 239.
[91] M. Ḳid. 4,13.
[92] Ḳid. 81a.

knowledge.[93] Throughout the ages no objection was raised to male instructors for a feminine class. But certain conditions were imposed, as we shall see in some of the community ordinances. R. Judah he-Ḥasid considers instruction for a girl obligatory upon the parents — of course, only elementary religious instruction — and agrees that a male teacher is perfectly satisfactory, provided, however, he be married. Otherwise, even private lessons in the girl's home under supervision of parents are prohibited.[94]

The tannaim, we have seen, objected to a woman teacher for boys. In and for itself the amoraim saw no objection thereto, except as it might open the way for intimacies between the female teacher and the pupils' fathers. Though the halakah as formulated in the codes prohibits the employment of female teachers on the basis of the amoraic view,[95] Jewish communities of the Middle Ages did not seem to take this prohibition seriously, probably because they had sufficient safety measures to insure against immorality. We have an account of the daughter of Samuel b. 'Ali of Bagdad at the end of the twelfth century having assisted her father in teaching the students Bible, giving her lectures through a window in the house to the students assembled outside so that she could not be seen by them.[96] Another woman, daughter of R. Eliezer of Worms of the same period, is said to have held public discourses on the Sabbath.[97] Maimonides reports a woman who made her living as a school teacher for boys.[98] Yet another woman at the end of the fifteenth century maintained a school for boys, and gave her lectures from behind a curtain.[99] From the facts that only rare records of women teachers have come down to us, that theoretical halakah has little to say on the subject, and that community ordinances practically never refer to it, we must conclude that on the

[93] Maimonides, Responsa, 384, ed. Freimann, Jerusalem, 1934.

[94] *Sefer Ḥasidim,* 835.

[95] Yad, I. B. 22,13; *Ṭur* E. H. 22 at the end. According to *Perisha, Ṭur,* ibid., a woman may not even teach girls.

[96] *Travels of R. Petaḥya,* ed. Grünhut, p. 10. See Mann, *Texts and Studies,* Cincinnati, 1931, I, p. 219, note 42; Abrahams, *Jewish Life,* p. 343.

[97] Abrahams, ibid.

[98] Responsa, 182.

[99] Kayserling, *Die jüdische Frauen,* Leipzig, 1879, p. 138. See Abrahams, ibid.

whole it was not usual for women to be school teachers, but that the condition was determined by the social and cultural position of women, not by the code of sex morality.

As liberal as has been the Jewish attitude to male teachers for girls and female teachers for boys, so opposed has been the attitude towards coeducation. There is no mention in the literature of the early Middle Ages of coeducational classes, and the assumption must be that such did not exist and were never thought of by the teachers. As late as the seventeenth century, when we first meet the problem, the possibility of mixing sexes in one class appears unthinkable. For we read among the community enactments in the city of Nikolsburg, toward the end of the seventeenth century, that a teacher conducting the instruction of five girls may not have a Bible class for boys, and if he teaches boys Talmud he may not teach even one girl. This restriction applies even if the girl or girls come there to be taught handicrafts by the teacher's wife, and even if they take their instruction in a separate room, unless it be in a different part of the building.[100]

In the last century, the education of girls, both religious and secular, has taken on larger proportions. The pious Jewish communities long preserved the tradition of placing the sexes in separate schools, and also resisted employing women teachers for boys' schools. In the Orient the tendency to this day is to permit no scholastic mixing of the sexes. The influence of western culture, however, has kept weakening the Jewish tradition of segregation in western Jewish communities, so that in Europe and America today Jewish religious schools, especially in elementary departments, are on the whole coeducational and, of course, there is no prescription as to whether the teacher shall be male or female, except for personal bias on the part of school boards.

V. SEGREGATION AT WEDDINGS AND FUNERALS

The mingling of men and women at weddings and funerals closely followed the course of their association at worship and at public discourses. Women were part of the Jewish public,

100 Güdemann, *Quellenschriften zur Geschichte des Unterrichts,* Berlin, 1891, pp. 270 and 281.

and weddings and funerals were public functions. Hence they were there as of right. In fact, they were singers and dancers at weddings and wailing choruses at funerals. It was considered unsocial for a woman to be absent from a wedding or a funeral in the neighborhood.[101] We know of no official restriction against mingling at these functions, even during the prudish period of the Second Commonwealth. In the Temple and in the academy, so at the marriage feast or in the house of mourning, women took their place beside the men and no mark of separation was required. The probabilities are that the men assembled in one corner and the women in another, not because of any legal requirement but out of natural modesty and shyness. This condition continued to the last days of the tannaitic period.

A late tannaitic text reports an established custom of having the women ahead of the coffin in the funeral procession and the men in the rear, or vice versa.[102] Likewise, in another late tannaitic text reference is made to the custom of men assembling within the house and women outside, or vice versa, which probably refers to feasts, particularly wedding feasts.[103] In amoraic days this separation was already conscious and legal, with lines of demarcation.[104] In the Orient the separation probably continued unchallenged, but in Europe the social standards of the general population impelled Jews also to permit free mingling at wedding feasts. Rabbi Judah he-Ḥasid, seeking a halt to this practice, ruled that the blessing at wedding feasts for the joy of the occasion not be recited if men and women were together.[105] R. Mordecai Yaffa, rabbi in Prague at the beginning of the seventeenth century, records that people ignored the stricture of R. Judah, explaining, "that mingling of men and women is usual now and therefore arouses no uncleanness of thought."[106] His

[101] M. Ket. 7,5.

[102] San. 20a.

[103] Ḳid. 81a.

[104] Ibid. See Rashi, s. v. *gulfe.* See also Suk. 52a on top, showing the consciousness on the part of early amoraim of the problem of the separation of sexes at funerals.

[105] *Sefer Ḥasidim,* 1176.

[106] *Lebush ha-Hod,* at the end, section on Minhagim, 36.

contemporary, R. Joel Sirkes, rabbi in Cracow, finds that at the main wedding feast, where the guests are many, the women are separated from the men, but at the minor feast held on the second night of the wedding, when the guests are few, men and women sit together.[107] A preacher of the eighteenth century, however, accepts no excuses and yields to no compromise, but warns his people most sternly that no mingling of the sexes may be permitted at any joyous occasion — "The serpent dances in their midst." [108]

VI. FEASTS AND PUBLIC CELEBRATIONS

Most family feasts in olden days had both a religious and a semi-public character, but the women could not be excluded from them, both because they belonged to the family circle, be it large or small, and because religious observance could not be denied them. The Bible, therefore, assumes the presence of women at such occasions without restriction.[109] A more public and religious feast was Passover, when several families joined to eat the pascal lamb. Nevertheless, this too was of the nature of a family gathering, and women sat freely at the festive table with the males.[110] Only one reservation was made — if the women in the family were not at the family table, they could not have a feast of their own with the male slaves, for that might lead to improper intimacies.[111] The feast over the pascal lamb came to an end with the destruction of the Temple, but the Passover feast continued, and at no time was any attempt made to separate the men from the women at this celebration.[112]

Other religious festivities of a public nature were conducted by the Jews in connection with the feast of Purim, at the birth or circumcision of a male child, at the redemption of the first-born, and (in post-talmudic days) at *bar-*

[107] *Bet Ḥadash,* E. H. 62, 12.
[108] *Ya'arot Debash,* p. 97a.
[109] See, for example, I Sam. 1:45; Job 1:4.
[110] M. Pes. 7,13; 8,1.
[111] Pes. 91a.
[112] Pes. 116a; Yad, Ḥameẓ u-Maẓah, 7,3; O. H. 473,7.

miẓwah, or confirmation.[113] From talmudic sources one feels that these festivities were meant for men only. Where women joined in the celebration, the rule of the Babylonian amoraim to keep them separate from the men [114] was probably observed. Personal observation at a *bar-miẓwah* of a sephardic family in Jerusalem and of a circumcision in Damascus showed the men assembled in one room and the women in another. This probably was the general rule among oriental Jews everywhere. In western lands the practice of separating men from women at such public religious functions was urged by moralists, even as they insisted on such separation at weddings. But the tendency among the masses was to resist segregation because non-Jewish European standards did not favor it. Naturally, in the long run the moralists lost out, and free mingling of men and women on such occasions in European lands is the rule rather than the exception.

Public festivities of a strictly social nature were also held among the Jews, but the sexes celebrated by themselves. To this category belongs the virgins' dancing festival outside Shiloh, where the youth of Benjamin captured wives for themselves.[115] When in the Second Commonwealth this festival was duplicated by the assemblage of youths and maidens in the vineyards outside Jerusalem, some progress was evident in that young men participated in the celebration; nevertheless, the men and the women were arranged in separate groups, close enough only to hear one another's voices.[116] When the festival was discontinued at the end of the Second Commonwealth, it is a fair guess that this was because the moralists of that day looked with suspicion even on that form of mingling. This standard of morality was evidently observed even in the Persian court of Ahasuerus, where men were feasted by the king, and the women by the queen in her own apartments.[117] It was not observed, however, by Belshazzar, who invited his consorts and concubines to the

[113] B. Ḳ. 80a. See also Tosafot at bottom. B. B. 60b; Meg. 7b; Yer. Ḥag. 77b; *Yam Shel Shlomo,* B. Ḳ. 7,37.

[114] Ḳid. 81a.

[115] Judg. 21:21.

[116] M. Ta'anit 4,8; Ta'anit 31a.

[117] Esther 1:9, 12.

feast,[118] nor by Herod, who took great pride in his daughter's dancing before the assembled guests.[119] It was maintained by the common people, who conducted their social festivities at the proper seasons, or irregularly on special occasions, where men celebrated with men, and women with women.[119a] Social affairs for men and women together, as we have them now, were never known in the old Orient; these are distinctly European inventions. The oriental standard, also close to the hearts of the European Jewish moralists, was for men and women never to conduct joint social functions; and when they gathered at communal religious or semi-religious celebrations, to keep distinctly apart and distant from one another.

VII. SONG AND DANCE

Public functions in antiquity were celebrated with song and dance, and women were prominent in the performances. They formed part of the religious choir, to sing the praises of God; [120] they joined in song and dance to pay tribute to a national hero; [121] they furnished the music for the celebration of seasonal public festivals; [122] they entertained bride and groom and guests at wedding feasts; [123] and they led funeral processions to the tune of their dirges.[124] These musical performances before a male audience were considered perfectly proper for women, even in the days of the Second Commonwealth. Moreover, no objection was raised to the mixing of sexes in choral or orchestral groups.[125]

The Bible also mentions professional male and female musicians maintained by the luxury-loving rich as entertainers.[126] These people would hold lavish banquets at their homes, where hilarity ran high together with winebibbing

118 Dan. 5:2.
119 Mark 6:22.
119a *Tarbiz*, I, 1, p. 97; *Pardes*, p. 196; *Ozar ha-Ge'onim*, Suk. pp. 69–70.
120 Exod. 15:20; Ps. 68:26.
121 Judg. 11:34; I Sam. 18:6–7.
122 Jer. 31:4, 13.
123 Ps. 45:15.
124 II Chron. 35:25.
125 Ps. 68:26.
126 II Sam. 19:36; Eccl. 2:8; Ezra 2:65.

and professional musical entertainment. Sirach fulsomely praises the elegance of these affairs. "As a signet stone of carnelian on a necklace of gold, is a concert of song at a banquet of wine; as settings of fine gold and a seal of carbuncle, is the sound of music with the pleasance of wine." [127] Distinguished from the musical performances of the harlot,[128] these home parties were considered decent even though there were females among the entertainers.[129]

At the end of the Second Commonwealth popular objection rose against these hilarities. A mishnah reads: "With the dissolution of the Sanhedrin an end came to music at drinking feasts." [130] It is clear enough that the mishnah did not consider the immorality of mixed choirs or orchestras, for it records the objection even to male music at these functions. Two possible motives can be read into this interdiction. One, hilarity may have become objectionable to Jewish taste of that period as leading to loose morals, and a few generations later R. Akiba expressed that sentiment in the statement: "Merriment and levity lead a man to lewdness." [131] More, the calamity that befell Israel saddened the people to such an extent that, like mourners, they denied themselves the luxury of music at their banquets — which sentiment, too, is abundantly expressed by later talmudists.[132]

[127] Sirach 32 (35):5–6.

[128] Is. 23:15–16; Ez. 33:32.

[129] It should be remarked that women's participation in public festivals, religious or communal, can be accounted for even for the period of the Second Commonwealth. See p. 80 above. But permission of women singers for the amusement of men can hardly be understood, unless these female singers were slaves who were considered below the level of sex morality. See note 19 of previous chapter.

[130] M. Soṭah 9,11; Tos. Soṭah 15,7. Halevy (*Dorot ha-Rishonim,* I, 3, p. 62 f.) maintains that this mishnah refers to the year 57 C. E., but Hoffmann (*Jahrbuch der jüdisch. liter. Gesellschaft,* V, 1907, p. 225 f.) argues against it. See Boaz Cohen, Responsum of Maimonides Concerning Music, in *The Jewish Music Journal,* II, 2, note 1. Commentators — Me'iri, Soṭah 48a — are inclined to render *bet ha-mishta'ot,* the wedding feast. This interpretation is not accepted by the halakah, as we shall see later, and is disproven by the fact that song and music at weddings did continue later as seen by M. B. M. 6,1, etc. It seems evident that secular drinking parties are referred to in this mishnah.

[131] Abot 3, 17.

[132] B. B. 60b. The former motive is given by R. Ḥisda and the latter by R. Huna in Yer. Soṭah 24b.

In the further development of this restriction against song both motives are discernible, but it may also be noted that the motive of moderation in luxury was stressed in Palestine during the amoraic period, while in Babylonia the motive of mourning for Zion was more prominent. In Palestine, after destruction of the Temple, a tendency toward asceticism developed which displeased the rabbis.[133] Their very attempt at stemming that trend rendered the rabbis cautious in their prohibitions. The Palestinian amoraim, therefore, offered no objection to song as such, but only to instrumental music in connection with drinking of wine at feasts; and based their objection on the verses in Isaiah (5:11–12): "Woe unto them that rise up early in the morning that they may follow strong drink; that tarry late into the night till wine inflame them. And the harp and the psaltery, the tabret and the pipe, and wine in their feasts."[134] Evidently the moral aspect alone is here revealed. In Babylonia, on the other hand, the rabbis had no cause to fear the danger of asceticism if mourning after Zion were freely allowed, because they were geographically too far removed from the scene of the calamity and because they lived under more favorable economic conditions than the Jews of Palestine. Therefore they restricted music expressly on the basis of the biblical verse (Hosea 9:1): "Rejoice not, O Israel, unto exaltation, like the peoples," with emphasis on the sentiment of mourning. Hence, their prohibition included vocal as well as instrumental music, and also song or music as private entertainment even where there was no drinking of wine.[135]

The restrictions of the Babylonian amoraim against music went beyond reasonable limits. Rab invoked a curse upon the "ear that hears music"; Raba predicted that destruction would overtake any house wherein music was played. Even the singing of laborers at their work was scrutinized; that of boatmen and ploughmen was permitted as stimulants to greater efficiency in their work, but that of the tanners was

[133] B. B. ibid.

[134] Soṭah 48a.

[135] Giṭ. 7a. See Yer. Meg. 74a, where this principle of Mar 'Uḳba against music is applied to the exilarch who entertained himself with music at the time of his lying down to sleep and at the time of rising up.

prohibited, since it had no purpose but to keep them cheerful. R. Huna completely eliminated music at feasts or any other social gathering and created a crash in the meat market because there were no buyers; then R. Ḥisda lifted the ban and caused a run on fowl.[136] A concession like that of R. Ḥisda was made apparently not so much out of disregard of the prohibition, but through compulsive public demand for social entertainment. Such conflicts between abstract law and public desire in the field of social morality is a recurring experience in Jewish history, with victory generally on the side of the public.

It should be emphasized that these restrictions against music were concerned with purely secular social functions, but did not cover music at public worship or holiday celebrations, or weddings or funerals. This point is the basis of a question directed to R. Hai Gaon by the scholars of Kairowan, who wonder how prohibition of music at weddings may be posited, since the Talmud accounts it a duty to entertain bride and groom. The gaon agrees that music at nuptials is permitted, that no Jew would think otherwise. But the important distinction is not the kind of occasion but the kind of music. Songs in praise of God or such as convey good wishes to the principals at a joyous occasion are permitted; but love songs or those in praise of beauty or of heroic achievement, whether vocal or instrumental, are prohibited both at banquets and at weddings.[137] All the codes from Alfasi to Karo have followed this ruling of R. Hai.[138] Song in itself without religious purpose is always prohibited[139] — both as a token of mourning for Zion and as a measure of moral discipline. It is a passion, according to

[136] Soṭah 48a.

[137] B. M. Lewin, *Ginze Ḳedem,* V, 5, pp. 33–35; *Oẓar ha-Ge'onim,* Soṭah, pp. 272–3; *Teshubot ha-Ge'onim,* Assaf, Jerusalem 1928, pp. 105–6; *Teshubot ha-Ge'onim,* Harkavy, 60, pp. 27–8; Freimann, *Teshubot ha-RMBM,* 370, pp. 338–9; Yad, Ta'anit 5,14; Tosafot Giṭ. 7a, s. v. *zimra.*

[138] Alfasi, Ber. ch. 5 at the beginning; Yad, l. c.; SMG, positive rabbinical command, 3; *Ṭur* O. H. 560; O. H. 560,3.

[139] See Freimann, *Teshubot ha-RMBM,* 370. R. Hai advises eliminating even beating of drums for keeping time — *Ginze Ḳedem,* l. c. *Ba'er Heṭeb* (O. H. 560,6) cites an opinion that singing at work, as women usually do, is also to be discouraged.

Maimonides,[140] that should be disciplined and suppressed, and Baḥya [141] adds that it detracts from fulfillment of God's commands and the exercise of good deeds. A later moralist, wailing over the low state of Israel and the frequent misfortunes befalling the people, exclaims: "That has been brought about by the corrupt ways of the young people drinking wine and beer and wasting their time on voluptuous music directed toward lust and indecency, thus bringing upon themselves the fire of passion to ravage their hearts." [142]

Different is the case of religious music, such as songs recited or played at worship or at weddings. Music helps give inspiration and joy and exaltation to prayer.[143] Like the Levites in the Temple, so do cantors and choirs in synagogues chant the psalms and benedictions to glorify the name of God, as it is written: "Serve ye the Lord with joy, come into His presence with song." [144] To the cabalist, "Song in connection with the recitation of Scripture causes the soul to cleave unto God." [145] Likewise music at weddings, though it need not maintain that exalted tone, brings joy to the newly wedded pair, in itself a religious duty. As a religious act it is so important that, contrary to standard Sabbath regulations, the law permits hiring of gentiles to play instrumental music on the Sabbath of the wedding week for entertainment of bride and groom and guests.[146] The importance of nuptial music is further illustrated by the following case from the responsa literature. In a certain German territory music was temporarily forbidden, as token of mourning for a personage of high nobility. At that time a Jewish wedding was to be held there, and this meant a marriage without music. The rabbi whose opinion was sought decided that music was essential at a Jewish wedding, and that the ceremony be moved therefore to another town.[147]

140 *Teshubot ha-RMBM,* ibid.

141 *Ḥobot ha-Lebabot,* Lemberg, 1837, II, p. 44.

142 *Eshkolot Merorot* by Habashush, ed. Gotein, *Ḳobeẓ 'al Yad,* XII, Jerusalem, 1936, p. 205.

143 *Teshubot ha-RMBM,* l. c.

144 Ps. 100:2.

145 *Reshit Ḥokmah,* Ahabah, 10, p. 44a.

146 O. H. 338, 2. See Boaz Cohen, o. c. pp. 20–21.

147 *Mahril,* 'Erube Ḥaẓerot, ed. Warsau, 1874, p. 31b.

Needless to say, Jewish practice to this day permits music at weddings and, at least, vocal music at worship. The desire for musical entertainment among young people was too mighty a force to be halted by the legalists and moralists who constantly protested against popular and secular and frivolous songs.[148] The rabbis had to close their eyes to this uncontrollable violation of tradition, and they did so for so long a time that in our day the talmudic prohibition against secular music is lost in oblivion.

Maimonides takes a secular gathering for musical entertainment, and analyzes it into five possible violations of tradition. If there is unseemly language, you have one violation. If there is singing, another. If instrumental music, still another. If there is drinking of wine, there is one more, because of the combination of wine and song. Finally, if women do the singing or the playing, the fifth violation is attained because of immodesty.[149] Every one of these prohibitions is of interest to us as an item in the code of public morality, but most closely related to our subject is the last, the exclusion of women from participation in musical entertainment.

As far down as the tannaitic period, we have not the slightest indication that mixed choruses of men and women were prohibited or that it was considered immodest for women to sing to a male audience. And the omission of such a reference in the tannaitic sources is significant, for women were always leaders both in vocal and instrumental music. However, we have hints from the later tannaim that in their time there was a sense of immodesty about mixing of the sexes at musical performances. One tanna insists that at the crossing of the Red Sea Moses sang with the men and Miriam sang with the women.[150] Another does not wish to take literally the biblical statement that male singers and female singers participated in the funeral dirges of King Josiah, but believes that "male

[148] Abrahams, *Jewish Life*, pp. 137, 197, 253–5; Güdemann, *Geschichte des Erziehungswesen*, II, p. 209; Leopold Löw, *Die Lebensalter*, pp. 309–12.

[149] *Teshubot ha-RMBM*, l. c.

[150] Mekilta, Shirata, at the end, ed. Lauterbach, II, p. 83.

singers and their wives" (who did not sing) were meant by the biblical author.[151]

The early amoraim considered a woman's voice a stimulus to impure thought.[152] At first this may have been only a moral maxim without legal implication, except perhaps to prohibit the reading of the *Shema'* when a woman's voice was heard. During the third generation of amoraim, that is to say at the end of the third and the beginning of the fourth centuries, definite administrative action was taken against conduct that did not attain these higher moral teachings. It is then that we note the strict separation of the sexes at all festive occasions, as indicated above.[153] From the same period comes the ruling that mixed choruses be as far as possible suppressed by administrative authority. Two kinds of choruses are described, one where the melody is carried by the men to the accompaniment of women, the other where women carry the tune and men accompany. The former is merely immodest; the latter kindles passion like fire consuming flax.[154]

The separation of men and women at musicals, according to post-talmudic interpretation, meant not only prohibition of mixed singing but also of mixed orchestral performances, not only of mixed audiences at these performances but also of men singing or playing for women audiences and women singing or playing to male audiences.[155] Music came to be regarded not only as levity but also as flirtation, and musicians were considered addicted to moral laxity.[156] It is surprising, says an Italian rabbi, that women retain any modesty when they are brought up from childhood on songs of love and romance.[157] In the same spirit, a later German rabbi declares

151 Pirḳ. de R. E. ch. 17, at the end, in the name of R. Me'ir, commenting on II Chron. 35:25. See commentary of David Luria.

152 Ber. 24.

153 See p. 81 and note 63; p. 90 and note 104.

154 Soṭah 48a.

155 *Teshubot ha-RMBM,* l. c.; Responsum of R. Hai in *Ginze Ḳedem,* V, pp. 34–5, and the correction of the text by the editor in his note on p. 35; *Sefer Ḥasidim,* 57.

156 See Löw, *Die Lebensalter,* p. 311; Krauss, *Archäologie,* III, p. 99.

157 *Malmad ha-Talmidim,* Lyck, 1866, p. 126b.

it sinful for parents to hire teachers to instruct their daughters in music.[158]

On the whole, the Jews of the western community have toally lost conscience on the subject of women singing to male audiences or vice versa, in secular entertainment or amusement. Even at religious functions, such as weddings, mixed choruses and orchestras or women soloists are acceptable to Jews of standard orthodoxy. Only in the synagogue has the prohibition been preserved against mixed choirs. Reform Judaism has constantly pressed for abrogation of this prohibition; Orthodoxy has battled in its defense for over a century.[159] As yet, the resistance to mixed choirs under the influence of tradition is deep and wide-spread, but seems to be softening with the passing of time.

The dance was as popular in the group life of ancient Israel as was music, and the two were generally performed in combination, to celebrate festivals, rejoice over victories, honor military heroes, express worship and praise of God, and make merry at weddings and at private feasts.[160] From biblical days we know of male group dancing, and likewise of female dancers.[161] As to the relation of the sexes at the dance, we gain the impression that in biblical times there were public dances in which men and women participated — perhaps in separate groupings — that men never hesitated to dance in the presence of women, that women sometimes held dances exclusively for their sex, but that not infrequently they danced in the presence of men.[162] This condition continued to the end of the Second Commonwealth.[163] One new form, however, came into Judea towards the end of that period, the female solo dance as a form of entertainment at private feasts, and that came from the Greco-Roman tradition.[164]

In the talmudic period the question of sex morality in-

[158] R. Joseph Hahn Nordlingen, *Yosif Omeẓ,* 889, 890.

[159] *Ḥatam Sofer,* Ḥoshen Mishpaṭ (H. M.), 190.

[160] See Benzinger, *Archäologie,* pp. 131, 244.

[161] Male: e. g. Ps. 149:3; 150:4; II Sam. 6:5, 14. Female: e. g. Exod. 15:21; Judg. 11:34, 21:21; I Sam. 18:6; Jer. 31:13.

[162] Löw, *Lebensalter,* p. 320.

[163] M. Suk. 5,4; M. Ta'anit 4,8; Ket. 16b–17a.

[164] Mat. 4:6. See Benzinger, o. c. p. 131.

volved in dancing was practically passed over in silence. The solo female dance, of foreign origin, apparently did not penetrate Jewish life to any degree, certainly not during the period of hostility to Rome. The group dancing of males and females was not objectionable to the rabbis, because it was public and because the men and the women danced in separate groups.[165] A Babylonian amora permitted himself to execute a bridal dance with the bride carried on his shoulders. This was, of course, unusual and caused comment among his colleagues. He explained, however, that he felt superior to the temptation of evil thought, and was inspired only by the *miẓwah* of participating in the wedding festivities.[166] Implied in this rabbinic statement, therefore, is a general condemnation of mixed dances even in connection with wedding festivities.

This implication was accepted by post-talmudic teachers.[166a] Whereas in talmudic days it constituted no problem, because the then style of dancing in the Orient did not require mixing of the sexes at the dance, in post-talmudic days, and in western countries in particular, the people did not take kindly to a prohibition of mixed dances, insomuch as the non-Jewish standard of morality permitted it. As early as the thirteenth century in Germany we find communal enactments against promiscuous dancing of men and women.[167] A rabbi of Corfu at the beginning of the sixteenth century reports an enactment forbidding mixed dancing except of husband and wife, father and daughter, mother and son, brother and sister. The cause of this ruling was the improper conduct of dancers, so that the dance hall was "becoming almost like a house of ill fame." Yet, despite this reason, sections of the community tried to free themselves from the restriction.[168] Resentment against these restraints gave the rabbinical and lay leaders no end of trouble. On festivals in particular, days

165 Krauss, *Archäologie,* III, p. 100, on top.

166 Ket. 17a.

166a *Tarbiẓ* I, 1, p. 97; *Oẓar ha-Ge'onim,* Suk. p. 70.

167 *Kol-Bo,* end of 66, citing R. Me'ir of Rothenberg.

168 Responsa of R. David of Corfu, 14; Responsa, *Binyamin Ze'eb,* 303; *Ohale Tam,* 168. See also enactment of Castoria, 1685, cited in *Peraḥ Maṭe Aharon,* I, 5.

of rest from labor, the young people craved recreation, and the public dance hall afforded them the most attractive form. Incidentally the local (non-Jewish) government was interested in having these young people frequent the dance hall, because the tax revenue on liquor was thereby increased. The rabbinical authorities and community heads, seeking to enforce the Jewish standards of morality and prohibit mixed dancing, had to battle both the young people and the local government. In one instance, the government forced the rabbis to rescind the *ḥerem* against mixed dancing. In another the rabbi argued the matter with the chief executive of the local government, who was versed in the Bible. The rabbi convinced him by biblical citations that separation of the sexes was an old Jewish tradition, and that the young people should be disciplined to follow the tradition of their fathers.[169]

Many are the legal and extra-legal objections to mixed dancing. First, separation of the sexes at public gatherings is a standard Jewish requirement. Next, looking at a woman is prohibited. In the third place, touching a woman, especially during her periodic defilement, is at least rabbinically, if not biblically, forbidden. Fourth, mixed dancing arouses passion and unclean thought. Finally, the intimacy begun at dances may lead to unchaperoned meetings and even to embracing or kissing or carnal sin.[170]

The rabbis took an unkindly attitude to mixed dancing even at weddings, but finding greater resistance to this prohibition, they were sometimes inclined to apply the principle, "Better that they sin in ignorance than in defiance." The community urge to join the bridal dance and talmudic compliance impelled greater rabbinical leniency toward mixed dancing at weddings.[171] With cautious admonitions that it was not the nicest thing to do, they permitted dancing with the bride but not with the female wedding guests. Yet even dancing with the bride was permitted only without

[169] Responsa, *Zikron Yosef,* I, 17.

[170] Ibid.

[171] *Shilṭe ha-Gibborim,* Beẓah 36b; *Zikron Yosef,* l. c.; *'Amude Shlomo,* Solomon Luria, end of Issure Bi'ah.

physical contact, which in olden times meant that the pair held two ends of a kerchief. But even this was a concession to the ignorant masses; the refined person should avoid mixed dancing in any form whatever.[172]

It was not to be expected that people would be as discriminating as the law required, and mixed dancing at weddings, not only with the bride but also with the guests and even with full bodily contact, was prevalent to an alarming degree. Legalist and moralist, preachment and enactment, excommunication and fines, were all thrown into the battle against this moral laxity. R. Judah he-Hasid, vehement in rebuke of mixed dancing, is willing to sacrifice the *miẓwah* of causing joy to the bride if the dancing and the hilarity are conducted in an improper manner. His principle, couched in a talmudic formula, is "Men by themselves and women by themselves" at all times.[173] Another moralist stresses the point that though participation in wedding feasts is meritorious, it should not be done if there be indecent jests or promiscuous mingling of men and women.[174] With greater or lesser success rabbis or administrative laymen of various communities tried to halt mixed dances at weddings, until they grew tired and the effort ceased.[175] Today apparently, in the western countries, we have gone beyond that trying period.

172 *Bet Ḥadash,* E. H. 21,5; *Pitḥe Teshuba,* E. H. 65,2; *Sede Ḥemed,* Ḥatan ve-Kalah, 12–13.

173 *Sefer Ḥasidim,* 60, 63, 1176, 1177.

174 *Orḥot Ẓaddiḳim,* Simḥah, p. 22b.

175 *Sede Ḥemed,* l. c.

CHAPTER IV

PRIVATE RELATIONS BETWEEN SEXES

So long as there was no morbidity among Jews on sex matters, and as natural human inclinations were not held under suspicion, law and custom meddled very little with the relations between men and women in their normal surroundings, as friends, as neighbors, or as kinfolk. Only flagrant violations of decency and the consequent anger of a jealous husband or a scandalized father were taken into account. Generally, with the exception of the law in Deuteronomy (25:13) wherein a penalty is prescribed for mere immodesty, the relation between a man and a woman was never conceived as alarmingly immoral until it resulted or was suspected to have resulted in carnal union. That was the situation during the First Commonwealth. But with the deeper sophistication of the Jews of the Second Commonwealth and with the development of greater rigor in the Jewish moral code in succeeding ages, the private relations between men and women became more and more restricted by new rules of conduct. Sometimes these sought to prevent even the remote possibility of carnality, and more often they were intended to establish and maintain high — exceedingly high — standards of sexual purity and innocence.

I. FLIRTATION AND LOVE MAKING

Only one kind of sinful flirtation was known during the First Commonwealth, that of the harlot. Isaiah laid such conduct to the daughters of Zion: "They are haughty and walk with stretched-forth necks and wanton eyes, walking and mincing as they go, and making a tinkling with their feet." [1] In addition, characteristic of the harlot is her loud ornamentation, over-done cosmetic effects, playing an instrument or

[1] Is. 3:16 f.

singing a song in the broad avenues of the city to attract attention.[2] Kissing, fondling, embracing, or other love making are not included as harlot's tricks in the literature of the pre-exilic period. Evidently harlotry was too professional to mask itself in the pretensions of love; and as for kissing and hugging, they were social formalities without sexual implication.

In the post-exilic period these sexual intimacies became fraught with illicit implications; love making became the most effective wiles of the harlot. Such is the description in the Book of Proverbs (7:13, 18): "She caught him and kissed him and with an impudent face she said to him. . . . Come let us take our fill of love until the morning, let us gladden ourselves with affection." Because of the sexual nature of these forms of love making the tannaim taught that the incestuous prohibitions in the Bible include not only intercourse but also kissing, fondling, and embracing.[3] A woman found kissing a strange man is held under suspicion of adultery and her husband is in duty bound to put her away.[4] A husband has a right to be outraged even when a eunuch kisses his wife.[5] When Jacob met Rachel at the well he kissed her and wept. His weeping, say the rabbis, was occasioned by his embarrassment, for he saw the shepherds whispering among themselves in resentment of such immoral conduct.[6] Throughout the ages the Jews have scrupulously followed the restriction against any display of affection toward a strange woman, and it is a standard prohibition in all the codes.[7] A story of the seventeenth century in Germany demonstrates the Jewish attitude. A woman posed as a strange man's wife in order to cross the border on his passport. The guard, suspicious, demanded that they prove the veracity of their statement by kissing each other. The couple refused to do this

[2] Is. 3:18 f.; 23:16; Jer. 4:30.
[3] Sifra, ed. Weiss, p. 85d; Ab. de R. N. ch. 2; Ex. R. 16,2. Maimonides accounts kissing a biblical prohibition, Naḥmanides gives it only rabbinical authority. See Yad, I. B. 21,1 and *Maggid* thereto.
[4] Yer. Ket. 31c.
[5] Yer. Sab. 6a.
[6] Gen. R. 70,12.
[7] E. H. 21,6.

indecent thing, thereby exposing themselves to severe penalties.[8] Some authorities maintain that a person is bound to accept martyrdom in preference to being forced to kiss or embrace a strange woman.[9]

In general, as said, the Jews accepted this restriction and observed it rigorously. There was one exception that greatly troubled the teachers, the intimacies engaged couples allowed themselves prior to their marriage. These liberties come to light in Central Europe in the sixteenth century, when not only the old restrictions against intimacies between engaged couples (such as will be recorded later) were thrown to the winds, but at every family gathering the couples were seated together and were permitted to indulge publicly in love play, with full approval of their parents and with no evident protest from the guardians of public morality. Prague seems to have been most guilty of this licentious practice, or perhaps the Prague rabbis were most zealous in the battle against it, for from that city came three generations of teachers that ruthlessly fought what they accounted violations of biblical law. R. Isaiah Horovitz (1565–1630) commands his family: "Be very careful that before nuptials the groom shall not sit near the bride, as is the custom in this wicked generation, when not only this is the case but he even hugs and kisses her. Woe unto the eyes that see this and the ears that hear of this. How surprising that the sages of our day allow this great sin to go on without calling a halt to it." [10] The practice apparently continued, and the challenge to the rabbis was thrown out later by an anonymous correspondent to R. Jonah Landsofer (1678–1712): "Scandal in the house of Israel . . . there is no one to make public protest . . . that habit has become second nature . . . a daily occurrence! From the time that the engagement is concluded between a boy and a girl they are seated together and given to hugging and kissing . . . under the encouragement of the assembled guests. Why are the leaders . . . who wear the crown of Torah silent? . . . Or should such a practice be permitted

[8] Responsa *Ḥavvot Ya'ir,* 182.
[9] Note of Isserles, Y. D. 157,1 and comment of *Sifte Kohen,* subsection 10.
[10] *Shene Luḥot ha-Berit,* Otiyot, p. 89a.

on the pretense that it is almost certain that the people will not obey nor accept any restrictions?" The rabbi answered: "We live at a time when it is better to be silent than to reprove," because it would do no good to correct the people; "but he who has the fear of God in his heart shall gird his loins like a warrior and shall set his forehead firm as brass to combat this practice of the masses." [11]

No wonder that R. Jonathan Eybeschuetz (1690–1764) had to face the same problem of public morality. He, however, had the courage to fight the evil, and accept the inevitable defeat. Powerful and voluminous preacher that he was, he let loose his oratorical skill against these infringements on Jewish standards of morality. He cries out: "Hearken now, ye holy people, holy in that we come not near unto the forbidden or the impure . . . even in respect to touch or word. . . . Why have ye taken hold of the other end of the cord in one respect, that at set times the groom visits the bride, embraces her and kisses her, and not a word is said? On the contrary, if he should fail to do this he would be counted a fool and the girl's parents would speak to him in anger that he does not know proper manners or he has ceased loving his bride. . . . See and behold what is being told us of our sinful ancestors who turned away from God and served idols, so that the fathers led their children to be burned by fire. Of them the prophet speaks (Jer. 7:18): 'The children gather wood and the fathers kindle the fire.' [12] . . . This parable applies to you, O God's people, for your transgression is greater than theirs. They slew their children and burned them unto a temporary death with a fire that in a moment is extinguished. But you burn your sons and your daughters with the fire of Gehinna, a fire that burns unto the grave, a fire of complete destruction, a burning of the soul unto eternity, while the father and the mother gather the wood . . . And what shall I do at such a time; 'the sons are my sons, the daughters my daughters,' my soul is distressed over them and mourns for them in personal grief. Therefore,

[11] Responsa, *Me'il Ẓedaḳah,* 19.

[12] The author takes the biblical sentence out of its context and paraphrases it.

I shall from now on endeavor with all my might to set up restrictions and I shall not permit the engagement contract to be written until both parties obligate themselves by solemn pledge that they shall not touch each other until their wedding." [13]

This preachment was considered a classic by R. Jonathan's successors in various parts of the world. It is quoted and reenforced by R. Raphael Meldola at Leghorn, Italy, at the end of the eighteenth century.[14] Evidently Meldola uncovered the same laxity of moral restraint against intimacies between brides and grooms in Italy that Eybeschuetz had found in Prague. It would not be surprising to learn that conditions in London, where he arrived at the close of the eighteenth century, were no better. Another scholar that leans heavily on the forceful sermon of R. Jonathan in an effort to improve moral conditions in his country is R. Hayyim Hezekiah Medini, who in the latter part of the nineteenth century was rabbi of Constantinople, Crimea, and Hebron in succession.[15] He does not speak of kissing, which apparently was unusual in the Orient, but of embracing in connection with the dances at the wedding, and there the violation is committed not only by bride and groom but also by the guests. He reports that he proclaimed a prohibition against the practice from the pulpit and that the community acceded to his demand.

Under the prohibition of kissing and hugging we must also include other affectionate or lustful approaches to a woman. The principle is: "A woman other than your wife you may not touch." [16] Holding her hand or putting your arm around her is sinful;[17] likewise, holding her on your lap or resting your head on her lap.[18] Reclining with her on a couch is prohibited even though both are fully dressed.[19] Accepting personal service from her that savors of intimacy,

[13] *Ya'arot Debash,* I, 3, p. 22a.
[14] *Ḥuppat Ḥatanim,* Ẓeni'ut.
[15] *Sede Ḥemed,* Ḥatan ve-Kalah, 12, pp. 12d, 13a–b, 14b.
[16] Ab. de R. N. ch. 2; Ex. R. 16,2.
[17] Yer. Ket. 31c; Exod. R. ibid.
[18] *Ṭore Zahab,* E. H. 21,1.
[19] E. H. 21,7 and commentators.

such as washing hands, feet, or face, is also condemned.[20] One specific service of this kind known in the past was to finger through the hair of the head in search of lice; that was considered intimate and affectionate and could not be accepted at the hands of a strange woman.[21]

Granting that these intimacies between the sexes with lustful intent were immodest and prohibited, the law could not ignore the possibility of affectionate relations between men and women without sexual implication, such as greetings between close relatives. The Midrash infers from the fact that Jacob kissed Rachel (Gen. 29:11) that kissing a relative as a form of greeting is not prohibited.[22] The Talmud tells of R. Aḥa, a Babylonian amora, who used to fondle his granddaughter and hold her on his lap. She was very young, of course, but she was already married.[23] Another Babylonian amora, 'Ula, would greet his sisters with a kiss on the hand and chest.[24] On the basis of these talmudic references, Maimonides in his code words the prohibition against kissing a woman very carefully, so as to indicate the difference between lustful and innocent kissing. The former he declares a biblical prohibition punishable by flagellation,[25] while of the latter he says: "Hugging or kissing any woman who is within the incestuous degree of kinship, such as an adult sister or aunt, even if it be without lustful intent, is exceedingly ugly and immoral. . . . However, a father may kiss his daughter and a mother may kiss her son as long as they are minors." [26] This ruling has come down through our standard codes, wherein by further elaboration the following decisions have been made. A father may kiss his daughter or granddaughter whether young or adult, whether single or married; likewise a woman may kiss her son or grandson. Fondling or holding on the lap is prohibited to a father or grandfather if the girl

[20] Yer. Ket. 30a; E. H. 21,5.

[21] B. B. 58a; Responsa, Solomon Adret, I, 1188; Abrahams, *Ethical Wills,* II, p. 216; note of Isserles, E. H. 21,5 and commentaries.

[22] Gen. R. 70,11; Exod. R. 5, 1.

[23] Ḳid. 81b. A variant reading has Ḥanan b. Raba. Sab. 13a.

[24] 'Ab. Zar. 17a; Sab. 13a.

[25] Yad, I. B. 21,1.

[26] Ibid. 21, 6–7.

has attained puberty or is married. A brother may kiss his sister only if she is a minor and unmarried. As for other female relatives and likewise strange girls and certainly married women, kissing or fondling is thoroughly prohibited, even though they be mere children and even though it is definitely without lustful intent. But a man of piety would do well to kiss no woman, even his daughters and sisters.[27]

The oriental Jews had a special problem in connection with the ruling that even innocent kissing is prohibited. For a long time it has been their custom for men and women to greet their rabbis on Sabbaths and holidays by kissing their hands as a token of esteem. Accepting a kiss from a woman, innocent as it might be, could not in any way be justified under the rules of modesty here presented. Some rabbis, unable to break down the custom, found protection against the immodesty of feeling a woman's lips on their hands by wearing gloves in the summer as in the winter; and the gloves were thick enough not to permit penetration of the kiss to the skin. But Rabbi Medini was satisfied with no evasions and permitted himself no compromise, refusing to allow women to kiss his hand, even his own daughters.[28]

The mere touch of a woman's body, where there is neither lustful intent nor even a suggestion of affection, is in itself indecent, because it might lead to unclean desires or thoughts. As the nazirite must keep at a distance from the vineyard, so must the man keep far away from the woman; the mere touch, in the literal sense, is dangerous. The ordeal of bitter water for the woman suspected of unfaithfulness required that the meal-offering be lifted by the hand of the woman supported by the hand of the priest. The Palestinian amoraim could not understand how such immodesty was permitted, the priest's hand touching the hand of the woman. They suggested a cloth separation between the hands of the two, but that was not satisfactory. An attempt was made to limit this particular service to a priest too old for sexual excitement.

[27] E. H. 21,7 and commentators; *'Aruk ha-Shulḥan,* Ishut, 21,10; *Netibot ha-Shalom,* Moses Nehemiah Feiwish, section Orḥot Ḥayyim, 8, 21–25.

[28] *Sede Ḥemed,* Ḥatan ve-Kalah, pp. 13c–14b.

However, the immodesty of touching a woman's hand was readily acknowledged.[29] In the Babylonian Talmud we find no prohibition either expressed or implied against touching a woman's hand, but there can be no doubt that the teachers never thought of permitting the touch of a woman's body. In mediaeval Europe of the thirteenth and fourteenth centuries, the tradition was already established that touching a woman's hand was a sure act of immodesty.[30]

In the meantime, the halakic teachers of that period succeeded in raising that prohibition to the level of a legal injunction. We have referred above to a ruling of the law that intimacies with a woman of incestuous kinship is either biblically or rabbinically prohibted.[31] A woman under menstrual impurity is considered prohibited under the category of incest. Even greater emphasis was put upon this prohibition, at least in respect to the intimacies between husband and wife during her impurity, to the point of proscribing the slightest, most innocent juxtaposition. Rashi, for instance, would not hand the key of his house directly to his wife during her period of impurity.[32] Naḥmanides prohibits a physician feeling his wife's pulse at such a period.[33] The codes categorically declare the slightest contact of flesh prohibited.[34] But one might argue, as do many of the halakists, that any young woman of mature age falls under the same prohibition whether she be wife or not, for until she has had her ablutions she is incestuously prohibited to every male.[35] It is on this basis that the prohibition against touching a woman, married or single, gains in legal importance in Jewish law.

29 Yer. Soṭah 18c.

30 See Abrahams, *Ethical Wills*, II, p. 211; *Ba'al ha-Ṭurim* commentary ad Gen. 24:47 points out the virtues of Eliezer that he did not touch Rebecca's hand.

31 Maimonides, *Sefer ha-Miẓwot*, negative command 353 and Naḥmanides, comment thereto.

32 Tosafot, Sab. 13b on top.

33 *Bet Yoseph, Ṭur* Y. D. 195. But see note of Isserles, Y. D. 195,17.

34 Y. D. 195,2.

35 Responsa of R. Isaac b. Sheshet, 425. See *Bet Shemuel*, E. H. 21,9, interpreting the distinction drawn by Adret between a wife and another woman. See also *Maggid*, ad Yad, Ishut, 4, 12; *Ya'arot Debash*, p. 22a; *Sede Ḥemed*, Ḥatan ve-Kalah, 12 and 26.

This raised many problems in Jewish life. What was a physician to do who had to examine a woman patient, and how were the women to get along without male physicians where there were no female doctors? The law really could not hurdle that difficulty except by evasions and compromises, offering excuses that the doctor's mind was on his work and therefore free from sexual intent, or other explanations of equal weakness. But it did bow to human needs and willingly or unwillingly permitted doctors to go about their medical duties with female patients.[36] However, another problem arose, more of the social type, where the law refused to accept a compromise and rather braved defeat. The handshake as a manner of greeting was employed in Europe both by men and by women. To refuse shaking hands with a lady meant to be stamped ill-mannered, and an offense and humiliation to the woman. Yet the law refused to permit this. Some pious men wore gloves so as not to touch a woman's hand flesh to flesh; [37] others stood firm by the law, and refused to shake hands with a female, regardless of all embarrassment. The restriction is now very lightly heeded among western Jews, but it is still deeply rooted in the conscience of pious Jews in Eastern Europe and the Orient.

II. FAMILIARITY BETWEEN THE SEXES

Restrictions upon the relations between men and women, of course, were not limited to physical touch, but even distantly they were expected to have as little to do with each other as possible. Joining together in entertainment, in merrymaking, in games, is a breach of modesty, not so much for itself but for the familiarity thus established. Levity and merriment are altogether unwholesome for morality, even where there is no mingling of the sexes, for they lead to lewdness, or as another rabbinic formula has it, "It is the door by which carnality enters." [38] It was repeatedly urged upon men and it was an accepted standard of conduct for women,

[36] *Sifte Kohen*, Y. D. 185,20.

[37] *Sede Ḥemed*, l. c. p. 14a at the bottom.

[38] Abot 3, 17. D. E. Zuṭa, 3; Seder Eliyahu Rabba, ch. 13, ed. Friedmann, pp. 61–65.

that "the daughters of Israel are not given to merriment or play." The woman who conducted herself contrary to this standard was soon enough summoned to account by her husband, who would not hesitate to impose the command of jealousy on her, which meant that she was held suspect of unfaithfulness.[39]

Men who are frivolous with young girls, says a tanna, are responsible for the delay of the coming of the Messiah.[40] Under the general effort of the mediaeval teachers to segregate the sexes, as presented in a previous chapter, special stress was placed upon keeping them from joint play or merriment. It is made a rule of conduct by the moralists,[41] and formulated as a spiritual legacy by a saintly father to his sons and daughters.[42] R. Judah he-Ḥasid recounts that he saw corpses, in expiation for sins committed through life, harnessed to carts, like beasts of burden, and dragging a heavy load. He asked them for what sin this punishment was meted out, and they answered, "For the sin of playing with women and girls . . . for he who acts like a beast in this world is treated like a beast in the next." [43] This saintly teacher objected even to male and female children playing together.[44]

Wine drinking is synonymous in the minds of the teachers with levity and frivolity, since merriment was generally carried on over a cup of wine. Like levity, drink is in itself unwholesome to morals, but it has special danger in regard to sex morality. In the ordeal of the "bitter water," the woman suspected of adultery is put through a cross-examination, and it is suggested to her that perhaps she had succumbed to the influence of wine or merriment.[45] The rabbis further point out that the law of the nazirite is recorded in the Bible immediately before the law of the "bitter water," to indicate that the temptation of wine is closely connected

[39] Tanḥ. Naso, 2; Numb. R. 9, 8.

[40] Nid. 13b. The amoraim take it to refer to the sin of marrying girls before they have attained the child-bearing age.

[41] *Sefer ha-Yashar* of R. Tam. ch. 7, p. 27b.

[42] Testament of R. Eliezer of Mainz in Abrahams, *Ethical Wills,* II, p. 211.

[43] *Sefer Ḥasidim,* 63, 875–7.

[44] Ibid. 60.

[45] M. Soṭah 1,4.

with the temptation of sexual immorality.[46] The same sentiment is expressed by Sirach: "With a married woman sit not at table and revel not with her at the wine; lest haply thy soul turn aside unto her and with thy spirit thou slide into destruction." [47] Post-talmudic teachers have little to say on the subject of drinking wine in the company of women, but no doubt they include this under the general prohibition against associating too intimately with females (treated in a previous chapter [48]), or they include drinking of wine under the head of levity and merriment, the prohibition of which is formulated in the codes,[49] or they treat it, as did Maimonides, as part of the complex of wine, woman, and song.[50]

Certainly, familiarity with definite sexual implication is an offense to the Jewish moral sense. Winking at a woman or executing gestures of levity with hand or foot to attract her attention, admiring her beauty or smelling the scent of her perfume is sinful, and Maimonides rules that such practices should be punished by disciplinary flagellation.[51] Greater restrictions are set on a man in relation to a woman of easy virtue, in that the law prohibits him to pass her house within a distance of four ells, and for repeated violation flagellation is likewise prescribed.[52]

In the Orient when a man and woman walk, the man walks ahead and she follows behind. This was also the custom, apparently, in talmudic times. But the rabbis considered this not only a matter of proper oriental etiquette but a rule of sexual morality. Walking behind a woman gives the man the opportunity of lustfully surveying the female form, which may lead to lascivious thoughts or to temptation. Hence the rabbis taught, "It is better to walk behind a lion than behind a woman." Instances are cited from the Bible to prove that this standard also prevailed in biblical times; deviations, where hinted at in the biblical text, are explained away; and

46 Ber. 63a; Numb. R. 10,42 at the end.
47 Sirach 9:9; San. 100b.
48 See pp. 93 ff.
49 Yad, I. B. 21,2; E. H. 21,1.
50 See p. 98 and note 149.
51 Yad, I. B. l. c.
52 'Ab. Zar. 17a; Ḳid. 12b; *Bet Yoseph* ad *Ṭur* E. H. 21; E. H. 21, 1.

the one exception, that of Manoah, of whom it is said (Jud. 13:11) that "he arose and walked after his wife," is declared by them evidence of his vulgarity. When one finds himself walking behind a woman, it is the rule of law that he turn in another direction or hasten to get ahead of her or fall behind a distance of four ells, or even more if necessary, until he is unable to scrutinize her figure and her motion. And this rule applies, according to a late authority, even where the women are so clad that their figure outlines are concealed.[53] There is another consideration in this restriction, that it may arouse a suspicion in the minds of people that the man is following the woman to some rendezvous for illicit purposes, and therefore the prohibition applies even to a man walking behind his wife.[54]

Indulgence in small talk or repartee with a woman should be avoided as bordering on indecent flirtation. One of the ethical teachings of Jose b. Johanan, head of the Sanhedrin in the early Maccabean period, is: "Indulge not in conversation with womankind." [55] That this was not only a pious sentiment but an actual standard of morality is seen by the fact that more than two centuries later the disciples of Jesus "marveled" with uneasiness to find their master speaking with a Samaritan woman at Jacob's well.[56] An incident is also related in the Talmud of the amoraic period, that a man who was desperately in love with a woman begged for the privilege of at least conversing with her — perhaps in a flirtatious manner — and it was stated by doctors that if this desire were not gratified the man's life was in danger; but the request was not granted, as a measure for protecting the modesty of the daughters of Israel.[57] The motive of this restriction, as may be analyzed from the statements of later teachers, is that it is a waste of time that might be better used for the study of Torah; that, second, it leads to nonsensical prattle, which evinces a person's flippancy and brings

[53] 'Erub. 18b; Ḳid. 81a; Ber. 61a; Gen. R. 60, 13; Abrahams, *Ethical Wills*, I, p. 45; Yad, I. B. 21, 22; E. H. 21, 1 and *Ba'er Heṭeb* thereto, quoting RDBZ.

[54] Ab. de R. N. ch. 2; Ber. 61a; 'Erub. 18b.

[55] Abot 1, 5.

[56] John 4:27.

[57] San. 75a.

humiliation upon him; and last, that it leads to unclean talk and lascivious thought.[58] Taking all these considerations together, it is advised that one avoid unnecessary conversation even with one's own wife.[59]

It seems that the ancients considered it especially objectionable for a man to greet a woman. How rarely one can find — if at all — in Bible or in Talmud a direct greeting of "Shalom" uttered by a man to a woman. The one case that comes to mind, that of Elisha the prophet greeting the Shunamite woman (II Kings 4:26), would seem to indicate that they permitted themselves only indirect greeting, conveyed or extended through a slave. The Talmud formulates into a rule of conduct that a man may not greet a woman, and adds further that conveying greetings through another, be it even her husband, is prohibited.[60] This rigorous law has its counterpart in the moral restrictions of Persia, where even today "a European physician cannot without being considered indecent even ask about the health of a Muhammedan's wife and daughter, although they are ill."[61] Jewish law, however, according to the interpretation of European post-talmudic teachers, is not quite so strict. It does prohibit direct greeting of a woman or directly inquiring about her health. It also prohibits sending greetings to a woman, even by correspondence, through another — whether husband or stranger. But it does permit inquiring about a woman's health either from the husband or from a stranger, by mail or in conversation.[62] With greater severity the rabbis prohibited drinking a toast to a woman; they consider one who does such a thing unworthy of the gift of life and beyond the reach of the life hereafter.[63]

[58] Ab. de R. N. ch. 7; Ned. 20b; D. E. ch. 1.

[59] Abot 1,5; Ab. de R. N. ch. 7. Me'iri ad Abot ibid. maintains that only nonsensical and unnecessary conversation is prohibited but not serious conversation on matters of importance. Nevertheless, brevity is still required. See 'Erub. 53b.

[60] B. M. 87a; Ḳid. 70b.

[61] Westermarck, *History of Human Marriage,* I, p. 311, citing Polak, *Persien,* I, 224.

[62] Tosafot Ḳid. ibid. on top; *Ṭur,* E. H. 21 and *Bet Ḥadash* thereto citing Asheri and R. Solomon Luria; *Maggid* ad Yad, I. B. 21,5; E. H. 21,6 and *Ba'er Heṭeb* thereto.

[63] Kallah, ch. 3 and 5, ed. Higger, pp. 126, 129.

Even looking at a woman is an infraction of ancient standards of modesty. "The heart and the eye are two agents of sin; the eye sees and the heart desires." If only the eye could be controlled, the heart would be kept pure. This sentiment, though formulated in rabbinic times, had its beginning in the early post-exilic period. Job contends that he was righteous all of his life and proves it by exclaiming, "I made a covenant with mine eyes; how then should I look upon a maid?" [64] The Apocrypha repeatedly reverts to this rule of conduct and preaches: "Gaze not upon a maid lest thou be trapped in her penalties. . . . Turn away thine eye from a comely woman and gaze not on another's beauty." [65] The New Testament is more didactic on the subject: "Whosoever looketh on a woman to lust after her hath committed adultery with her in his heart." [66] To the rabbis of the Talmud, the biblical Joseph was the classical example of modesty, for as he was led in procession through the streets of the Egyptian capital city, the maidens sought to attract his attention by throwing jewelry and ornaments at him, but he refused to raise his eyes to look at them.[67]

Rabban Gamaliel II, apparently a worldly person of courage and independent spirit and one who maintained his own standards of public relations, sometimes in defiance of the law, also ignored this restriction against looking at a woman. He saw a beautiful gentile lady and pronounced a benediction in praise of God who had fashioned so exquisite a creature. Later generations of teachers considered this a misdeed and believed it could not have happened except in an accidental manner, when the rabbi, at a turn in the road, came upon the woman by surprise.[68] Despite Rabban Gamaliel's leniency in this matter, the law against gazing at a female gained in authority and severity in the later tannaitic and amoraic periods. The praise lavished upon

[64] Job 31:1; also Prov. 6:25. See also 'Erub. 18b; Ber. 61a; Ned. 20a; Kallah, ch. 1; D. E. ch. 1; Yer. Yeb. 3d; *Sefer Ḥasidim* 1100.

[65] Sirach 9:5–8; 41:20–21. See also Testament of Reuben 3:10 and Ahikar, Armenian version, 2:2; Syr. version 2:5; San. 100b.

[66] Mat. 5:28.

[67] Targum Yerushalmi, Gen. 49:22; Targum Jonathan, ibid.; Gen. R. 98, 23.

[68] 'Ab. Zar. 20a–b; Yer. 'Ab. Zar. 40a.

Joseph for not looking at women was also heaped upon a number of amoraic saints who matched Joseph in this high level of piety.[69] Gradually it became a rule of conduct promulgated by the amoraic teachers, that "One may not look at a virgin if he finds pleasure in her beauty, nor at a married woman even if she be ugly." [70] They buttressed this prohibition by the threat that "he who looks at a woman will eventually come to carnal sin . . . and he who passes a coin from his hand to hers (ostensibly in the course of business) with the intent of looking at her, will not escape the punishment of Gehinna." [71] And this prohibition, in the minds of the amoraim, does not mean looking at her face alone to notice her beauty, and certainly not at any hidden part of her body which might arouse sexual desire,[72] but even a glance at her little finger.[73] More than this, one may not even look at a woman's garments, whether on her body or hanging in the closet, because they might start an unwholesome train of thought.[74]

An exception to this rule was the long standing permission to view the bride on her marriage day. We have seen above that, contrary to the general rule for women, the bride was expected to expose her face to public view.[75] This practice is reflected in a halakic statement by R. Jonathan, of the first generation of amoraim, who teaches that one may look at the bride during the entire wedding week.[76] His contemporary, Rab, demands that the groom see the bride prior to betrothal, so that he go not blindly into the matrimonial bond.[77] Post-talmudic teachers, following this ruling of Rab and the older usage of exposing the bride to view, permitted ample opportunity in the ceremonies preparatory to the nuptials to give the groom and his family a glimpse at

69 Abba Umna, Ta'anit 21b; R. Hanina and R. Oshaya, Pes. 113b.

70 'Ab. Zar. 20b.

71 'Erub. 18b; Ber. 61a; Ned. 20a; Kallah, ch. 1; D. E. ch. 1; Sab. 64a; Yer. Yeb. 3d.

72 B. B. 57b; 'Erub. 18b.

73 Ber. 24a; Sab. 64b.

74 'Ab. Zar. 20b; *Sefer Ḥasidim* 38, 55; E. H. 21,1.

75 See above p. 45, note 92.

76 Ket. 17a. The decision of the law is against it.

77 Ḳid. 41a.

the bride. It was probably in disapproval of this practice that the Karaite teacher, Sahal b. Maẓliaḥ of the tenth century, wrote: "When you come to bless the bride, permit no man to see her, for such a practice never existed in the days of our fathers." [78] Rabbinic halakah, however, made it mandatory for the groom to see the bride prior to the marriage.[79] In certain European localities it was the custom to hold a special reception in the bride's home for the groom on the night before the wedding, at which time bride and groom were put together in a private room so that he might have the opportunity of having a good view of her.[80] Our present day custom of having the bride veiled prior to the nuptial ceremony by the groom himself, and not by the officiating functionary or the elders of the community, as was the custom in earlier days, is also said to provide an opportunity for the groom to see his bride before he marries her.

That a husband should be permitted to look at his wife can, of course, be taken for granted. The halakah does not challenge the right, although it demands reserve and refinement.[81] But the agadah speaks of Abraham as displaying special saintliness in that he did not look at his own wife Sarah and did not know how beautiful she was until they were about to enter Egypt, when by chance he saw her reflection in a stream of water they were crossing.[82] The Talmud tells a similar story of saintliness concerning a man who was married to a crippled woman and did not know of her physical defect till the last day of her life.[83]

III. CHAPERONAGE

As today, so in the remote past, private meetings of men and women without a chaperon were considered improper. If

[78] In his introduction to 'Anan's *Sefer ha-Miẓwot,* Harkavy, *Me'asef Nidaḥim,* p. 201.

[79] Yad, I. B. 21,3; E. H. 21,3; *Sefer Ḥasidim,* 1143. However, the latter contradicts himself in section 1134 without explanation.

[80] *Yad Ephraim,* notes on Y. D. 198.

[81] The question is raised only regarding looking at one's wife when she is in her period of impurity — Ned. 20a. But this, too, is permitted — E. H. 21,4.

[82] B. B. 16a. See Tanḥ. Lek Leka, 9 and note 70 of Buber.

[83] Sab. 53b.

the place or the circumstances of their meeting justified suspicion, the husband of the woman — if she were married — was honor bound to put her away.[84] The husband would warn his wife in advance to hold no tryst with any man he might single out as the target of his jealousy. This warning was known as "the command of jealousy." If she violated his command, even if there be no proof of unfaithfulness, she was assumed by the law to have committed adultery, and the ordeal of bitter water was administered to her.[85] In rabbinic times the law of chaperonage was definitely and firmly established, prohibiting private meetings between a man and a woman no matter what the place or the circumstances, no matter whether the husband approved of it or resented it. The amoraim believed the law had gone through three stages. Its earliest roots are in the Pentateuch, wherein chaperonage is required between a man and a married woman. The second goes back to the time of David, when Amnon violated Tamar, at which time the law was sharpened to prohibit unchaperoned meeting of a man and an unmarried Jewish woman. The final stage was reached through the legislation of the Hillelites and the Shammaites, prohibiting unchaperoned companionship between a Jewish man and a non-Jewish woman.[86]

In unchaperoned association, both the man and the woman are held guilty, for the restriction applies to each of them. The age of the persons involved is immaterial, provided, however, that the "man" in the case is above nine years of age and the "woman" above three.[87] Relatives are not exempt from the law of chaperonage. A man may not associate with his mother-in-law, sister-in-law, niece, or aunt without a chaperon; likewise a woman may not associate unchaperoned with her corresponding male relatives. Even brother and sister need a chaperon.[88] The only exceptions among relatives are

[84] Yeb. 24a; Yer, Ket. 31c.

[85] This subject is treated separately in a later chapter.

[86] 'Ab. Zar. 36b; San. 21b.

[87] Yer. Ḳid. 66b.

[88] Tos. Ḳid. 5,10; Ḳid. 80b; San. 21b. Yer. Ḳid. seems to indicate that unchaperoned meeting between brother and sister is permitted, but they may not occupy the same apartment. Babli does not record that distinction.

father and daughter or mother and son.[89] Yet even they are advised to know limits; they should not occupy the same apartment in a hotel, because of appearances.[90]

The law of chaperonage does not apply in public places where many men and many women mingle.[91] Likewise, the private meeting of a man and a woman in a house that has an opening to a public thoroughfare is not prohibited.[92] There is a view also that at the cemetery, in connection with burial duties, the law of chaperonage is considerably eased, on the assumption that people are not likely to indulge in frivolities in such a time and place.[93] The law is also less severe in the city and in the daytime than in the fields and at night.[94]

One man who is of good repute may be a chaperon.[95] This applies only to inhabited places. In the field or on the road two men are required and both must be of good repute, for one may have to relieve the other in case of need.[96] Men of ill repute, even a hundred of them together, cannot act as chaperons; therefore a woman may not be found in the company of men of questionable character, be they ever so many.[97] A heathen is never trusted as a chaperon. Hence, a woman may never be in the company of heathens no matter what their number. A Samaritan or a slave, on the other hand, is acceptable.[98] One woman is not satisfactory as a chaperon, because she lacks stability and firmness of character.[99] According to a certain view, two women or more are a good combination to constitute chaperonage, unless the man involved has built up a familiarity with women through his business contacts.[100] The severer view of the law, however, is that one

[89] M. Ḳid. 4,12 and the references cited in the previous note.

[90] Ab. de R. N. ch. 2; Numb. R. 10,22.

[91] Yad, I. B. 22,8; E. H. 22,6.

[92] Ḳid. 81a; Yad, ibid. 22,12. Certain authorities maintain that even there the law of chaperonage applies at night when traffic has ceased. See *Ba'er Heṭeb,* E. H. 22,9.

[93] Ḳid. 80b; Yer. Ḳid. 66b, the view of Abba Shaul.

[94] E. H. 22,5. Details will be presented in the succeeding pages.

[95] M. Ḳid. 4, 12.

[96] Ḳid. 81a; Yer. Soṭah 16d.

[97] Ḳid. 80b; 'Ab. Zar. 25b; Yer. Ḳid. 66b.

[98] Tos. Ḳid. 5, 9; 'Ab. Zar. 22a.

[99] M. Ḳid. 4, 12; Ḳid. 80b.

[100] Rashi, Ḳid. 82a, s. v. *Yityaḥed.*

woman may never be in the company of men nor one man in the company of women, no matter what their number, unless there be an especially watchful eye present.[101]

This especially watchful eye, which the law considers the chaperon extraordinary, may be the husband of the woman, who would allow no wrong,[102] or her mother-in-law, sister-in-law, step-daughter, or co-wife, who, if wrong were done, would tell.[103] Likewise, a little girl who is old enough to understand sexual immorality but not old enough to be trusted to keep a secret is an excellent chaperon.[104] As a matter of fact, it was customary for Jewish women, going about among gentiles or compelled to travel on the road with gentiles, to take a little girl along in fulfillment of the law of chaperonage.[105] The only good chaperon to see that the man behaves in the company of women is his own wife. It is a sad commentary on the position of women among the heathens that the rabbis rule the wife of a heathen unqualified as a chaperon, for the heathen will do wrong even in the presence of his wife.[106]

The law of chaperonage is enforced by disciplinary flagellation administered both to the man and the woman. Unless it be a violation of a husband's "command of jealousy," the law does not disturb the husband, if he has confidence in his wife, on account of her unchaperoned meeting with men.

[101] E. H. 22,5. The view is based on Ḳid. 81a, where Rab and R. Judah did not feel it was proper for them to have a woman in their company. But Isserles, there, gives the more lenient ruling.

[102] The view is expressed — Ḳid. 81a — that even if the husband is in the city she may meet privately with other men because the woman would be afraid that he might come in unexpectedly. To this a late authority remarks that she may meet other men only in her own house but nowhere else where she may feel confident he would not come.

[103] Ḳid. 81b. According to certain views a son is also a satisfactory chaperon to watch his mother. See *Pithe Teshubah,* E. H. 22,2.

[104] Ḳid. ibid.

[105] *Ba'er Heṭeb,* E.H. 22,4; *Pithe Teshubah* ibid. The problem of chaperonage for Jewish women who pursued business among gentiles was the basis of many community enactments. See, e.g. *Pinḳas Medinat Liṭa,* #133; an enactment of Prague in 1611, ed. by Isaac Rivkind in *Reshumot* IV (1926), pp. 348–9 and numerous others. See also an article by the latter, "Die yiddische Frau . . ." in *Die Zukunft,* Vol. 38, #2 (N. Y. 1933) pp. 110 ff.

[106] M. Ḳid. 4, 12; 'Ab. Zar. 25b. Certain authorities disqualify a daughter as chaperon for her father because she is unable to check him. See *Pithe Teshubah* l. c.

More than this, the married woman is even freed from disciplinary flagellation, in order to safeguard the good name of her children. There was a Babylonian magistrate who did inflict the penalty of flagellation on married women caught in unchaperoned companionship with men, but he made sure to make public announcement that the offense was only violation of the chaperonage law and not actual immorality.[107]

Certain rabbinic prohibitions stem from the desire to eliminate conditions which will throw the man and the woman into each other's company and where chaperonage will not prove practical. Thus, for instance, a widow may not board a student in her house; [108] a bachelor may not be a school teacher, lest through his pupils he come too often in contact with their mothers.[109] A business whose customers are mainly women should be carried on by a man only if his wife can be with him in the business; else he should seek to make a living in another manner.[110] A woman should not own male slaves [111] and a strange man should not be left in charge of a household of females.[112]

IV. SPECIAL PRECAUTIONS

In cases where the temptation toward immoral relations is too great, chaperonage is not recommended, but the law puts such restrictions upon the man and the woman as will keep them out of each other's way. Men are accounted guilty of sin if they only pass the door of a harlot; the law requires them to keep at a distance of at least four ells.[113] The tannaitic teachers declared it sinful for a man to marry the mother or

[107] Ḳid. 81a.

[108] 'Ab. Zar. 22b. Maimonides — Yad, I.B. 22,16 — interprets this to mean that a student may not live in the same apartment house with a widow where he may meet her in the hallway or court yard. See *Ba'er Heṭeb,* E.H. 22,11.

[109] M. Ḳid. 4,13. Bachelor male teachers, however, could not always be avoided, and when a married teacher could not easily be found, the bachelor was allowed to remain on his post but a special proclamation was made in the community prohibiting the mothers to visit the school house. See *Neveh Shalom* by Elijah Hazan, Alexandria, 1930, p. 50a.

[110] M. Ḳid. 4,14. See Yad, I.B. 22,8 and *Maggid* thereto.

[111] B. M. 71a. See Yad, I. B. 21,16.

[112] Ber. 63a.

[113] See note 52 above.

daughter or sister of a woman with whom he had had sexual intimacies, because this marriage would throw him into the company of the woman, who would now be incestuously prohibited to him.[114] A post-talmudic teacher rules, in the same spirit, that a man in love with a woman, if the woman marries another, may not live in the house occupied by this woman and her husband.[115]

In olden times, a son-in-law and his mother-in-law were held under suspicion of developing a fondness for each other that was not morally healthy. The fondness of a mother-in-law for her first son-in-law was noticed by the rabbis with particular apprehension.[116] For this reason talmudic law disapproved of a married couple living with the wife's parents. The sentiment is older than the Talmud which quotes a proverb of Sirach: "I have weighed everything on the scales and I found nothing lighter than chaff, yet lighter than chaff is the son-in-law who lives in his father-in-law's house."[117] The objection of Sirach may have nothing to do with sex morality. It may refer to solitary remnants in his day of the metronymic marriage, or to cases where the burden of maintaining the young couple was imposed on the bride's parents instead of being carried, in accordance with accepted social standards, by the parents of the groom. Be that as it may, there is no doubt that normally in Sirach's days, as for many centuries later, the married couple settled with the groom's parents; the very essence of the nuptial ceremony was taking the bride to the groom's home. In the time of the earliest amoraim, for the groom to live with his bride's parents was considered immoral. Rab imposed the penalty of flagellation therefor, and R. Sheshet sentenced a groom to be flogged for merely passing the door of his parents-in-law.[118]

In the course of time the family structure and economic conditions changed, and the parents of the girl, who were anxious to see her married, had to take on responsibility for the couple's maintenance. In rare events they could provide

114 Tos. Yeb. 4.5. See Epstein, *Marriage Laws*, p. 300 and note 102.

115 *Sefer Ḥasidim*, 70.

116 Pes. 113a.

117 B. B. 98b.

118 Ḳid. 12b.

a separate home for the newlyweds; in most cases the young folk took up their residence with the bride's family. The law was lenient because of economic necessity. It was explained that evil intent on the part of the mother-in-law or the son-in-law could not be suspected, for everybody knew their economic conditions had forced them into living together.[119] It was also suggested that so long as a separate room was assigned the young couple there was no objection to their living with the wife's parents.[120] In the earlier codes the prohibition is still recorded without prescribing a penalty for violation,[121] but in the later codes it is passed over in total silence. In practical life the Jews ignored this prohibition completely, since about the twelfth century, and in more recent times, it became customary for the most pious families who desired to acquire a bright talmudical student as a son-in-law to offer him, in addition to an attractive dowry, a set period of maintenance at his father-in-law's home, technically known as *"koest."*[122]

The law is particularly suspicious of a divorced couple meeting in privacy, on the psychological assumption that their intimacies during their married life have broken down all inhibitions when the opportunity for sexual contact offers itself. This assumption has severe and complicated bearing on some legal points in respect to divorce. It is ruled by the Hillelites that a divorced couple who have associated privately under conditions favorable to sexual contact are considered remarried and must go through the ceremonies of another divorce.[123] This special suspicion of a divorced couple accounts for the law which prohibits them living under the same roof, or in different houses opening on the same court yard, or in the same street, and in the case of a small place, even in the same village.[124] The woman is always compelled

119 Tosafot Ḳid. ibid., s. v. *be-kulhu.*

120 Note of RABD ad Yad, I. B. 21,15.

121 Yad, ibid.; SMG, negative precepts, 126.

122 See Abrahams, *Jewish Life,* pp. 174–5.

123 M. Giṭ. 8, 9.

124 Sifre Deut. 24:2; Ket. 27b–28a; Semaḥot 2,12; Yer. Giṭ. 49d. This rule applies only to a couple divorced after nuptials, not if divorced after betrothal. It applies always to a priestly couple, because remarriage, after divorce, is impossible for them. In the case of an Israelitish pair, the law is severe where

to move away from the man, unless the house occupied by them while married belongs to the woman, in which case the man is made to move.[125] Furthermore, they are restricted against doing business together or appearing at litigations together; they can do these things only through agents or representatives.[126]

Much offense was caused the Jewish sense of morality by the liberties of betrothed or engaged couples. The Talmud saw no special problem therein. Prior to betrothal, even though they were already engaged, the couple were considered legal strangers, and were not permitted to associate privately, under the law of chaperonage. After betrothal they were legally husband and wife; therefore the law of chaperonage could not apply to them. Hence two practices existed side by side in Palestine in tannaitic days: in Judea the couple were permitted private companionship before nuptials, in Galilee they were not.[127] If cohabitation took place between the betrothed, even though this constituted a violation of rabbinical law,[128] it did not seem to trouble the Judeans either legally or socially. The amoraim, in explaining this laxity, believed that the Judeans recited nuptial prayers at the betrothal ceremony which might be said to sanction marital relations after betrothal.[129] In Galilee these prayers were reserved for the nuptial ceremony, and prior thereto, by accepted standards, the couple were not permitted to associate without a chaperon.

The Galilean custom became the norm for Jewish life in Babylonia under the teaching of the amoraim. In the blessing over the cup of wine at betrothal, they inserted the phrase,

---

the woman is remarried, but the law is uncertain where the woman is still free. According to some the restriction goes only so far as to prohibit their living in the same house. See *Peri Ḥadash,* E. H. 119, 7. According to others, all restrictions apply to them, even if the divorced wife is not remarried. See *'Aruk ha-Shulḥan,* E. H. 119, 25–28. Interesting are the two interpretations of Yer. Giṭ. ibid. Cf. *'Amude Yerushalayim* commentary thereto. See Yad, I. B. 21, 27, and *Leḥem Mishneh* thereto; E. H. 119,7.

125 Ket. 28a; Yer. Giṭ. 49d; Semaḥot 2, 14; Midr. Tannaim, Deut. 24:1.

126 Ket. ibid.; E. H. 119, 8–9.

127 M. Ket. 1, 5; Tos. Ket. 1, 4; Ket. 12a.

128 Kallah 1, 1; Yer. Ḳid. 64b; Ket. 7b.

129 Ket. 7b.

"and He prohibited to us our betrothed." [130] A report has it that Samuel, of the first amoraim, ruled that bride and groom who had cohabited were to be given disciplinary flagellation.[131] More telling, however, is the ruling of Samuel that a child born to a betrothed maiden from contact with her groom is a doubtful *"mamzer,"* and the severer view of his opponent, Rab, that he is a positive *"mamzer,"* for as the girl has shown herself immoral in relation to the groom, she probably has done so also in relation to others.[132] In the geonic period, as in amoraic times, Babylonian Jewry maintained the same standard of conduct for bride and groom and permitted them no unchaperoned association.[133] However, no disciplinary action was taken against those who violated the standard,[134] and it seems that violations were not unusual. But where they became too frequent, the teachers thought it best to have the nuptial benedictions recited at the betrothal ceremony, so as to give partial sanction to the possible prior cohabitation of bride and groom, exactly as was done in old Judea. The geonim were asked whether they approved that Judean practice for Babylonian Jewry; one gaon saw no objection whatsoever, but the dominant geonic teachers thoroughly disapproved of it.[135]

Approximately the same attitude as that of the geonim was maintained by the rabbis in Europe through the mediaeval period. Private association between bride and groom prior to nuptials occurred not infrequently, and sometimes even cohabitation. Prohibitions were pronounced, and public opinion condemned the practice. The talmudic law of chaperonage, which legally did not apply to bride and groom, was declared as applicable to them as to any strange couple.[136] Disciplinary flagellation was prescribed for violators.[137] Communal enactments with additional restrictions and penalties

130 Ket. ibid.
131 Yer. Ḳid. ibid.
132 Yeb. 69b; Ḳid. 75a.
133 Lewin, *Oẓar ha-Ge'onim,* Ket. pp. 18, 19, 20; ibid., Yeb. p. 166.
134 Ibid. p. 18 and note 4 thereto.
135 Ibid. pp. 17–20.
136 *Mordecai,* Ket. 132; REBJH, ed. Aptovitzer, I, p. 220.
137 Yad, Ishut 10, 1; E. H. 55, 1.

were recommended by the teachers.[138] It was proposed also that bride and groom not be permitted to live in the same apartment house, because this would lead to unchaperoned meetings between them.[139] Where it seemed impractical to make one of the parties move, the rabbis suggested that the nuptial benedictions be recited at betrothal.[140] But apparently Jewry of Central Europe did not grow excited about the problem. They were satisfied to leave it to the conscience of the people and to the moral force of the law to keep brides and grooms in innocence and purity before their nuptials. Hence, they did not employ communal enactments to impose restrictions on social relations between brides and grooms. "Ashkenaz" was therefore designated by a fifteenth century scholar as one of the places where lovemaking between bride and groom prior to nuptials was permitted.[141] A contemporary scholar reports for Egypt, too, that there bride and groom were "encouraged" to meet privately prior to nuptials, in order to break down their shyness and inhibitions in each other's presence.[142] The country that is singled out in Jewish literature as the classical example for sexual liberties between bride and groom is Romania, where the old Judean custom was introduced in full, freedom of association between bride and groom and the nuptial benedictions at the betrothal ceremony. The "Minhag Romania" apparently spread throughout the Byzantine empire and extended even into Sicily and Southern Italy.[143] Things went so bad there that "most brides came to the nuptials in full bloom of pregnancy." [144]

Naturally, where moral laxity is most pronounced communal effort to counteract it is most likely. This rule has proven true also in respect to communal enactments setting up restrictions against free social relations between bride and

138 Responsa, Asheri, 37, 1.

139 TSBZ (b. Ẓadoḳ) 44, 8; *Kol-Bo,* 75, quoted in notes of Isserles, E. H. 55,1.

140 *Mordecai,* Ket. 131, quoting R. Elazar b. Nathan (REBN).

141 Responsa, Elijah Mizraḥi, 4.

142 Responsa, RDBZ, III, 525.

143 Assaf, *Jubilee Volume for Prof. Krauss,* pp. 169–176.

144 Report of R. Obadiah Bartenoro, quoted by Assaf, ibid.

groom. The earliest of these enactments brought to our attention is that of Candia on the island of Crete, formulated under the influence of R. Baruk b. Isaac, a European scholar who halted there on his way to the Holy Land in the year 1238. The enactment reads: ". . . no groom shall be permitted to enter the house of his father-in-law until nuptials. If for some compelling reason he must enter the house, he shall be obliged to take two of the officers . . . or any two other people with him. Those who are studying with their fathers-in-law . . . they alone shall be permitted to enter the houses of their fathers-in-law, for the power of the study of Torah is mighty to subdue the power of the tempter." [145]

Sometimes the zeal of community leaders for moral purity among the young people impelled them to enact unreasonable restrictions, which caused quarrels and schisms within their constituency. The community of Arta in Southern Greece furnishes a classical example of such a case. It served as a refuge for the Jews after the expulsion from Spain, and was settled by three immigrant groups, who together with the native group made up the four sections of the community, each with a separate synagogue. The moral laxity among the young was disturbing to all groups, and they joined in conference to legislate against it. The majority, comprising three groups, agreed upon an enactment which seemed to those of the fourth too harsh and unreasonable. They refused to recognize the validity of the enactment and the community sued them on the grounds of communal authority. Leading rabbis of the day were drawn into the controversy, some supporting the community, others declaring the right of the minority group to accept or reject the general enactment.

The act provided that the groom might not enter the house of the bride or any room in it, even if there be a hundred, and even if her father and mother were present to guard their conduct. No exception to this prohibition was made if the father-in-law or mother-in-law fell sick and the son-in-law wanted to visit to inquire about their health, in the company of other members of the community. Nor was it permitted

[145] Finkelstein, *Jewish Self-Government,* p. 279. See also *Sefer Takkanot Kandia,* Artom and Cassuto, Jerusalem, 1943, Nos. 8, 19, 64.

for the groom to enter the house at a public celebration or a house party in honor of a visitor, where many people were assembled. Even the wedding could not be held in the bride's house, since the groom was not permitted to enter it. The minority group was willing to accept the restraint against the groom's entering the bride's house without a chaperon, but was unwilling to drive the restriction too far.

The majority of the leading rabbis of that day declared the enactment binding even on the minority group.[146] A few, however, supported the minority in their protests. One scholar records the results of such an unreasonable set of rules. Since the groom cannot enter the house, he comes close enough to it, and the bride puts her head out through the window. Thus in the open street and in the sight of all people they indulge in kissing and hugging. The gentiles who see wonder over the lack of modesty on the part of the young Jews, and they are told that kissing must be done only outdoors according to Jewish law, because it is prohibited indoors. Else, the pair make clandestine appointments to meet in the park and there carry on their love affair beyond the bounds of decency.[147] Another scholar justifies the minority in their protest but pleads for peace in the community, suggesting that the enactment be modified to provide moderate restrictions such as were employed in his own community — that the groom may visit the house of his parents-in-law only on the Sabbath and then, too, only in the company of his father or older brother; that the visit must have a general social character; that the groom is not to accept an invitation for a meal with his parents-in-law, except when they have a social affair to which they invite many other people; that any negotiations or communication between the groom and the bride or her family be done (if on week days, when he may not enter) through the open door of the house, except that close to the time of nuptials the groom may enter the bride's house as often as he wishes in order to carry out preparations for the wedding.[148]

146 Responsa, Binyamin Ze'eb, 303–8.
147 *Ohale Tam,* in *Tumat Yesharim,* 168–170.
148 Responsa, Moses Trani (MABIT), III, 77.

These regulations, being based on community enactments, have only local validity and do not represent universal Jewish halakah. In addition the picture has gradually changed. By a process of evolution, the two moments in the Jewish marriage, betrothal and nuptials, have come to be celebrated jointly in one ceremonial. Thus the problem of the betrothed couple has ceased to exist. What remains is only the problem of proper relations between an engaged couple prior to betrothal, who in the eyes of the law are legally still strangers to each other. For them, the standard law of chaperonage is prescribed by Jewish law, with an additional prescription, according to certain authorities, that they may not live in the same house.[149]

[149] Notes of Isserles, E. H. 55,1.

CHAPTER V

NATURAL AND UNNATURAL SEX CONDUCT

MORAL law and natural law, both the product of the one Creator, could not, from a religious view, be in conflict with each other. The assumption may be made, therefore, that one who follows out the moral law can never be guilty of doing anything contrary to the dictates of nature. The reverse, however, cannot be said, that one whose life is thoroughly consonant with the laws of nature does, as a matter of necessity, fully observe the moral law. If that were the case, there would be no need for Revelation and Torah once Creation were accomplished. The religious view is that nature, while basically good and sound, lacks in refinement, in sensitiveness, in nobility. It is the groundwork of the good life, but it does not rise above the ground. The moral law supplies that refinement and nobility and builds the ladder for the higher climb into the realm of the ideal, the exalted, the holy. But it may be said with certainty that to defy nature's law is to violate the revealed law of morality. What nature abhors the law prohibits.

I. SEX PERVERSIONS

At the various stages of biblical legislation the prohibition is recorded against buggery with a beast. The law is more fully formulated in Leviticus: [1] "And if a man lie with a beast, he shall surely be put to death; and ye shall slay the beast. And if a woman approach any beast and lie down thereto, thou shalt kill the woman and the beast: they shall surely be put to death; their blood shall be upon them." Together with other unnatural connections, the Bible speaks of this perversion as belonging to the abominations of the heathen, more

[1] Lev. 20:15–16. See also Ex. 22:18; Lev. 18:23; Deut. 27:22.

especially the former inhabitants of Canaan.[2] Beyond doubt there were infringements of this law among Jews also, but on the whole it would seem that this was not one of the vices which the Jews learned from their neighbors, for beyond the bare statement of the law, the Bible is thoroughly silent on the subject; and the prophets, who generally did not spare their people in denunciation of evil, never once charge them with such unnatural lust. In post-biblical times, even the licentiousness and debauchery of Rome did not thus infect the Jewish people. When R. Judah b. 'Illai, a tanna of the second century, wanted to prohibit young unmarried Israelites from engaging in shepherding, out of fear that they might commit buggery with the animals under their care, his colleagues protested, "Israelites are above suspicion of buggery."[3] The law therefore knows no restriction against raising animals, against isolated companionship with them, or even against fondling and petting them. However, finer taste and greater scrupulousness among the ancient teachers displayed careful avoidance of these things.[4] At least, the public is often more suspicious than the law, and it behooves people in certain circumstances to be careful about their reputation; therefore the law teaches that a widow may not have a pet dog.[5]

The Bible itself rules that the penalty for contact with a beast is death both for the human and the beast. By hermeneutic derivation the rabbis deduce that the death penalty intended by the Bible is that of stoning, provided the offender be of the age of majority. The animal, too, is killed by stoning, provided the contact was with a human male above nine years and a day, or a human female above three years and a day, for below that age male and female respectively have no sexual status at all. The execution of the animal presents a moral problem to the rabbis, especially when the female animal is attacked by a male human, for the animal has not sinned, since it has no code of morality and particularly since

[2] Lev. 18:24. Hittite Code declares bestiality a capital crime, except with a horse or mule. Hittite Code, 187; 199; 200A.

[3] Ḳid. 82a.

[4] Ḳid. 81b; Yad. I. B. 22,2.

[5] 'Ab. Zar. 22b; B. M. 71a; Tosafot, ibid. s. v. *lo*.

it has been the passive object of a human crime. They believe, however, that the law is justified in executing the beast because it served as a tool for the downfall of a human being; more so because the recollection of the crime and the human criminal is focused on the beast, whose execution would cut that memory short.[6]

The Talmud considers this moral injunction against copulation with beasts applicable to all human society and binding also upon heathens.[7] It constitutes for the talmudic teachers one of the seven moral laws which are obligatory for Noahides.[8] A heathen under Jewish jurisdiction committing the crime of buggery suffers the death penalty by the hand of the Jewish court. His case, however, differs from that of a Jewish offender in two ways. First, his death penalty is execution by the sword, not by stoning; [9] in the second place, the beast is not slain together with him, because basically, as said above, the beast has no moral guilt.[10]

Unlike the Jew, the heathen in biblical and talmudic days was not above suspicion of this particular form of sex perversion. The suspicion does not go so far as to stamp any animal raised by him as unfit for sacrifice, but it does prohibit an Israelite giving his animal to a heathen shepherd or lodging it with a heathen innkeeper.[11] The amoraim, despite the fact that some of them report most revolting sex atrocities committed by their heathen contemporaries,[12] softened that suspicion somewhat, declaring that heathens of various localities had different moral standards and the law must recognize these differences.[13] On this basis a teacher of the fourteenth century declares those restrictions and suspicions at an end among the gentiles of his day, whose morality is above crimes of this nature.[14]

Sodomy, or copulation between male and male, was an evil

[6] San. 54a–b; Yad, I. B. 1,16–17.
[7] Ḳid. 82a.
[8] San. 58a; Yad, Melakim, 9,5.
[9] San. 57b; Yad, Melakim, 9,14.
[10] San. 55a–b; Yad, Melakim, 9,6.
[11] 'Ab. Zar. 22a–b.
[12] Ibid. 22b.
[13] Ibid. 14b.
[14] See *Maggid* ad Yad, I. B. 22,5.

practice in ancient times more prevalent than buggery with beasts. It belonged to the same class of sex perversion, but evidently it was accepted as a pardonable indulgence for licentious rulers and as a natural form of debauchery for pleasure-seeking common folk. Its prevalence comes to light in the biblical stories of the atrocities of Sodom and those of the town of Gibeah, in both of which the mob demanded to be given the visiting strangers for male copulation.[15] At the same time, from these stories we get a reflection of the revulsion which decent Jews felt to such an act; in either case the host offered his daughter for rape in exchange for the strangers, pleading that "so vile a thing" be not committed. It may be taken for granted therefore that from very ancient days sodomy was considered among the Hebrews a severely immoral act. Yet no direct legislation is found against it either in the Covenant Code or in Deuteronomy. It is only in Leviticus that the law specifically prohibits sodomy and declares it a capital crime. "If a man lie with a male as one lieth with a woman, both of them have committed an abomination; they shall surely be put to death, their blood shall be upon them." [16]

In the Bible and the Talmud sodomy and buggery are treated as similar sex crimes, and the assumption is that the one like the other had its origin in the licentiousness of the heathen Canaanites. Again, both from biblical and talmudic evidences, we should be inclined to say that sodomy was also one of the vices which the Hebrews did not adopt to any extent from their heathen neighbors. This statement might be true, were it not for the fact that sodomy was sometimes part of the heathen worship, with male sacred prostitutes known to the Hebrews as *ḳedeshim* (*s. ḳadesh*), ministering sexually to the worshipers; and the Hebrews who refused to accept immorality in secular form succumbed to it more readily when draped in religious garb. Thus sacred sodomy, alien and hateful to the ancient Hebrew cult, penetrated into Judea at the time of the early kings from the idolatry of the Canaanites. Under Rehoboam, and probably due to the in-

[15] Gen. 19:5; Judg. 19:22.
[16] Lev. 20:13. See Lev. 18:22.

fluence of his Ammonite mother, idolatry became rampant in Judea "and also sodomites were in the land." [17] His grandson Asa tried to cleanse the Temple in Jerusalem of that practice; a further effort was made by his great-grandson Jehoshaphat; but sodomy in the Temple was not eradicated until the vigorous reforms of the righteous king Josiah.[18] It was then followed up by the deuteronomic legislator, who set down the specific prohibition that "There shall be no *ḳedeshah* among the daughters of Israel nor shall there be any *ḳadesh* among the sons of Israel." [19] This prohibition, it should be noted, differed from the later levitical law in two ways. First, it stressed the crime of sodomy not as a sexual crime but as a form of idolatry, saying nothing concerning secular sodomy. Second, it prohibited it on the same level as prostitution but did not consider it a capital crime. The levitical law went the whole way and was evidently quite effective in eradicating sodomy among the Jewish people.

In rabbinic times, the *ḳadesh* in the original connotation, as a sacred sodomite, was entirely out of existence. The deuteronomic law was sometimes understood as a prohibition against marriage with a slave,[20] but more often as containing nothing more than what is implied in the levitical law against secular sodomy. To the rabbis, therefore, sodomy is sodomy no matter what the circumstances, and the law applies in all cases, sacred as well as secular, condemning both male participants to death. The death penalty is by means of stoning, provided neither one of the culprits is below nine years and a day old, for copulation with a boy below that age is not considered a sexual act in the law. However, though not a capital crime, sodomy with a minor below that age is punishable by flagellation as a matter of public discipline.[21]

Like the injunction against buggery, the prohibition of sodomy is taken by the rabbis to be universal in character, applicable to Noahides as well as to Jews. The death penalty in the case of a Noahide, however, is not stoning but slaying

[17] I Kings 14:24.
[18] I Kings 15:12; 22:47; II Kings 23:7.
[19] Deut. 23:18.
[20] Targum Onkelos, Deut. 23:18.
[21] M. San. 7,4; San. 54b; Yad, I. B. 1,14.

with a sword, exactly as in the case of buggery.[22] In talmudic as well as in biblical times, the heathen was held under suspicion of committing this crime when the opportunity was afforded him. The Roman standard of sex morality known to the rabbis of the Talmud did not by any means undo that suspicion. To take an example offered by Josephus, Herod refused to send his young brother-in-law Aristobulus to the Roman court at the request of Antony, because "he did not think it safe for him to send one so handsome as was Aristobulus, in the prime of his life, for he was sixteen years of age, and of so noble a family; and particularly not to Antony, the principal man among the Romans, and that would abuse him in his amours, and besides, one that freely indulged himself in such pleasures as his power allowed him without control." [23] No wonder then that the rabbis prohibited a Jewish father giving his male child to a heathen for instruction or for training in a vocation, and generally allowed no situation to arise wherein a Jewish youth should find himself in seclusion with a heathen.[24] They explained the heathen's leaning toward unnatural lust as follows. The serpent infected Eve (and through her mankind) with lasciviousness; Israel was cleansed of it by the Sinai experience, but the heathens who were not at Sinai remained addicted to those passions.[25]

The superior morality of the Jew, thus, is ground for the rabbinic principle that "Jews are above suspicion of committing sodomy." If the law prohibits an unmarried man to be a teacher for boys, it is because of the visits of their mothers to the schoolhouse, not because of his association with the boys themselves.[26] Post-talmudic authorities, however, advised as a matter of special piety, that there be no solitary association between males without chaperonage,[27] and R. Joseph Karo, the famous codifier, adds: "Especially in this generation, when immoral persons have become more numerous, it is proper to

[22] San. 57b–58a; Yad, Melakim, 9,5, 14.
[23] Josephus, *Antiq.* XV, 2, 6.
[24] Tos. 'Ab. Zar. 3, 2.
[25] 'Ab. Zar. 22b.
[26] Ḳid. 82a.
[27] Yad, I. B. 22,2; E. H. 24,1.

avoid unchaperoned association between males."[28] It is more than mere piety but actually moral necessity, some rabbis teach, not to permit young people to sleep together in one bed, because it is putting temptation in their way.[29]

Amours between females is not prohibited in the Bible. The rabbis record it as a practice among the heathens and find it implied in the general levitical injunction, "After the doings of the land of Egypt wherein ye dwelt shall ye not do; and after the doings of the land of Canaan whither I bring you shall ye not do, neither shall ye walk in their ordinances."[30] R. Huna, a Babylonian amora, considered such homosexual practice equal to harlotry and would declare a woman who indulged in it unfit for marriage with a priest. The law, however, does not treat the practice so severely, but accounts it an unseemly, immoral act,[31] which Maimonides advises should be disciplined by flagellation, declaring also that women known to be addicted to this vice should be excluded from the company of decent women.[32] It is reported that Samuel's father, a saintly Babylonian amora of the third century, did not permit his daughters to sleep together, probably to avoid homosexuality among them.[33] The final halakah, however, condemning the act and imposing disciplinary penalties, did not recognize the restriction of Samuel's father or any other restriction against private association between woman and woman.

II. DESPOILING NATURE

The law prohibits castration either of man or beast or fowl. The rabbis assume that this prohibition is of biblical origin, and they derive it from the levitical verse which reads: "Ye shall not offer unto the Lord that which is bruised or crushed or broken or cut (in its genitals); neither shall ye thus do in

28 E. H. ibid.

29 *Ḥelkat Meḥokek,* E. H. ibid.

30 Lev. 18:3. See Sifra, Lev. ibid.

31 Yeb. 76a.

32 Yad, I. B. 21,8. See also E. H. 20,2.

33 Sab. 65a–b. The Talmud interprets the mind of Samuel's father as desiring not to have his daughters become habituated to the feel of another (male) body in bed.

your land." [34] They interpret the second half of the verse to mean that causing these defects in animals, such as are enumerated in the first half of the verse, is prohibited; and by their hermeneutic rules of derivation, they infer that the prohibition extends to all animals whether intended for sacrifice or for domestic purposes, that it includes man as well as beast, and that it applies everywhere, in Palestine as in any other land.[35] Furthermore, some rabbis believe that the prohibition is meant for Noahides as well as for Jews.[36]

It seems definite that the castrated person was despised in biblical times, for he was not accepted in marriage in Jewish families, as the castrated animal was not acceptable as an offering upon the altar. It is not improbable, therefore, that the rabbis were right in declaring that the prohibition against castration was of biblical origin. But definite proof for this view cannot be found in the biblical verse itself, for it is altogether indefinite as to its meaning and, in the second place, it may refer specifically to sacrificial animals and not to humans at all. If the rabbinic view is granted, we shall have to assume, however, that this law is of post-exilic origin and was passed as a reaction to the prevalence of eunuchs in Persian society. True, eunuchs were known before and in Judea as well,[37] but it seems that post-exilic Jews were more offended by this practice than their ancestors, and no doubt their experience in the land of their exile taught them to fear lest the evil take root and spread in their rebuilt home in Judea.

Josephus considers castration a despicable practice, whether of man or of beast, and even designates it as a capital crime.[38] This can be but an exaggeration in order to impress his non-Jewish readers, for in no other source do we find a suggestion that castration is punishable by death. The rabbis treat this prohibition as an ordinary negative biblical injunction, punishable by flagellation. And the prohibition, in the biblical sense, is very narrowly limited, according to their interpretation. In the first place, it applies only to the males of man

[34] Lev. 22:24.
[35] Sifra, Lev. ibid.; Sab. 110b.
[36] San. 56b–57a. Not accepted by the halakah.
[37] See II Kings 24:15.
[38] Josephus, *Antiq.* IV, 8, 40; *Apion,* II, 38.

or beast but not to the females. In the older tradition the distinction must have been based on the fact that the female eunuch was unknown, but the rabbis, thinking of castration of humans specifically, base the distinction upon the fact that the law imposes the duty of procreation only on the man and not on the woman. Maimonides, however, is responsible for a ruling, which has been accepted in the final halakah, that castration of a woman is rabbinically prohibited.[39] In the second place, castration in its legal definition means a surgical act by the offender upon the victim's genitals. Causing a male to become sterile by any other method than that of cutting off his genitals is not a case of castration but of sterilization.[40]

The sterilization method most prevalent in the time of the Talmud was that of drinking down a potion consisting of equal parts of Alexandrian gum, liquid alum, and garden crocum, which came to be known as "the sterilizing potion." [41] Maimonides speaks of placing a man in snow or ice until his genitals were frozen as another method of sterilization.[42] It is doubtful whether the modern technique would fall in the category of sterilization or castration — probably the former. Now, there is admittedly no biblical prohibition against sterilization of male or female, man or beast, but there is a rabbinic prohibition applicable only to the male of man or beast, but not to the female.[43] Here again, the rabbis have in mind the human species especially and permit sterilization of women, because the duty of procreation does not fall upon them.[44] As to the man, even though his duty of procreation is fulfilled when he has one son and one daughter, piety requires that he beget as many as possible. Therefore no matter how old he is or how many children he has, the rabbinical pro-

[39] Sab. 111a; Sifra, Lev. 22.24; Yad, I. B. 16,11, and *Maggid* thereto. See Tos. Mak. 4,4. In contrast to the Jewish sentiment, Time Magazine, N. Y. July 31, 1944, p. 75, records a custom especially prevalent in Italy in the 17th and 18th centuries of castrating young boys with beautiful soprano voices so as to preserve their voices.

[40] Yad, I. B. 16,12; E. H. 5,12–13.

[41] Sab. 110a.

[42] Yad, I. B. 16,12.

[43] Tos. Yeb. 8, 2; Yad, ibid.

[44] Yeb. 65b; Sab. 111a.

hibition against sterilization continues.[45] The penalty for violation is disciplinary flagellation.

Celibacy is prohibited in Jewish law. The rabbis consider procreation the first command recorded in the Bible and they refer to the verse in Genesis (1:28): "And God blessed them and God said to them, Be fruitful and multiply and replenish the earth." They stress the importance of this command, accounting the unmarried man as no man at all; surely he is no man of achievement or blessing or happiness or peace. Celibacy, in the agadic way of thinking, is a crime of the nature of bloodshed; and because it diminishes the number of souls who would be born to worship God, it is accounted an interference with the Kingdom of Heaven.[46] The halakah prescribes no penalty for celibacy, but in the Middle Ages under Jewish self-government the rabbinic courts would employ the powers vested in them, by corporal punishment, fines, or excommunication, to compel the bachelor to get married. After the fifteenth or sixteenth century, however, the rabbinic courts no longer interfered with the individual who desired to remain single.[47]

Marriage and study of Torah are put ahead of all other religious obligations, so that while one may not sell a scroll of the Law to finance any religious project, no matter how holy, he may do so for the purpose of making possible marriage or the study of Torah.[48] As between the two, however, study takes precedence over marriage. We have that judgment expressed in a biographical note of Simon b. 'Azzai, a tanna of the second century. He spoke eloquently of the sacred duty of marriage, yet he was a celibate all of his life. It was thrown up to him by his colleagues that he preached well but that he did not practice what he preached, and he said in answer, "What shall I do? My heart desireth Torah; let the world be

[45] Sab. ibid. See Tosafot, Sab. 110b on top.

[46] Yeb. 61b–64a.

[47] *Ṭur* E. H. 1; E. H. 1, 2 and note of Isserles thereto. However, exceptions to this rule are found in local communities. A communal ordinance of Jerusalem of 1745 corroborates an older enactment that an unmarried man between the ages of 20 and 60 may not live in the city. If he cannot find a suitable match he must move away and seek his livelihood outside. See *Sefer ha-Taḳḳanot* by Eliashar, Jerusalem, 1883, section 53, p. 41.

[48] Meg. 27a.

maintained by others."[49] In Palestine, where economic problems were severe in amoraic days, and it was impossible for a married man to give himself fully to the study of Torah, it was taught that students might remain unmarried as long as necessary, neglecting the command of procreation for the sake of study. But in Babylonia, under better economic conditions, students were advised to marry in proper time and to study Torah after marriage, seeing an advantage in that the student's mind would be free from impure thoughts.[50] By the example of Simon b. 'Azzai and in accordance with the Palestinian practice, our final halakah permits a scholar who dedicates his life to study to remain unmarried or to postpone marriage indefinitely.[51]

Celibacy is condemned in the law for two reasons; first, because of the neglect of procreation, second, because of immorality in thought or action to which the unmarried man falls a victim. The duty of procreation requires a person to have at least one son and one daughter.[52] Once he has fulfilled this duty, strictly speaking, the law should have no further concern whether he be married or not. But it is understandable that a superior sense of obligation should require that he do more than the bare minimum in the fulfillment of God's command. Therefore the law insists that a man be married and continue to beget children as long as he is physically capable of reproduction.[53] The difference between the childless man and one who has already met the legal requirement of procreation is that the former may not marry a barren wife while the latter may. Considering, however, that piety requires the maximum reproduction, not the minimum, the pious person would hesitate to marry a barren wife, even after he had already raised a family, if not out of legal considerations, at least out of a superior religious conscience.[54]

The second objection to celibacy, that it constitutes a

[49] Yeb. 63b.
[50] Ḳid. 29b.
[51] Ḳid. ibid.; Yad, Ishut, 15,2; E. H. 1,3–4.
[52] Yeb. 61b.
[53] Yeb. 62b.
[54] Yeb. 61a; Yad, Ishut, 15,7; Epstein, *Marriage Laws*, pp. 292–4.

temptation to immorality, ignores completely the question of procreation. Any marriage is therefore satisfactory, regardless whether the wife be capable of bearing children or not. On this basis, celibacy is condemned in any man, no matter what his age and no matter how large the family he has already raised.[55] Even the scholar cannot be permitted to be celibate or to postpone marriage beyond the proper time, unless he is self-assured that the purity of his mind will not be disturbed thereby.[56] What is the proper time for marriage? Logically puberty should be the right age, for then one becomes bound to fulfill the law of procreation and then also temptation for immorality develops. The rabbis would ordinarily have recommended that age, or perhaps, taking into account the year set aside from betrothal to nuptials, they would have agreed on marriage by males at the age of fourteen. But due to a number of social influences, men were wed in tannaitic days at the age of eighteen.[57] The law would therefore hold the man guilty of immorality if not married at eighteen. Twenty, however, is declared to be the outside limit for marriage, if one is not to violate flagrantly the Jewish code of sexual purity.[58]

The law does not account the unmarried woman guilty of sin. Basically this is due to the fact that the bachelor woman was unknown in talmudic days. But the halakah has another explanation — that the duty of procreation does not fall upon the woman.[59] However, one would expect the celibate woman to be condemned by Jewish law on the basis of her being exposed to immoral temptations; yet the law does not even agree to that. Evidently it considers the many social restrictions set upon woman's conduct sufficient guarantee that she will not violate her chastity.[60] Nevertheless, the law urges the woman too to be married lest she be suspected of immoral conduct.[61]

[55] Yeb. 61b; E. H. 1,7.
[56] Yad, Ishut, 15,3; E. H. 1,4; *Bet Shemuel* ad E. H. 1,3.
[57] Yeb. 62b; San. 66b; Ḳid. 29b; Abot 5,24
[58] Ḳid. ibid.; Yad, Ishut, 15,2.
[59] Yeb. 65b; Yad, I. B. 21,26.
[60] See *Ba'er Heṭeb*, E. H. 1,2,27.
[61] Yad, Ishut, 15,16; Isserles, E. H. 1,13.

III. WASTING NATURE

The purpose of intercourse is procreation. Nature has so ordained it by withholding complete satisfaction in copulation until it produces the seed of reproduction. By human design, nature's purpose may be frustrated by the deliberate waste of nature's power. The classic example of that wickedness is the biblical story of Onan, recorded in the following words: "And Onan knew that the seed should not be his, and it came to pass when he went in unto his brother's wife that he spilt it on the ground, lest that he should give seed to his brother." [62] From this derives the term onanism. The rabbis describe it euphemistically as "threshing within and winnowing without." There is no definite inference from the Bible itself that onanism as such was considered a severe sin, for the death penalty suffered by Onan was not due to his waste of nature, but for refusing to raise seed for his deceased brother in accordance with the levirate requirement. But the rabbis treat such an act as moral depravity in and for itself, a wasting of nature. They prescribe no penalty, but account the offender as under automatic excommunication until he ceases the practice.[63]

Marrying a woman who is incapable of child-bearing has been considered above under the heading of the duty of procreation. It was said also that even when the duty of procreation has been fulfilled, piety forbids marrying a barren wife. Now we have another motive for avoiding marriage with a barren woman, that intercourse with her amounts to a waste of nature on the part of the man. Philo takes this motive seriously, considers it a real violation of Jewish law, and

[62] Gen. 38:9.

[63] Yeb. 34b; Yad, I. B. 21,18. Under this heading belongs also intercourse *shelo ke-darkah,* also condemned by most authorities as a wasting of nature. See Yad, I. B. 21,9; *Shene Luḥot ha-Berit,* Otiyot, p. 89b; Tosafot Yeb. 34b s. v. *ve-lo.* The final view of Tosafot accounts it no sin unless it becomes a habitual practice. Dr. Moses Lutzki of the Jewish Theological Seminary Library brought to my attention a passage in *Sefer Ḥaredim,* at the end of section 3 of chapter on Teshubah (ed. Venice, 1601, p. 65a) where the rabbis — including R. Joseph Karo — ruled to impose severe penalties on the man for such a practice — "they wanted to burn him with fire, but finally drove him out of Palestine."

argues that such cohabitation is outright lustful indulgence.[64] To Philo, this would constitute a prohibition against marrying any kind of woman incapable of child-bearing, whether too young or too old or physically defective. The rabbis do not wholly agree with Philo on this point. Granted that piety requires a man to beget children as long as he can and that therefore he should marry only a wife who is fruitful, nevertheless intercourse with a barren wife, so long as it is legitimate and natural, is no sin.[65] The problem does arise in the law where the wife has a vaginal obstruction which makes natural intercourse impossible, in which case, by a ruling of Asheri, cohabitation between husband and wife is prohibited since it constitutes a factual waste of nature.[66] The law defers to the opinion of Asheri only in the case where the intercourse becomes unnatural, but where it is natural, though definitely non-productive, the law recognizes no prohibition.

The foregoing may reveal to us the rabbinic attitude to contraceptives. Of course, any contraceptive employed for the sake of birth control runs contrary to the basic ideal of Judaism. It is sufficient to reflect on the teaching of the law that a person should beget as many children as he is capable of, and further to recall how in biblical as well as in talmudic times the parents of a large family thought themselves especially blessed, to be convinced that planning for a small family, even without artificial contraceptives but by means of regulating intercourse, is a violation of Jewish standards. If the economic problem be offered as an argument for birth control, Judaism would be quick to retort that it behooves the person of faith to trust in Him who giveth children that He will also provide for their maintenance.[67] The only time a person may or rather should permit economic considerations to limit his reproductive efforts is when there is a general famine, where the unborn would encroach upon the insufficient food of the living.[68]

The question that Jewish law would consider at all would

[64] Philo, *de spec. leg.* III, 36, ed. Cohn, Vol. II, p. 194.

[65] Isserles, E. H. 23,5. See Tosafot Yeb. 12b on top.

[66] Asheri, Responsa, 33,3; E. H. 23,5.

[67] *Sefer Ḥasidim,* 1913–14.

[68] Ta'anit 11a.

be the use of contraceptives for purposes medically justifiable. The Talmud permits the insertion of an absorbent in the vaginal canal in order to prevent conception in case the wife is too young or in a condition of pregnancy or if she is a nursing mother.[69] Post-talmudic law is surprisingly lenient on the question of contraceptives for medical purposes on the basis of this talmudic law, permitting artifices of various kinds even where the problem is not danger to health, but medical tests on the fertility of the male or research to improve fertility.[70] Where there is no medical purpose in the contraceptive it would seem that the law would prohibit these artifices. Nevertheless there are two views on the matter. One declares that the woman, like the man, is prohibited from wasting nature; therefore, without medical necessity any artifice in any form calculated to make the seed unproductive is prohibited. The other view is that a woman is not included in the prohibition of waste of nature, since she is not included in the duty of procreation. Therefore, anything the woman can do after the act of cohabitation to destroy the seed is perfectly permissible, so long as the intercourse was natural and normal. But nothing may be done to make the intercourse useless to begin with.[71]

The worst offense in this category is self-abuse, or waste of nature without sexual contact. R. Ishmael taught that the command, "Thou shalt commit no adultery," includes lewdness by means of the hand as well.[72] Another tanna applied to those who practice self-abuse the biblical phrase, "Your hands are full of blood." [73] More explicit is R. Johanan, a Palestinian amora, who says he "is guilty of a capital crime." [74] The Zohar, quoted in our code, accounts it the severest sin of all recorded in the Scriptures.[75] The ethical literature of post-talmudic days, down to the latest centuries, endlessly

[69] Yeb. 12b and parallel passages.

[70] *She'elat Ya'bez,* I, 43; *Zofnat Pa'ne-ah* II, Warsau, 1935, 164; *Melamed le-Ho 'il,* III, 18.

[71] Tosafot Yeb. 12b on top.

[72] Nid. 13b.

[73] Is. 1:16; Nid. ibid.

[74] Nid. 13a.

[75] E. H. 23,1.

harps on the severity of this sin, exhorts its avoidance, points out its danger to health, threatens dire punishment in the day of reckoning, and pleads for penitence and expiation.

Involuntary waste of nature, of course, cannot be prohibited by law, since it is unintentional. Yet the law does not consider the man a helpless, innocent victim in every case. He must carry part of the responsibility for this involuntary occurrence in so far as it is in his power to prevent sexually stimulating situations which may bring it on. Thus, the law would have men of piety avoid reaching down with their hands below the belt, in accordance with the example set by R. Judah ha-Nasi.[76] Better still if they followed the example of the same saint and did not permit themselves to look at sexual members, either their own or another's.[77] The law definitely prohibits touching one's genitals — the unmarried man never, and the married man only in connection with urination.[78] The rabbis also advise men not to sleep face up but recline somewhat to the side, believing that the supine pose suggests luxury and induces sexual excitement.[79] Likewise they advise against wearing trousers that are too tight around the loins, and also against riding on animal bareback.[80] But the most general and far-reaching rabbinic injunction is to avoid lascivious day-dreaming or anything that may set the mind thinking on sexual matters.

[76] Nid. 13b; Sab. 118b; Yer. 'Ab. Zar. 42c.
[77] Sab. ibid.; Yer. 'Ab. Zar. ibid.
[78] M. Nid. 2,1; Nid. 13a.
[79] Nid. 14a.
[80] Nid. 13b–14a.

CHAPTER VI

PURITY OF MIND

A CODE of sex morality, such as the Jewish, blending legal precepts and ethical ideals and aiming not only at rectitude but at saintliness, must regard purity of mind both as elemental in stimulating proper conduct and at the same time as the goal and objective of proper conduct. It is both a means and an end in our code of morality.

The many precepts of our code so far discussed may be divided into three groups, according to their intent and purpose. (a) The code prohibits certain acts because they are in themselves evil. Nakedness, the extremer forms of exposure, and the more intimate forms of love-making border closely on this territory, but sex perversions, despoiling and wasting of nature, dealt with in the previous chapter, and prostitution, rape and seduction, and adultery, discussed in succeeding chapters, are true representatives of this category. (b) The code prohibits certain acts which make it possible for those of evil intent to welcome the opportunity for sin, or for those of weak moral fibre to be tempted into sin. Many precepts in our code have this purpose: the prohibition against wearing garments of the opposite sex, the walls of separation between the sexes, chaperonage, and the more rigorous rules for separation of the divorced or betrothed couple. (c) Most of the rules, however, have the purpose of keeping passions down, temptations out of the way, the eye out of sight of sexual stimulants, and thus the mind free from indecent thoughts. To this end are directed the rules of modesty in dress for women; in fact, their entire conduct is calculated to keep the minds of men as well as their own pure. The prohibitions against levity and song and wine and dance and the severer prohibition against mixing the sexes at these entertainments, that against touching a woman, looking at her or her garments, walking behind her, or listening to her voice — all these aim at purity of mind in the man, and, according to a post-talmudic authority, similar prohibitions are intended for women in order to keep their minds pure.[1]

To these precepts should be added a few more which in the minds of the rabbis have special bearing on purity of thought. They teach that a person must avoid the sight of copulation either in man, beast, or fowl.[2] An exception is made in the case of breeders of live-stock, who go about their business in a professional way and in whom the sight of copulation between animals does not arouse unclean thoughts.[3] A later teacher prohibited taking note of a bed used by husband and wife, which is associated with copulation.[4]

The rabbis undoubtedly would say that the importance of purity of mind consists not so much as an end in itself as a means to proper conduct. Given a pure mind, proper conduct is practically assured; in an impure mind is rooted all the evil that man commits. The heart and the eyes are the two agents for promotion of sin — the eyes see and the heart lusts.[5] The biblical injunction, "Thou shalt keep thyself from every evil thing," is paraphrased in the Talmud, "Thou shalt avoid lascivious thoughts by day so that thou shalt not be defiled at night." [6] We are already familiar with the rabbinic dictum, "The thought of sin is worse than sin itself." [7] This is the rabbinic way of expressing a sentiment current in the literature of the Second Commonwealth and formulated in the New Testament, "Whosoever looketh on a woman to lust after her hath committed adultery with her already in his heart." [8] The severity of the sin of unclean thoughts is so great, according to one amora, that he who is guilty thereof will be forever barred from admittance into the presence of God.[9]

[1] *Sefer Ḥasidim*, 59.
[2] 'Ab. Zar. 20b; Midr. Tannaim, Deut. 23:10, p. 147.
[3] 'Ab. Zar. ibid.; B. M. 91a.
[4] *Reshit Ḥokmah*, Ḳedushah, ch. 8, p. 134b.
[5] Yer. Ber. 3c.
[6] Ket. 46a; 'Ab. Zar. 20b.
[7] Yoma 29a.
[8] Mat. 5:28. See also Lev. 6:25; Ahikar, Syr. version, A, 2:5.
[9] Nid. 13b.

Much more, however, was made of the ideal of purity of mind by post-talmudic moralists, philosophers, and cabalists. They have a common conception that the desire of the heart is to a physical act what the soul is to the body; in fact, the desire belongs, for the greater part, to the soul, while the act belongs to the body. But the soul is more important than the body, hence the *kawwanah* is more important than the deed. A sinful act soils the body, but a sinful thought detracts from the perfection of the soul. Thus, argues R. Judah he-Ḥasid, if you turn a corner and come suddenly upon a beautiful woman and you find pleasure in beholding her beauty, if you had no desire of the heart to look upon her beauty, you have committed no sin.[10] R. Israel Ba'al Shem has even a better suggestion concerning such an unpremeditated sinful act. "When it happens accidentally and unexpectedly that a man beholds the sight of a beautiful woman . . . he should immediately reason with himself whence cometh this beauty if not from the divine power that emanates into the world? Hence the source of beauty is in the upper spheres. Why, then, be attracted by the part; better be attracted by the All, which is the root and the source of all the beauty in the parts?" [11]

The evil of unclean thought is pernicious; seldom, if ever, can a man escape it. Early marriage is highly recommended for purity of mind. One who marries beyond the age of twenty, says a Babylonian amora, remains burdened all his life with unclean thoughts.[12] Another amora makes the observation that hardly a single human being is free from some sinful thought every day.[13] In fact the greater the person the more vicious his evil *yeẓer*.[14] What, then, should a man do to control his mind? The rabbis answer: concentrate on Torah. The Talmud formulates it thus: "If the ugly one (the evil *yeẓer*) meets thee, drag him into the house of study. If he be stone he will crumble, if he be steel he will melt." [15]

[10] *Sefer Ḥasidim*, 54.
[11] *Testament of BESHT*, Abrahams, *Ethical Wills*, II, pp. 297–8.
[12] Ḳid. 29b.
[13] B. B. 164b. See Tosafot, 'Ab. Zar. 20b, s. v. *shelo*.
[14] Suk. 51a.
[15] Ḳid. 30b; Suk. 51b. See also Ber. 5a. Yad, I. B. 21, 19, applies this rab-

Uncleanness of speech is akin to and derived from filthy thought. Even in a jocular fashion it is prohibited as indecent, in addition to the fact that joking in itself is prohibited as levity. Like unclean thoughts, *nibul peh,* or filthy speech, is a vice from which few individuals are free, and in every generation special condemnation is pronounced anew. Isaiah complained of his generation that "every mouth speaks indecently," and for this he threatened the unceasing wrath of God.[16] The rabbis of the Talmud offer a classical preachment: "On account of the sin of unclean speech great misfortunes and evil decrees keep on recurring; the youth of Israel perish, orphans and widows cry out and there is none to help them. . . . Everyone knows why a bride goes into the nuptial chamber, but he who gives himself to filthy talk causes a heavenly decree of seventy years of happiness to be turned into a decree of misery . . . yea, Gehinna is deepened for him. . . . This is true of him who listens to indecent conversation as well." [17]

---

binic statement specifically to the way of escaping the temptation of unclean thoughts.

[16] Is. 9:16.

[17] Sab. 33a. The law takes the attitude that cleanness of speech is a matter of ethical standard rather than legal prescription. Yet among the enactments of Candia is found one against *nibul peh* wherein definite penalties are formulated for violation. See *Sefer Taḳḳanot Ḳandia,* Artom and Cassuto, Jerusalem, 1947, No. 100.

CHAPTER VII

HARLOTRY

THE complex rules of modesty were designed to hold the sex impulse within the confines of the marriage bond, but they proved to be no match for that savage impulse. The sex urge refused to be tied down by matrimonial strings and sought freedom in indulgence outside of marriage. There were various channels for such satisfaction of sex desires, but one stands out as an institution like marriage itself, namely, prostitution. It has the dignity of great antiquity and the social dignity of having been maintained and regulated frequently as a public utility; it has a distinctive character, a historic evolution, and persistence throughout the ages. Jews like all other groups have had their share of prostitution, and can tell their own story of its history and progress.

I. SACRED PROSTITUTION

The story begins with sacred prostitution. In the oriental scene, the Hebrew people found this rooted from most primitive days. It existed in one of two forms, the priestess-prostitute and the lay prostitute. There were women votaries attached to the temple of worship as priestesses, who conceived of themselves as married to the deity, and who gave their bodies to worshipers for carnal union as part of the temple rite. Corresponding to the female priestess, there were male votaries who served female as well as male worshipers in like manner. The second form of sacred prostitution was less a temple rite and more a holy traffic. Women would spend a few weeks in harlotry, giving themselves for hire to anyone who would pay the price and dedicating the gain thereof to the sanctuary. These women were not priestesses, but pious members of the cult who offered the gain of their bodies to their deity.

Sacred prostitution flourished in the Orient, the land of sanctities, and Israel met it with varying reactions. The Hebrew term was *ḳedeshah* for the female and *ḳadesh* for the male. The practice proved quite a lure to the ancient Hebrews in their contacts with their heathen neighbors, so much so that it was sometimes adopted in the worship at the sanctuary of Jehovah. The sons of Eli are said to have employed their priestly office in the rite of sacred prostitution, "lying with the women that assembled at the door of the tabernacle of the congregation."[1] This conduct saddened their aged father, the high priest, and is recorded by the author of the First Book of Samuel with vehement protest; to that sin he ascribes the defeat of Israel before the Philistines, the capture of the ark of the Law, and the death of Eli and his sons. We do not hear of sacred prostitution in the time of Saul, David, and Solomon, but Rehoboam, son of Solomon, through the influence of his Ammonite mother, introduced the practice into the Temple of Jerusalem.[2] His grandson Asa[3] and his great-grandson Jehoshaphat[4] attempted to eradicate it, yet it lingered in suppressed form until the wicked king, Manasseh, carried it into full life again. At length the saintly King Josiah brought it to an end through his assault upon all idolatrous practices in the sanctuary at Jerusalem.[5] Out of this period came the Deuteronomic injunction: "There shall be no *ḳedeshah* among the daughters of Israel, neither shall there be a *ḳadesh* of the sons of Israel."[6] Following this period, sacred prostitution as part of Temple worship came to an end, for we hear no more of it,[7] though it is not improbable that for many decades

[1] I Sam. 2:22.
[2] I Kings 14:24.
[3] I Kings 15:11.
[4] II Kings 22:47.
[5] II Kings 23:7.
[6] Deut. 23:18.
[7] Later the *ḳedeshah* and the *zonah* seem to have merged together. Post-biblical authors have altogether lost the technical sense of *ḳedeshah*. Septuagint, Deut. 23:18, makes it synonymous with harlot and idolatress; Onkelos interprets it as sex relations between free-born and slaves; Jonathan trans-

individuals participated in that lustful activity at the shrines of their heathen neighbors.

The second form of sacred prostitution, carried on as street traffic for the benefit of the temple treasury rather than as a temple rite, also found its way into the ancient Hebrew camp. The patriarch Judah mistook his daughter-in-law, Tamar, for that kind of *ḳedeshah*.[8] He did not hesitate to go in unto her, nor to make his act known among the neighbors. The Hebrew term for that sort of prostitute is also *ḳedeshah,* but more often she is called *zonah,* that is, a simple harlot, stripped of her sanctity, despite her pious motives. Our Hebrew sources do not tell us where the institution came from, but we know, albeit from later sources,[9] that the Hebrews found it among their Canaanite neighbors. Nor do we know to what extent it was ingrained in Hebrew life except that it constituted a sufficient menace to the moral fibre of Israel to necessitate the deuteronomic legislation: "Thou shalt not bring the hire of a harlot (*zonah*) or the price of a dog into the house of the Lord thy God for any vow; for even both these are an abomination unto the Lord thy God." [10]

A third form of sacred prostitution deserves mention here. The ancients in their savage state held festival orgies as part of their idolatrous public celebrations. This practice was widespread in antiquity both in the Orient and the Occident, and the Hebrews were also drawn into that form of sacred debauchery. The Midianite incident that brought Phineas fame as a zealot for slaying Zimri, the arch offender, was one of the saturnalia of the Ba'al Pe'or cult.[11] Because this temptation constituted so pernicious a moral danger to the children of Israel, the lawgiver found no milder way of eradicating it

---

lates it by prostitute. Philo, *de. migrat. Abrahami,* at the end, agrees with this translation, and believes that the rape of Dinah was a typical case of *ḳedeshah.* The halakah has accepted this translation, and so have the exegetical writers. See Ḳimhi, I Kings, 14:24; Rashi, ibid.; Naḥmanides commentary, ibid.; Yad, Ishut, 1,4; Karaite, *Keter Torah,* Gen. 38:15.

[8] Gen. 38:21–2.

[9] Test. of Judah, 12:2; Baruch 6:43; Herodotus, I, 199; Justin, *Hist. Philippicae,* 18,5; Westermarck, *History of Human Marriage,* I, 208–14.

[10] Deut. 23:19.

[11] Numb. 25:1 f.

than by commanding that all adult females of the Midianites be put to death.[12] The whoredom at mountain tops and under green trees, accompanied by the pouring of oil and offering of sacrifices, referred to by the prophets,[13] probably represents the usual sex orgies in celebration of heathen festivals. We have no record of such orgies held in connection with Jehovah worship. The Jew who yearned for licentiousness had to join a heathen festival. Therein consisted the lure of idolatry and therein may be found the basis for the extreme intolerance the Bible displays toward the original inhabitants of Canaan.

A derivative of sacred prostitution is the ritual defloration of virgins, prior to their marriage, by men other than the groom. This has its origin in many primitive concepts and motives. It is a form of offering to the deity, of magical blessing of the womb, or of superstitious fear of undoing virginity. Defloration was usually performed by the head of the tribe or by the priest, sometimes by a person of lesser dignity or even by a number of the male guests at the nuptials. It was in vogue for a long time in the East; [14] in the West, out of this early sacramental origin, it developed into the *jus primae noctis,* or the law which granted the resident government official the right to the first night with every virgin bride.

One would assume that the Jews never had anything to do with this primitive practice, for throughout the Bible the state of virginity is regarded with a special sense of purity; a high value is set upon the maid entering the nuptial chamber untouched by any male, so that a price is paid by the groom who enjoys the virgin legitimately, and a penalty is imposed upon any one who takes that enjoyment by force and illegitimately. Deception as to the bride's virginity involves a crime serious enough for capital punishment.[15] Yet, as in the case of sacred prostitution, possibly also in the case

[12] Numb. 31:16–17.

[13] Is. 57:3 f.; Jer. 2:20; 3:6; Hosea 4:13.

[14] Herodotus, *History* (London, 1875), IV, 168; Wellhausen, *Die Ehe bei die Arabern,* p. 464. Westermarck, *Marriage Ceremonies in Morocco,* p. 271. See Ibn Ezra, Haggai 2:12.

[15] Deut. 22:13 f; 22:28–29; Ex. 22:16.

of defloration, the biblical ideal was one thing and life's actuality another. The Bible reflected the native and higher Jewish ideal, while the routine of life fell a prey to the foreign influences which the people picked up from their neighbors. One word in the Bible betrays that defloration was not an unknown and uncommon practice among the Jews. The word is *ḥalalah* (חללה) and the Bible has a number of references to it. A father may not make his daughter a *ḥalalah;* [16] a priest may not marry a *ḥalalah.*[17] The word is generally translated a "profaned one," leaving the term indefinite and confusing. This definition is prompted by the fact that the same term is used for "profaning" the Sabbath, the priesthood, or the name of God,[18] but one may wonder what there is in common between a profaned Sabbath and a profaned maiden. The rabbinic attempt to define *ḥalalah* as the maiden who by the sin of her mother or by her own sin has become unfit for marriage to a priest [19] is evidently artificial and begs the question. The Bible could not have had that in mind. Is it not more than likely that the term is employed in its strictly literal sense, "a perforated one," one pierced through, one who has been deflowered? [20] The earlier forms of defloration being performed by male contact, the deflowered girl is therefore accounted by the Bible as equivalent to the *zonah,* the harlot; and where, as in the case of the high priest, virginity is insisted upon, the deflowered girl becomes prohibited as the direct antithesis to the virgin.[21] To what extent defloration was practiced among the Jews of biblical times is not known, but evidently to a sufficiently large extent to give the legislator cause to combat it by various injunctions. In the rabbinic period the practice of defloration was apparently unknown among the Jews, except the *jus primae noctis,* which they tried to evade. However, at the end of the amoraic period we hear that Palestinian Jews

[16] Lev. 19:29.

[17] Lev. 21:7, 14.

[18] Ex. 31:14; Lev. 10:10; 20:3; 21:9; 22:15.

[19] Sifra, Lev. 21:7; Ḳid. 71a. The Talmud has also a male *ḥalal* of which the Bible does not know.

[20] See L. Ginzberg, Beitrage zur Lexicographie des Aramäischen, in *Festschrift Adolph Schwartz,* p. 354, s. v. *ḤRF.* See also *Miḳra ki-Peshuṭo,* Ehrlich, Lev. 21:7 and Epstein, *Marriage Laws,* p. 322.

[21] In Lev. 21:13–15, *ḥalalah* is contrasted with *betulah.*

practiced artificial defloration, without male contact,[22] an ugly lesson which they seem to have learned from their contemporary neighbors.

The *jus primae noctis* was never exercised by Jewish government dignitaries over their own people, but was one of the bitterest annoyances imposed by foreign rulers — and how seldom it was that the Jews were not subjected to foreign rulers! It is reported that the Maccabean war started in protest against this outrageous demand for the first night with every Jewish virgin bride by the Greek rulers of Judea. Under Roman subjection the *jus primae noctis* was again imposed upon Judea, but the Jews were now too weak to defend the honor of their daughters. They did the next best thing. They schemed to hide from their Roman officers any knowledge of Jewish weddings; they changed the wedding day from the customary Wednesday to Tuesday; they omitted the writing of the ketubah and other public ceremonials; they permitted copulation between the betrothed pair prior to the nuptials, so that the bride would be non-virgin at the time of the wedding.[23]

The story of sacred prostitution in all its forms and with its derivatives as here told makes clear the fact that not one phase of it was of native Jewish origin, but was either imported into the Hebrew camp by their own wicked rulers from idolatrous neighbors or was forced upon them by foreign despots. All told, it presents the picture of a battle between the native Hebrew aversion to carnality in the name of religion, and the heathen groups, one after another, who made a religion of carnality. Legislator and prophet, warrior and rabbi, fought the battle for purity, both purity of the worship of Jehovah and purity of sex life. Despite some casualties, inevitable either in the conflict of ideals or in the conflict of powers, Judaism was steadily victorious.

II. SECULAR PROSTITUTION

While sacred prostitution and ritual defloration were foreign imports into Judea, secular prostitution was born on

[22] Pirḳ. de R. E. ch. 16; Yer. Ket. 25b; Yeb. 34b; Gen. R. 51, 11. See also Joel Miller — *Ḥiluf Minhagim,* Vienna, 1878, #40.

[23] See the brief article on *Jus Primae Noctis* in Jewish Encyclopedia.

native soil. The Jews no more than any other racial group could claim freedom from the social evil, particularly in the remote past when the family was less intimate and romantic, when the level of sex morality was lower, and when the position of woman was more servile. Aside from irregularities in sex relations, such as betrayal of innocent maidens or occasional adulterous amours, there was a regular and professional traffic in prostitution, integrated within the social life of ancient Israel.

The Hebrew prostitute was called *zonah,* which means the "faithless one." The original connotation is fraught with a variety of social implications, as we shall see, but the biblical authors always refer to the term with condemnation. When Simeon and Levi avenge themselves on Shechem for the rape of their sister, Dinah, they justify themselves with the exclamation, "Shall one treat our sister as a *zonah?*"[24] The strongest term of reproach the prophet could apply to Israel for unfaithfulness to God was *zonah.*[25] Yet the Bible itself betrays traces of a remoter past, when the term *zonah* was not so thoroughly opprobrious, and conveys the impression that not all cases so designated had the same social standing or the same moral disapproval. Some were thoroughly condemned as criminals, others were social outcasts, still others half respectable.

In our judgment, the respectable *zonah* is the oldest of her namesakes. She was not a harlot at all, but a metronymic wife. Among the Arabs, too, the metronymic wife was called *zina.*[26] In remote antiquity the Hebrews had a metronymic family organization, wherein the husband does not own his wife, nor does he take her to his tribe, but she remains with her own kin and he stays with her for a prolonged period, even permanently, or for shorter visits. The man may enter into two marriages of different orders; he may have a patronymic wife at home who has become part of his household, and a metronymic wife away from home

[24] Gen. 34:31.
[25] Is. 23:15, et passim.
[26] W. Robertson Smith, *Kinship and Marriage in Early Arabia,* p. 151; Epstein, op. cit. p. 51.

who retains her independence. The patronymic wife is subject, is faithful, does his bidding, and cannot free herself without a release from him. The metronymic wife does not subject herself to her husband, retains her freedom from her husband's domination, and, when displeased with him, sends him off and takes on another as his successor.

When the Jews were close to the scene of metronymic marriage, the woman was respectable in their eyes. She was like a concubine, even though they sometimes called her *zonah.* But as the metronymic order receded into the past, her reputation suffered. She did not at all meet the standards of faithful wifehood. The husband visited her away from his home, she was free to go off with another man at will, the children begotten by her were not his but counted to her own tribe.[27] They considered her, therefore, just a sexual luxury that did not fit into the accepted family frame. She was not condemned, but was only half respectable. Of this type of *zonah,* the metronymic wife, we find a few biblical examples — the mother of Jephthah,[28] the two women litigants before King Solomon, each claiming the living child as her own,[29] and probably also the first wife of Hosea.[30] The biblical command that a priest may not marry a *zonah* probably also intended to prohibit a priest from entering into a metronymic marriage, for thereby the offspring were alienated from the holy order of priesthood, since they were counted after their mother.[31]

Less respectable than the metronymic wife was the "inn-

[27] Kimḥi, Judg. 11:1, quotes a *targum* which explains the term *zonah* as one who is married out of her tribe and is thereby disinherited. It is more likely that diverting the lineage of the children is of greater importance than turning the line of succession to property; and because in a metronymic marriage the lineage of the children is turned, the man's family call the woman a *zonah.*

[28] Judg. 11:1.

[29] I Kings 3:16.

[30] Hosea 1:2. New significance is attained by the phrase, *eshet zenunim ve-yalde zenunim,* meaning probably a metronymic wife and children.

[31] Lev. 21:7. Significant is the expression, *velo yehalel zar'o,* Lev. 21:15. One is tempted to say that while the term *zonah* is used to designate a harlot, the expression *ishah zonah* is mostly used in the technical sense of a *zonah*-wife, or as we would say, a metronymic wife.

keeper," who also fell into the category of *zonah*.[32] Possibly she also had her origin in the metronymic family organization, with the significant distinction that she was the metronymic wife of many husbands. It is believed that at one time there existed in the Orient a kind of family organization that we now call "nair polyandry," that is, a metronymic family headed by the wife, who maintains her own apartment in the midst of her own tribe and has a number of husbands visiting her successively for a specific period of time.[33] One can easily see how by multiplying husbands, by calling any visitor a husband and any husband a visitor, this metronymic family apartment could be looked upon as a public inn. The Jew, to whom nair polyandry was a strange conception, could understand this situation only in the illicit commercial sense, simply as a brothel. Starting from the other angle of the simple commercial necessity of providing lodging for wayfarers, and together with food and shelter also entertainment and refreshment, we arrive at the logical consequence of including sexual comforts for the visitors in the service of the hostelry. Thus it is that both from the commercial angle and that of the metronymic family the inn ultimately becomes a house of ill fame and the innkeeper a *zonah*.

The natural location of the inn was at the gate of the city, since its traffic was among wayfarers, and probably a sign or emblem of its trade was displayed in the form of a colored cord or lantern.[34] When the inn became a brothel, it continued the tradition of segregation in a separate street, possibly at the end of the city but not necessarily at the gate.[35] It also continued the traditional display of a red emblem.

The innkeeper as a woman of easy virtue is recorded as early as the Code of Hammurabi, which teaches that a devotee entering an inn suffers the death penalty.[36] The Jews first came into contact with the profession when Joshua's

[32] Some biblical commentators derive the word *zonah* when used in this sense from the root *zun*, to feed. *Ḳimhi*, Joshua, 2:1.

[33] W. Robertson Smith, *Kinship and Marriage*, ch. 5; Westermarck, *History of Human Marriage*, III, p. 154.

[34] Josh. 2:15, 18. See *Miḳra ki-Peshuṭo*, ibid. and ad Gen. 38:14.

[35] See Ket. 64b: *shuḳ shel zonot*.

[36] Code Hammurabi, 110.

spies were sheltered by Rahab the innkeeper at the gate of Jericho.[37] The Bible has no special term for the innkeeper other than the general unsavory appellation, *zonah,* but Josephus makes sure that we include the innkeeper in the biblical condemnation of the *zonah.*[38] However, the Targumim employ the technical term *pundeḳita,* the exact equivalent of innkeeper, to translate the biblical *zonah* in that sense,[39] and the Talmud follows that terminology.[40]

The other professional prostitute, equivalent to the innkeeper in the eyes of the law and also designated as *zonah* but apparently inferior to her socially, was the street woman. In fairness it should be recalled that she was originally a sacred prostitute who was not connected with the temple but offered herself for hire and dedicated that gain to the sanctuary. Out of that sacred calling developed the secular streetwalking prostitute. She was a "singing girl," [41] who used song as a means of attracting the attention of men. The "song of the harlot" brought a familiar picture to the audience of the prophet Isaiah.[42] The more gifted would use a musical instrument to play forth her invitations to men; the fewer her personal charms, the more energetically she strummed her musical solicitations. She was all about the city and kept herself in evidence in the marketplace, her face uncovered,[43] her attire gaudy, her manner vulgar, "walking with stretched forth neck and wanton eyes, walking and mincing and making a tinkling with her feet." [44] In the Targumim and Midrashim she is technically designated as *nafḳat bera,* a street walker.[45] This term has lingered through all these centuries, so that in our own day *nafḳa,* an abbreviation from *nafḳat bera,* is still employed to designate a harlot.

[37] Josh. 2:1.
[38] Josephus, *Antiq*. III, 12, 2.
[39] See Targum ad Josh. 2:1; Judg. 11:1; I Kings 3:16; Ez. 23:44.
[40] Yeb. 122a.
[41] Test. of Judah 23:2.
[42] Is. 23:15.
[43] Assyr. Code, I, 40, forbids a prostitute to veil herself. The passage in Gen. 38:15 which gives the impression that the *zonah* had her face covered is correctly explained by the commentators.
[44] Is. 3:10 f.
[45] Onkelos, Gen. 34:31, et passim.

There is no denying that the Jews had their share of secular professional prostitution, else the laws against it would not have been written. But it must have been a rarity. The Jewish brothel as a social institution seems to have been nonexistent in the biblical and talmudic periods. There is sufficient evidence in the fact that the law has nothing to say on the subject of regulating the traffic, either in respect to the ritual purity of the inmates, or as to community ordinances concerning such establishments. Furthermore, there is hardly any mention in the Bible, Talmud, or Midrashim of a Jewish prostitute maintaining a brothel. Almost as rare as the brothel was the street-walking prostitute. Probably at no time were the Jews free from this type of fallen women, but their presence in Jewish society must have been rare at all times. The purity of womanhood was an ideal highly prized among Jews throughout history. Social condemnation of harlotry was so severe that only an abnormal woman could defy such social and moral forces. The rarity of the harlot in Jewish society, perhaps, justifies Philo in believing that according to Jewish law a prostitute "is not even allowed to live." [46]

Even in post-talmudic times we do not hear of Jewish brothels or prostitutes until the fourteenth century. The Church had decreed a death penalty for a Jew who visited a brothel of Christian women, but Jewish young men, apparently, disregarded this danger. Whereupon certain communities, especially in Italy, thought it their duty to provide Jewish houses of prostitution for the foolhardy young people within the walls of the ghetto, under proper supervision as to hygiene and ritual purity. The question was debated before the rabbinate, and the verdict was against it.[47] Not that the rabbis could entirely stamp out Jewish prostitution, but they could not permit the community to give it sanction,

[46] Philo, *de Josepho,* 43, ed. Cohn, I, p. 167. See also *de spec. leg.* III, 51, ed. Cohn, II, p. 198. He may have read Deut. 23:18: *lo teḥayeh,* there shall not *live* instead of there shall not be. So in the Samaritan Targum. He has further evidence from Gen. 38:24 and Deut. 22:21. See Ritter, *Philo und die Halacha,* pp. 91–3.

[47] See Responsa, R. Judah b. ha-Rash, 17; Arama, *'Aḳedat Yiẓḥaḳ,* va-Yera', ed. Warsau, 1904, p. 114a; Bernfeld, *Dor Tahapukot,* p. 30.

no matter what the reason. Under such circumstances, however, it would not be surprising to find the Jewish streetwalker, as few as there may have been, prosper in her illicit trade.[47a] In the latest centuries, with the congestion of Jews in big cities and the general break-down of moral discipline among young people, professional Jewish prostitutes, even though fewer than justified by the proportion of Jews to the general population, are no longer rare or unusual. Interesting is a legal question that arose in Egypt in the last century, about Jewish prostitutes who donated a Torah cover and other holy objects to the synagogue; the authorities wanted to know whether they might be accepted or used in the synagogue. The rabbis did not like the idea but could cite no legal objection. However, one of the harlots, in making her contribution to the synagogue, had had her name woven into the Torah cover in golden letters. This was too much for the rabbis. They felt it would have a demoralizing effect on young people, because apparently her name was well known, especially to those who visited her.[48] The cover was ordered to be put away and never used.

III. PROFESSIONAL HARLOTRY

For legal purposes, whether we deal with biblical or rabbinic law, we need not go into the finer distinctions between one kind of harlotry and another. Whether sacred or secular, whether in the brothel or on the street, they share one common characteristic; they are professional harlots. The Bible may have had in mind a special punishment for the *ḳedeshah* — perhaps a death penalty, because her profession was bound up with idolatry. Nevertheless, she was a *zonah* at the same time. Post-biblical literature, including the Apocrypha and Talmud, no longer know of the *ḳedeshah* and think only in terms of *zonah,* the professional prostitute.

Because of the historic connection of prostitution with the idolatrous cults of the Canaanites, the Bible first legislates

[47a] Hence we find occasionally communal enactments for the purpose of eliminating prostitution. See, e.g. *Sefer Taḳḳanot Kandia,* Artom and Cassuto, Jerusalem, 1943, Nos. 31 and 113, and *Taḳḳanot haḳehillot deḳahal Ashkenuzim,* Amsterdam, 1737, No. 71.

[48] Raphael Aaron. b. Simeon, *Nehar Miẓrayim,* p. 12.

against prostitution in connection with the Temple or the priesthood. It prohibits sacred prostitution as such in the command referred to above. It further prohibits bringing the gain of a harlot to the sanctuary as an offering.[49] Again, it forbids a priest to marry a harlot.[50] In addition, the levitical law prohibits parents giving their daughters into harlotry.[51] Especially severe is the offense of a priest's daughter who takes to prostitution; she is sentenced to death by burning.[52] One more biblical law relating to harlotry should be cited, that of the bride who is found to be non-virgin. Deuteronomy legislates that "if this thing be true and the token of virginity be not found for the damsel, then they shall bring out the damsel to the door of her father's house, and the men of the city shall stone her with stones that she die, because she hath wrought folly in Israel, to play the whore in her father's house." [53]

The biblical attempt to stamp out harlotry among the Jewish people is definite enough. The question may be raised, however, concerning the penalty the Bible had in mind for violation of the law. The specific death penalty is prescribed for the girl who takes to harlotry without her father's knowledge — burning to death, if she be a priest's daughter, and stoning, if the daughter of a layman. Does this mean that harlotry under all circumstances was a capital crime? The Book of Jubilees takes that position, ruling that any Jewish harlot is to be burned to death.[54] Philo states that among the Jews a harlot is not allowed to live, and indicates that her penalty is death by stoning.[55] The Book of Jubilees evidently generalizes the biblical law of the priest's daughter,

49 Deut. 23:19.

50 Lev. 21:7.

51 Lev. 19:29.

52 Lev. 21:9.

53 Deut. 22:20–21. The Assyrian Code, I, 55, under similar circumstances, gives the father the right to punish his daughter in any manner he pleases.

54 Jubilees 20:4. See Albeck, *Das Buch der Jubiläen und die Halacha*, pp. 26 f. That the author of the Book of Jubilees prescribes for the harlot of an Israelitish family the same penalty which the Bible prescribes for the priest's daughter, may be due to a theological assumption of their sect that the sanctity of priesthood went over to all Israelites, since all are a "kingdom of priests."

55 Philo, *de special. leg.* III, 51, ed. Cohn, II, p. 198. See note 46 above.

while Philo apparently generalizes the law of Deuteronomy concerning the non-virgin bride. Both are, no doubt, mistaken. There could be no law in the Bible concerning the marriage of a harlot (to a priest), if the law required her to be put to death. The two instances where the Bible prescribes capital punishment for harlotry represent not the sexual sin as such but sex liberties taken by the daughter in disregard or in defiance of parental authority. They are the female counterpart of the "rebellious son," for whom Deuteronomy also prescribed the death penalty.[56] As adultery for the married woman constitutes unfaithfulness to her husband, her master, so harlotry in the unmarried girl constitutes unfaithfulness to her father, who prior to marriage is her master. It may not be far-fetched to assume that for such defiance of parental authority the original penalty was death by burning in all cases, but that the sentence was modified by the deuteronomic legislator in two ways, in requiring court action before sentence was imposed, and in reducing the penalty to stoning. The priestly caste, however, more jealous for the purity of priestly families and at the same time more persistent in preservation of old traditions, retained the old usage of executing the harlot who had defied parental authority by burning. The death penalty, we feel, is specific for these cases; the ordinary case of harlotry was not penalized by death. The man who cohabits with a harlot is not accounted by the Bible guilty of sin, because he is never professional unless he is a *ḳadesh.*

Rabbinic law agrees that there is no death penalty for prostitution, no matter what kind. The patriarchal authority of parents over children had come to an end in the early days of the Second Commonwealth, and the death penalty in the case of harlotry in defiance of parental authority, as here explained, could not apply in the rabbinic period. The rabbis, therefore, interpreted these two instances of capital punishment as cases where not harlotry but adultery was involved. That is to say, the priest's daughter who commits adultery, and the Israelite's daughter who at the time of her first contact with her husband is discovered to have com-

[56] Deut. 21:18 f.

mitted adultery after betrothal, are put to death, the former by burning, the latter by stoning.[57] This interpretation, though in many points forced and artificial, was not impossible for the rabbis of the Talmud, because the term *zonah* in Hebrew applies equally to the adulteress as well as to the harlot. They consider prostitution, therefore, simply a violation of a negative biblical command, for which the standard penalty is flagellation. The negative biblical command which they have in mind is either the levitical law against giving a daughter to prostitution[58] or the deuteronomic injunction against the *ḳedeshah*,[59] for to the rabbis the *ḳedeshah* is a plain harlot.

Josephus declares that a priest may not marry a harlot; so does Philo. Both are supported by R. Akiba of the Talmud.[60] Both are correct in presenting the original intent of the levitical law. But the later rabbinic halakah rejects this natural interpretation and gives a special definition of the term *zonah* in respect to the law of priestly marriage, as a woman who has had contact with a gentile, slave, or a man of incestuous kinship. The harlot, therefore, who gives herself for hire to all men but avoids her kin and gentiles and slaves, is according to later halakah fit for marriage to a priest.[61] Josephus, however, is alone in declaring that a harlot is not even permitted to marry an Israelitish man.[62] The natural interpretation of the biblical verse on which he bases his decision does not support his view, and rabbinic law definitely denies that a Jewish harlot may not be married to a Jew.

In respect to marriage, therefore, the halakah is distinctly lenient to the professional harlot. On the other hand, it is quite severe in regard to unmarried contact with a harlot. Not only does the harlot herself suffer the penalty of flagel-

[57] Both cases will be treated more fully in the chapter on adultery.

[58] Lev. 19:29; Sifra, ed. Weiss, p. 90d; Tos. Ḳid. 1, 4; San. 76a.

[59] Deut. 23:18; Targum Jonathan, Rashi, Naḥmanides, Ibn Ezra, ibid. So also Sifre, Deut. ibid. according to a reading quoted by RABD, Yad, Na'arah Betulah, 2,17. So also Philo, *de migrat. Abrahami* at the end. So also Maimonides, Yad, Ishut, 1,4 and Na'arah Betulah, 2,17.

[60] Epstein, *Marriage Laws*, p. 323.

[61] Ibid. p. 324 f. Note that *SMG* takes exception to this ruling.

[62] Josephus, *Antiq*. IV, 8, 23. See Epstein, ibid. note 181.

lation for her conduct, but also the men who visit her, for they share the guilt of whoredom with her.[63] As previously mentioned, the law forbids a man to pass by the house of a harlot within a distance of four ells, and if the man is seen too often about the house of a woman of ill repute, he must suffer disciplinary flagellation.[64] Even catching a whiff of the perfume of a harlot is a sin, for it is sure ultimately to undermine one's moral resistance.[65]

IV. NON-PROFESSIONAL HARLOTRY; FORNICATION

The Bible does not seem to consider non-commercial and unpremeditated sexual contact between a man and an unmarried woman as harlotry. In fact, the Bible has no prohibition against it, either for the man or for the woman. It takes up this subject only in connection with the rape or seduction of a virgin, and there it is treated not as a moral crime but as a civil case against the man for theft of virginity. That the family was outraged by such an act, there is no doubt, and in the older law the case was left to the family to square it with the offender, upon whom was visited the full horror of the ancient blood revenge.[66] But from the time of the earliest formulation of biblical law, the family could do nothing but demand payment for the stolen virginity or give the girl in marriage to the ravisher. This done, the girl was not a harlot and the man was not a criminal.

During the Second Commonwealth, the age of exaggerated moral discipline, when even innocent sociability between the sexes was condemned, any unmarried contact between a man and a woman was, of course, cause for public outrage. But there is no legal verdict against the practice until the age of the early tannaim, when R. Eliezer taught that any unmarried contact between a man and a woman constituted harlotry. The dishonored maiden, therefore, is the biblical *zonah,* who is not admitted into marriage with priests,[67] and who, if a priest's daughter, is executed by burn-

[63] Yad, Ishut, 1, 4; Na'arah Betulah, 2, 17. See notes 58, 59.
[64] See note 52, p. 114 above.
[65] B. Ḳ. 16b.
[66] Gen. 34; II Sam. 13.
[67] Yeb. 61b.

ing for her indiscretion.[68] Furthermore, if the father was aware of the mishap to his daughter and failed to prevent it, he is guilty of a sin for which he suffers flagellation.[69]

The view of R. Eliezer did not prevail in the halakah, however, and his contemporaries as well as successors drew a clear distinction between the prostitute who gives herself to many men either for gain or for gratification of passion, and the girl who succumbs to the temptation of intimacies with a lover. Unmarried cohabitation of the latter kind, in their view, does not constitute a violation of biblical command; the man, the girl, and her father, if he consented to it, suffer no penalty on the basis of the biblical injunction against prostitution,[70] although they may be penalized by local community authorities for immoral conduct. This peculiarly lenient view of the Talmud toward unmarried sex relations between lovers has never been challenged or modified by post-talmudic teachers on any legal grounds. The impression was created by a certain statement of Maimonides [71] that he considered such unmarried relations as biblically prohibited under the head of *ḳedeshah,* and would therefore prescribe flagellation for violations. But in reality Maimonides condemns as harlotry permanent unmarried relations between a man and a woman, a "mistress" or a concubine.[72] But he makes it clear that "there is no flagellation where cohabitation took place as a matter of accident . . . and where the girl had not premeditated it, for that has no permanency and is not usual." [73]

However, the legal leniency toward non-professional harlotry should not mislead us into believing that the Jews tolerated unmarried relations between the sexes. The Jews have a super-halakic standard of morality, the agadic standard, evidences of which we have seen abundantly through all the preceding chapters; that standard obtains its authority from

[68] Sifra, ed. Weiss, p. 94c. His view could not be understood by the amoraim. See San. 51a–b. Josephus is in full agreement with him. *Antiq.* IV, 8, 23.

[69] Tos. Ḳid. 1,4.

[70] Sifra, l. c.: *yakol 'al ma'ase yeḥidi;* Yeb. 61b.

[71] Yad, Ishut, 1,4.

[72] See Epstein, *Marriage Laws,* pp. 70 ff.

[73] Yad, Na'arah Betulah, 2, 17 and *Kesef Mishneh* thereto.

public sensibilities and often proves more potent than the law. The various restrictions set up against the mingling of the sexes, the constant watch by the community over the conduct of young people, all were intended to prevent unmarried sex relations so that the bride might be virgin and the groom pure at their marriage. It may be repeated here that in amoraic times, the court put a person's life in danger rather than permit him unmarried intercourse with a maiden.[74] Philo assures us that in his day Jewish girls, practically without exception, entered their nuptials in complete innocence and purity.[75] This testimony is again and again corroborated by rabbinic records, with a sense of pride in the purity of Jewish girls as compared with those of the heathens.[76] Total elimination of premarital unchastity was, of course, never to be expected. Thus a Babylonian amora complains that Messiah has not come because there is too much of unmarried sex relations going on in his city, Nahardea.[77] We have mentioned above the trouble of certain Jewish communities in keeping bride and groom from prenuptial sex contacts.[78] But certainly the effort to stop such practices was not lacking, and the severity of communal enactments and their measures of enforcement had a telling effect. It is no exaggeration to say that down to the present time pre-nuptial sex relations among Jewish women has been a rare occurrence, and when such a mishap has occurred, the girl has felt herself disgraced for life beyond redemption.

Men, it may be assumed, were never as pure from prenuptial sex indulgence as were women, and the social stigma against offenders among them was never so sharp as against women. Yet the standards of sex morality presented in the foregoing chapters definitely assume that men can be expected to be as pure as the weaker sex. In fact, most provisions of our moral code were directed to control of the conduct of men. Philo boasts that Jewish men in his day enter their nuptial chambers as innocent as the brides they

[74] San. 75a; Yer. Sab. 14a; Yad, Yesode ha-Torah, 5, 9.
[75] Philo, *de Josepho,* 43, ed. Cohn, I, p. 167.
[76] 'Erub. 21b.
[77] Yoma 19b.
[78] See p. 126 above to the end of chapter 4.

marry.[79] Perhaps he exaggerated, having in mind the average well behaved young man, and closing his eyes against the few exceptions. It is sufficient, however, to hear such praise of Jewish young men in Alexandria twenty centuries ago. Even the small kernel of truth in his exaggeration is enough to show a much higher level of sex morality among Jews of his day than we now permit ourselves to hope for. Early marriages, watchful parents, small communities, Jewish self-government, communal discipline, and the influence of religion, all contributed to the purity of men as of women. To the extent to which some of these influences have continued in Jewish life today, the level of sex morality of Jewish men still remains high. But modern influences emanating from city life, from realism in literature and on the stage, from secularization of life, from the self-expression fad in education, from the breakdown of all social walls of separation between the sexes, and of all authority in private life, whether that of parents or State or church, all these things have brought down the level of sexual purity among Jews as among men of other racial groups.

V. GENTILE AND SLAVE

The distinction between professional and non-professional prostitution vanishes in the case of a gentile or a slave, because marriage between Jew and gentile, or Jew and slave, is not valid; therefore the sexual contact is of the nature of harlotry whether commercial or romantic. Another reason is the fact that probably the heathen woman, and certainly the slave girl, were held under the legal suspicion that in giving themselves to man for sexual satisfaction they so acted with more than one man and in a commercial spirit. With this in mind, we now have the simple question before us: What has the law to say about prostitution with a gentile woman or slave girl?

There is no biblical legislation on the subject, because, as for the woman, the Bible does not legislate for the gentile or the slave, and as for the man who visits her, the assumption may be made that he is free from guilt because, as said

[79] Philo, l. c.

above, the man is never considered professional unless he be a *ḳadesh.* In post-biblical law, however, considerable attention is given to sex relations between gentiles and Jews because of the moral degradation suffered thereby by the Jewish community. The story of Phineas, who slew Kazbi the Midianite and her Jewish partner in the act of harlotry, was taken as a precedent in the law as to treatment of a Jew cohabiting with a gentile. The rabbis call it "the lynch law," that is, the fornicator can be put to death without trial by any zealot who feels outraged by his act.[80] This law is presented as a Sinaitic revelation, which means, incidentally, that it was recognized by the rabbis as having great antiquity.

In the Greek period of Jewish history there were evidently too extensive sexual relations between Jews and heathens. At the same time, with the Maccabean victory there was a resurgence of national pride and separateness and a new condemnation of sexual intimacies with the heathen. Tradition therefore ascribes to the Hasmonean court a new or renewed enactment prohibiting sexual contact with non-Jewish women. This enactment was again promulgated and reenforced at the time of the fall of the Jewish state, apparently because of the greater need for building up Jewish resistance to the assimilative influences from without. The authorities for this legislation were the schools of the Hillelites and the Shammaites.[81] The penalty is not specified either in the enactment of the Hasmoneans or in the ordinance of the Hillelites and Shammaites, and it is felt that it was to be determined by local authorities as they saw fit for the purpose of community discipline, which meant generally that flagellation was administered to the offender to the amount and in the manner ordered by the local court.[82]

[80] San. 82a. The precedent, it should be noted, represented sacred prostitution, but we have already mentioned the fact that in post-biblical times the distinction between sacred and secular prostitution ceased to exist.

[81] San. ibid.; Sab. 17b; 'Ab. Zar. 36b; Yad, I.B. 12,2. According to amoraic interpretation, the "lynch law" refers to public prostitution with a heathen woman; the Hasmonean ordinance stressed the offense of private sexual acts; the last enactment includes a prohibition against intimacies with a gentile woman even where the carnal act was not committed. See Josephus, *Antiq.* XII, 4,6.

[82] Yad, I. B. 12,2. Some authorities feel that since professional prostitution with a Jewish woman is biblically prohibited (see notes 58 and 59 above), the

In view of the fact that Jewish prostitutes were so rare, sex relations with non-Jewish prostitutes became a grievous problem to the Jewish community. The problem was most acute in mediaeval Europe. Under the rule of the Church in mediaeval times, it became part of the general problem of Jewish-Christian relationship. The Church saw in sexual intimacies between Jews and Christians a danger to Christianity, not so much in their immorality, but more so in the possibility that friendships might thereby be established leading to apostasy from the Church. The famous or infamous badge was ordered to be worn by Jews under Church decree for the one reason above all others, that the gentile prostitute thereby recognize her visitor as a Jew and be warned to avoid him.[83] If, however, despite the badge, intimacies did occur between a Jew and a gentile prostitute, the Jew was burned alive in the public square.[84] This danger, no doubt, was an effective deterrent to offenses with non-Jewesses. We find a reflection of the fear of Jewish men carnally approaching non-Jewish women from a ruling of R. Judah he-Ḥasid, who teaches that a Jewish woman who finds herself in the presence of immoral Jewish young men may conceal her Jewish identity and claim to be Christian, may don Christian clothes, probably displaying a crucifix on her chest, in order to intimidate the men against molesting her.[85]

To the Jews, sex relations with non-Jews was not a question of rivalry between synagogue and Church but a purely moral problem. The danger to life threatened by the Church was only of secondary interest to the rabbis; the primary interest was the corruption of the soul.[86] They had the talmudic preachment before them that he who cohabits with a gen-

---

same biblical prohibition should apply also to prostitution with a gentile woman, which always has the status of professional prostitution, since marriage is impossible. But the halakah does not recognize this view. See *Maggid* ad Yad, Ishut, 1,4 and *Be'er ha-Golah,* E. H. 16, note 4. It becomes a biblical violation only if a priest visits a heathen prostitute. Cf. Yad, I. B. 12,3.

[83] See Solomon Grayzel, *The Church and the Jews in the XIII Century,* p. 62, note 101, and documents cited in note 99.

[84] Abrahams, *Jewish Life,* p. 94 and note 5.

[85] *Sefer Ḥasidim,* 261.

[86] Responsa, Judah b. ha-Rash, 17: *muṭab she-yistakenu ha-gufim min ha-nefashot.*

tile woman will not be released from Gehinna,[87] and they added exhortations of their own, trying to build up moral resistance against the evil. But preachment alone did not satisfy them. They employed the power of disciplinary flogging quite generously,[88] and if conditions required, went beyond their powers and administered penalties unheard of in Jewish courts. In Spain of the fourteenth century a widow was charged with having sex relations with a gentile, and the Jewish court under the sanction of the leading rabbi ordered her nose cut off so as to disfigure her and make her no longer acceptable to her lover.[89] In Italy, we are told that the Jewish community was troubled with laxity in sex matters between Jews and gentiles during the fifteenth century, and a sharp protest arose from the rabbinate, resulting in severer community enactments and restrictions. With the breakdown of Jewish self-government and with the free mingling of Jews and gentiles socially after the days of the emancipation, the problem of prostitution with non-Jewish women as against relations with Jewish prostitutes has ceased to exist. Both have merged in the consciousness of the Jew in the one problem of sex morality for the community as a whole. For the greater part it is dealt with by the State, and the Jews have ceased to think of it as a Jewish problem.

The female slave constituted a special problem in sex morality. A good deal of immorality among Jews, as among other racial groups in antiquity, had its root in slavery. This does not imply only that a morally degraded slave class in the midst of the population contributed to laxity in sex matters. It means also that the very basis of slavery had its implications of sexual immorality. The female slave was a sex tool beneath the level of moral considerations. She was an economic good, useful, in addition to her menial labor, for breeding more slaves. To attain that purpose, the master mated her promiscuously according to his breeding plans. The master himself and his sons and other members of his

87 'Erub. 19a.

88 Ber. 58a; Responsa, *Sha'are Ẓedeḳ,* 13.

89 Responsa, Asheri, 18,13. Adret opposed this practice. See *Besamim Rosh,* 192.

household took turns with her for the increase of the family wealth, as well as for satisfaction of their extra-marital sex desires. Guests and neighbors too were invited to that luxury. In the place of lending and exchanging wives, practiced by other oriental peoples, the Hebrews complied with those standards of hospitality by the use of their female slaves.

The Bible raises no protest against this condition. It assumes that such is the nature of slavery, and since it takes for granted the institution as such it also takes for granted promiscuity with female slaves as a concomitant. The Jewish slave girl alone stands superior to promiscuity, for she is to become the slave-wife of her master or his son; else she goes free.[90] But as for the heathen slave girl, the Bible leaves her just where it found her, a tool for sexual gratification. Perhaps Amos senses the immorality of this when he complains that "a man and his father go in unto the same maid to profane my name." [91] Other than that there is no suggestion of disapproval in the entire Bible of promiscuity with female slaves.

Ezra's antagonism to mixed marriages had no direct bearing on promiscuity with slaves; this did not endanger the purity of the Hebrew stock, since the children born of such unions counted as slaves, not as Israelites. It may be supposed, therefore, that promiscuity with female slaves continued after Ezra as before him. But his teaching had an indirect bearing in that it ultimately developed a conscience on the subject among the more refined people. Sirach calls down shame upon the person who is "over busy with his maid," and commands him "come not near her bed." [92] An old tradition ascribed to the Hasmoneans declares that contact with a Samaritan woman is prohibited because she is both gentile and slave,[93] implying that the prohibition of contact with a female slave was then already taken for granted. The Mishnah also takes this prohibition for granted when it teaches that one who has had intimacies with a female slave may not marry her even after she is freed.[94] The Mishnah

[90] Ex. 21:7–11.
[91] Amos 2:7.
[92] Sirach 41:22.
[93] San. 82a.
[94] M. Yeb. 2,8.

teaches that even promiscuity between slave and slave is prohibited, that while marriage between them has no legal validity, their sex relations must nevertheless be of an enduring nature.[95]

The source of the prohibition against contact with a female slave cannot be traced; it has no origin in biblical legislation. Onkelos in his Targum makes the *ḳedeshah* synonymous with the female slave and the *ḳadesh* with the male slave.[96] Onkelos is no teacher of law and his view is not corroborated by the Talmud nor taken seriously by post-talmudic teachers.[97] The talmudic teachers did not class the female slave with the harlot, though her loose morals were well known to them; they could not prohibit her on the basis of her being gentile in origin, because the female slave was considered a half-convert to Judaism. They did prohibit her to the priest and called her a statutory *zonah* only because of her non-Jewish origin.[98] Though the prohibition was definite and clear in their minds, they never refer to any formal legal enactment. One is inclined to believe that it is a legislative act of public opinion rather than a court enactment, and that it was initiated by extreme nationalists who constituted a religious or political party but who never attained to the dignity of court authority. Slave owners did not take them seriously, but the populace was gradually won over to their views, and thus an unwritten law came to be, which in talmudic times was already taken for granted. The beginnings of this unwritten law probably belong, as the talmudic tradition suggests, to the Hasmonean period.

This law, like many others, had its struggle against not infrequent violations. Promiscuity was too much ingrained within the institution of slavery to be easily eradicated. Violations seem to have reached scandalous proportions in the

[95] M. Temur. 6,2. The amoraim (Tem. 30a) did not recognize the distinction between enduring sex relations with a slave and promiscuity, either in respect to a Jewish male slave or to a non-Jewish one. But see the view of R. Akiba in Mekilta, Ex. 21:4, ed. Lauterbach, III, p. 10, where the view is recorded anonymously and not in the name of R. Akiba. See also Nid. 47a.

[96] Onkelos, Deut. 23:18.

[97] Except *SMG,* negative command 80.

[98] M. Yeb. 6,5; Yeb. 61b.

eighth and ninth centuries in Mohammedan lands.[99] From that period and those lands we get the famous legal case of Bostonai. To Bostonai, first exilarch under Arabian rule, the Caliph presented a war captive, a Persian princess. He lived with her and begot children, who claimed the right of succession to the exilarchate of their father. The opposition argued that since their mother was a foreign captive and had the status of a slave the children begotten by her were legally slaves. Their status, of course, also affected the status of their descendants, who were to be legally counted as slaves as well. The controversy continued for three centuries. Apparently the Bostonai family was too powerful and their descendants too many and the case too serious to be dealt with by the bare letter of the law. The courts evidently went out of their way to assume that an illustrious personage like the exilarch would not commit the sin of living with his female slave but must have freed her legally before he had relations with her. This formed a legal presumption which gave all the descendants full legitimacy.[100]

As breach of this law against contact with a female slave became conspicuous, the rabbis of that period in those lands began exaggerating the severity of the violation. One rabbi says that "for sexual intercourse with a female slave a person is guilty of the violation of fourteen biblical injunctions, and his penalty is to be extermination by heavenly decree." [101] A minor treatise of the Talmud belonging to the same period calls the children born of a union of Jew and female slave "like bastards, though not quite bastards." [102] The exaggeration of the offense gradually turned into exaggerated

[99] See Büchler, Die Schneiden des Haares, WZKM, 19.

[100] Lewin, *Oẓar ha-Ge'onim,* pp. 38–42 and 350–51; Eisenstein, *Oẓar Midrashim,* I, pp. 73–4; *Jewish Encyclopedia,* s. v. Bostonai; Yad, Naḥalot, 4,6 and *Maggid* thereto.

[101] D. E. ch. 1; *Halakot Gedolot.* 253. Büchler, l. c., believes that the original reading was "gentile" instead of "slave," as the Yalḳut, Numb. 22, 531 has it. He argues that the change was made to stem the intimacies with slaves which became prevalent in geonic times. However, see Lev. R. ch. 9 and ch. 25: "They who permit themselves intimacies with female slaves. . . . God will hang them by the tops of their heads in the world to come."

[102] Kallah, ch. 10, ed. Higger, p. 138–9.

forms of punishment for violators. The offender was compelled to free the slave girl, or to purchase her freedom from her owner, and thereafter to marry her; if marriage was not deemed advisable, because of legal objections, the purchase price of the slave, when sold on the market, was distributed among the poor in the community; and in addition the offender's head was shaved in order to expose him to public disgrace, he was put under ban for thirty days, was given a disciplinary flogging, and was declared subject to the "lynch law" applying to a Jew consorting with a gentile woman.[103]

Maimonides rules that the lynch law does not apply to one who has contact with a female slave, because she is a half-convert. He orders disciplinary flagellation for the offense and makes a strong moral plea to his generation: "Let not this sin be light in thine eyes because the Bible did not prescribe the penalty of flogging for it; for by that . . . the offspring is caused to turn away from God, for the son of a slave woman is a slave and not an Israelite; thus one causes holy seed to be profaned and become slaves." [104]

Ultimately the evil was practically eliminated even in those days when slavery still existed. But it was not the preachment and the threat of penalties in Jewish law that did it alone. The Jewish ideal of purity found two powerful allies, the wife and the state. The wife naturally did not like to share her husband with the female slave in the household. Anticipating such a possibility, she demanded a pre-nuptial agreement to be inserted in the ketubah "that he shall not retain in his household a female slave that is objectionable to her, that if he violate this stipulation he shall give her a legally valid bill of divorcement and pay her the ketubah in full." [105] The state under the influence of the Church objected to Christians being bought by Jews as slaves, because this led to conversions to Judaism. It objected more especially to Christian female slaves being owned by Jewish

[103] JQR, XIV, p. 244; *Sha'are Ẓedeḳ*, 13, p. 25a; Lewin, *Oẓar ha-Ge'onim*, Yebamot, p. 43, note 3; *Bet Yoseph, Ṭur*, E. H. at the beginning of Ḳiddushin; *Orḥot Ḥayyim*, I, p. 110. See also *Sha'are Ẓedeḳ*, 42, p. 28b.

[104] Yad, I. B. 12,13. See Responsa of Maimonides, 130 and RDBZ, IV, 225.

[105] Epstein, *Jewish Marriage Contract*, p. 272.

masters, for fear of sexual intimacies. If a Jew violated a government ordinance of this sort, excessive fines and severe corporal penalties were imposed on him.[106] Between the two, the wife and the state, the evil gradually came to an end.

[106] Grayzel, *The Church and the Jews*, pp. 209, 315; Abrahams, *Jewish Life*, pp. 96–100.

CHAPTER VIII

RAPE AND SEDUCTION

VIOLENCE to an unmarried girl was not an uncommon occurrence in the primitive days of human civilization. It constituted an actual fear to the girl's family, and the greater the girl's charms the more serious the fear. Sirach spoke of this when he declared, "A daughter is an illusory treasure to her father; she causes him fears that give him no sleep at night . . . while she is young, lest she be dishonored." In his day too the practice obtained of keeping girls cloistered indoors, especially virgins. This practice was interpreted as a standard of modesty for women, but it was equally a measure of safety for them lest they be violated. The rabbis were quite right when they pointed out that Jacob's daughter, Dinah, was raped because she "went out" — as the biblical verse has it — beyond the shelter of her home. Strangely enough, the Hebrew term for modesty is *ẓeni'ut,* which literally means being hidden, thus perpetuating linguistically the connection between sex morality and sex safety.

I. BIBLICAL LEGISLATION

Violation of a girl caused great humiliation to the girl herself,[1] constituted an affront to the family,[2] and, of course, meant a loss of value in the defloration of the virgin. In the narrative portions of the Bible we have two cases of rape, that of Dinah, daughter of Jacob,[3] and of Tamar, daughter of King David.[4] In both cases the civil action for the loss of virginity is entirely ignored and the emphasis is laid on the criminal side of the attack, the affront to the girl and to her family. The matter is not taken to court but, apparently in accordance with older usage, the brothers of the girl take

[1] II Sam. 13:13.
[2] Gen. 34:29.
[3] Gen. 34.
[4] II Sam. 13.

it in their own hands and make the ravisher pay with his life. In both cases the father disapproves the action of the brothers, which indicates that while blood revenge for rape was still in operation, saner judgment condemned it.

In pre-biblical codes the *lex talionis* was invoked to avenge a case of rape, that is, the ravisher's wife or daughter was given over to the family of the betrayed maiden for rape. That law still obtained in the Assyrian Code (I, 54) where, in addition to making the ravisher marry the girl or pay triple her bride price, it is prescribed that "the father of the virgin shall seize the wife of the adulterer and give her to be raped; he shall not return her to her husband; he shall take her." In Jewish law the *lex talionis* is nowhere suggested as a penalty for rape. The earliest biblical legislation on the matter is exceedingly lenient; it makes an end to any corporal punishment and to any act of revenge against the offender by the girl's family. It treats the incident as a civil case, similar in nature to theft, for rape, in civil terms, is theft of virginity of a maiden; the restitution required by the Bible, then, is payment of "the price of virginity" and, if agreeable to the family, marriage of the dishonored maiden.

Logically it is possible that this biblical prescription is intended only to take care of the civil action as between the ravisher and the girl's family, but that the moral aspect, the infringement on the rules of chastity, was treated separately by the elders or the local court as a criminal offense, imposing fines and corporal punishment. To some extent we are forced into such an assumption, else the person who violates a widow or divorcee, where there is no loss of virginity, would be entirely free from punishment. Yet the Bible has no indication that any other punishment was levied upon the offender than payment of the bride price and compulsory marriage, and no punishment is indicated for ravishing a widow or divorcee. However, Philo, perhaps from old unwritten law, states that local tribunals exercised their authority to inflict corporal punishment or impose fines on any one who corrupted a widow or a divorcee; and that likewise in case of rape of a virgin, where a biblical fine was provided, the courts imposed additional fines and penalties.[5] The Talmud, as will be seen later, carries on the tradition of imposing higher penalties than those prescribed in the Bible.

The biblical legislation on the subject is recorded in two verses, one of which by traditional interpretation is supposed to treat of seduction, the other of rape. In the Covenant Code we have: "And if a man entice a virgin that is not betrothed and lie with her, he shall surely pay a dowry for her to be his wife. And if her father refuse to give her to him he shall pay money according to the dowry of virgins." [6] The Book of Deuteronomy has the following law: "If a man find a damsel that is virgin, that is not betrothed, and lay hold on her and lie with her and they be found, then the man that lay with her shall give unto the damsel's father fifty shekels of silver and she shall be his wife because he hath humbled her; he may not put her away all his days." [7]

No one can deny that the two verses are worded so as to give the impression that the first deals with seduction, where the girl was *enticed* and gave her consent to the corruption, and that the second deals with rape carried out by violence, the man *laying hold* of the damsel. The Septuagint preserves this distinction in its translation of these passages. Yet we wonder how seriously we are to take this distinction between enticing and laying hold. In a social sense the distinction was perhaps evident to the biblical author, but it is hardly conclusive that it constituted any legal difference. It cannot be said with certainty that this differentiation between rape and seduction was known to the other ancient systems of law.[8] Philo and Josephus treat of rape and seduction without any legal difference.[9] Internal evidences argue against ascribing legal distinctions to the mind of the bib-

[5] Philo, *de special. leg.* III, 64, ed. Cohn, II, p. 202, and note 3 thereto. See also p. 204 and note 1.

[6] Ex. 22:15–16.

[7] Deut. 22:28–29.

[8] Assyr. Code I, 54, according to a conjectural reading mentions force, but that reading is uncertain; I, 55, in our judgment, treats of "harlotry in her father's house." The Attic Law is not clear in that distinction — see Heinemann, *Philon's Griechische und jüdische Bildung*, p. 287, note 3.

[9] See Philo, l. c.

lical legislator. Logic is against it. If the guilt of the girl in giving her consent were considered, the difference would, of course, be significant. But the girl is free from guilt in either case; the only question is the loss of property to the girl's father. Again, can the girl's consent matter very much, since she does not own herself, and when she gives herself gives what she does not own? Furthermore, the girl is said to be a minor virgin not yet betrothed, which in biblical times meant that she was of a very tender age. How can her state of mind make any legal difference? In the second place, if the Bible does take the consent of the girl seriously, why does she escape punishment in the case of seduction, or even the death penalty prescribed for the virgin who commits harlotry in her father's house? [10] Third, if the law in Exodus (seduction) and the law of Deuteronomy (rape) are not synonymous, then both laws are incomplete; Exodus does not state that the offender may not put her away, and Deuteronomy does not say that the girl's father may withhold consent to marriage between the girl and her ravisher. While it is conceivable that the Covenant Code had not yet reached that stage of development of law positing the possibility of interfering with a husband's right to divorce his wife at will, it is uterly impossible to believe that the deuteronomic legislator meant to deny the father the right to object to the girl's marriage to the ravisher, for that is contrary to the older biblical tradition.[11]

A fair conjecture on the basis of the foregoing is that the Bible treats rape and seduction as one phenomenon legally, blaming both on the man, because a young girl is considered as helpless before a love-making young man as before one who uses physical force. In both cases the girl is free and the man is guilty. The opposite of both is the girl who "commits harlotry in her father's house," having clandestine relations with men behind her father's back. In that case the guilt falls entirely upon the girl; the man is free.[12] These

[10] Deut. 22:21.

[11] As in the case of Dinah, Gen. 34, the father and brothers are given the choice of accepting or rejecting marriage.

[12] Deut. l. c.; so in Assyr. Code I, 55. See pp. 164–5 above.

laws, therefore, that of Exodus and that of Deuteronomy, supplement each other and make up one set of rules for rape and seduction alike. The price of virginity is paid to the father; this amounts to fifty shekels. Marriage is compulsory on the offender but subject to consent of the girl's father. If the girl be given in marriage to the offender, he may never divorce her. Probably additional fines and penalties were imposed on the offender, not prescribed or standardized by any code but by the authority of local courts as a measure of discipline against immorality. This general treatment of rape and seduction remained in force to the end of the Second Commonwealth.

II. TALMUDIC LAW

The Talmud makes a clear distinction between rape and seduction, based on the difference in phraseology used in the Bible, and the distinction is legal. Disregarding the tender age of the girl, the rabbis see significant legal import in the fact that in rape the offender violates both the will of the girl and the property rights of her father, while in seduction only the father's rights are violated but not the girl's. The law of rape in Deuteronomy and the law of seduction in Exodus are, therefore, separate and independent legislation. They have certain things in common; in both the fine is fifty shekels and the father may object to marriage. But in many essential points they differ. In rape marriage is compulsory and divorce is denied; in seduction marriage is optional and divorce is permitted.[13] In the case of rape, according to rabbinic interpretation, the offender has to marry the girl *and* pay the fine; while in the case of seduction he *either* marries her *or* pays the fine.

In biblical times this distinction did not mean very much. In terms of shekels it meant the same thing, for he never paid twice and never less than once. If he married her he paid *mohar,* which is the bride price; if he did not marry her he paid the fine, which is the price of virginity. In both cases the sum was fifty shekels; the difference in name did not mean anything, for both *mohar* and fine were paid to the father

[13] Mekilta, ed. Friedmann, p. 94a; Sifre Deut. p. 119b; Ket. 39–40a.

before the marriage. To the rabbis *mohar* and fine were different not only in name but also in essence; the fine was paid to the father, *mohar* to the wife herself; the fine was paid prior to marriage, *mohar* at the time of dissolution of the marriage. This difference arose from the post-biblical development of the institution of *mohar,* which we have presented elsewhere.[14] With this in mind the rabbis ruled that in rape, even if the offender marries the girl he pays the fine and not *mohar;* while in seduction, if the seducer marries the girl, he pays only *mohar* but no fine. He pays the fine only if he does not marry her.[15]

a) FINE. We have used the term fine in a non-technical sense, but in rabbinic law it becomes technical. In the Bible the payment of fifty shekels for rape and seduction was remuneration for the theft of virginity, just as *mohar* was payment for the purchase of virginity. That conception of the price of virginity was no longer pleasing to the taste of the people at the time of the tannaim. The rabbis therefore treated it as a punitive fine primarily and added that the man, secondarily, had received his money's worth in paying it by the fact that he had enjoyed intercourse with a virgin.[16] As a fine it had two judicial limitations. It was not payable if the culprit confessed before the plaintiff presented court testimony in support of his claim,[17] and it was not enforceable in Jewish courts outside Palestine.[18]

This fine of fifty shekels is paid by the offender only if the girl be a *na'arah,* that is, a minor girl, neither child nor woman, and only if she were a virgin. These specifications are contained in the wording of the law in the Bible, and the rabbis stand by them literally. R. Me'ir would say that the more exact definition of *na'arah* would describe the girl as between the ages of twelve and twelve and a half, between puberty and majority, but the prevailing view of the halakah applies the term in case of rape or seduction to any girl above

[14] Epstein, *Jewish Marriage Contract,* pp. 19 f. and 79 f.

[15] See Mekilta, Ex. 22:15; M. Ket. 3,4; Ket. 39a–b.

[16] 'Erak. 15a; Ket. 40b: "the pleasure of intercourse." The conception is similar to the German "Morgengabe." See Ket. 41a.

[17] M. Shebuot 5,4.

[18] B. Ḳ. 84b.

the age of three until she attains legal majority, twelve and a half. Prior to three she is a child, above twelve and a half she is a woman.[19] A girl of retarded development, called *'eilonit,* is a matter of controversy among the authorities; according to some the fine applies to her up to the age of twenty, according to others no fine applies at all as soon as she is diagnosed as abnormal.[20]

Rape or seduction of a non-virgin does not rate the biblical fine of fifty shekels, because the Bible specifies that she be a virgin and refers to the fine as the price of virginity. Therefore, the married woman, widowed or divorced, even if she has not yet lived with her husband, cannot demand a fine for rape or seduction.[21] However, if betrothed, widowed, or divorced, and not yet having entered nuptials, she is assumed to be a virgin and can claim the fine.[22] The minor orphan girl wedded to her husband by her brother and mother under authority of rabbinic enactment, though her marriage is not valid biblically, has the status of a non-virgin and cannot claim a fine for rape or seduction.[23] Rabbinic law has a list of "statutory non-virgins," that is, whose life has subjected them to such sexual liberties that they are assumed by law to be non-virgins. These are the gentile, the captive, and the slave. If they have been converted or ransomed or liberated, respectively, below the age of three, they are accounted virgins and can claim the fine, because loss of virginity at that age is not a permanent injury. But if they have remained in their heathen, captive, or slave state beyond the age of three, they are statutory non-virgins and can claim no fine for rape and seduction.[24] A girl, too, who has proven herself of easy virtue, who has offered herself to a man, even though her offer was spurned, belongs to the category of statutory non-virgins and can claim no fine.[25] It is a matter of controversy among later

19 Ket. 29a; Yad, Na'arah Betulah, 1,8; *Ṭur* E. H. 177. R. Ḥananel accepts the view of R. Me'ir, *Ṭur,* ibid.

20 See Yad, Na'arah Betulah, 1,9; RABD and *Kesef Mishneh* thereto, and *Ṭur,* ibid.

21 M. Ket. 1,4; Yad, Na'arah Betulah, 1,10.

22 M. Ket. 3,3. The prevailing view is that of R. Akiba.

23 Ket. 35b.

24 M. Ket. 3,1–2.

25 Ket. 36b.

teachers whether the girl deflowered by accidental injury without male contact has the status of a virgin in respect to the fine for rape and seduction.[26] It is also not settled among the teachers whether the mentally defective girl, the insane or the deaf-mute, has the status of a virgin, because she is not capable of taking care of herself.[27]

b) INDEMNITIES. The Bible assigns no other monetary compensation to the girl or her family than the standard fifty shekels. Post-biblical law imposes extra payments on the ravisher in connection with his offense. Philo speaks indefinitely of such additional fines, omitting details. Rabbinic law has a full analysis of these extra payments. The fifty shekels, as said, are considered by the rabbis a punitive fine, and are standard for all girls, the noblest and the humblest alike; [28] the extra payments are in the nature of indemnities for injuries inflicted and for losses sustained, and vary according to the nature of the case. They consist of three items, loss of value, humiliation, and physical or mental anguish.[29] By the first item is meant the girl's loss of market value as a result of the attack, and it is estimated by the court in the light of the difference between what the girl could be sold for on the slave market before the mishap and after it.[30] The second item, humiliation, varies with the station of the girl and of the man who dishonored her,[31] and is determined by the court's estimate what the girl's family would have been willing to spend in order to spare her that humiliation.[32] Physical and mental anguish, of course, has no standard market value, and is variable in accordance with the physical make-up of the girl and the man. The court may determine the amount by

[26] Ket. 36a; *Tur*, E. H. 177, where the views of RI and RMH are cited in controversy on the subject.

[27] Yad, Na'arah Betulah, 1,10, and opposed by RABD, note thereto.

[28] M. 'Erak. 3,4; 'Erak. 14b; Ket. 40a.

[29] M. Ket. 3,4; Ket. 39b.

[30] M. Ket. 3,7, wishes to calculate depreciation by her loss of market value as a slave. The amoraim think this estimate unfair and suggest an estimate of what her virgin state might be worth to a kind master who would choose a slave-wife for his male slave. Tosafists insist on taking her social position into consideration, even in this inadequate standard of values. See Ket. 40b and Tosafot, s. v. *kamah*.

[31] M. Ket. ibid.

[32] Suggestion of Maimonides, Yad, Na'arah Betulah, 2,5.

an estimate of what the girl's family would have been willing to pay to spare her that pain.[33] The first two items of indemnities prescribed by rabbinic law are paid by the offender in cases of rape as well as seduction; the last, physical and mental anguish, is paid only in case of rape but not in seduction, because the seduced girl has evidenced by her consent that the pleasure she derived outbalanced the pain she suffered.[34]

Philo knows of the extra indemnities above the biblical fine of fifty shekels only where no marriage has followed between the pair after rape or seduction. The rabbis consider the payment of indemnities independent of the question of marriage. They treat these indemnities as ordinary cases of torts and damages. They are to be paid whether the pair be married or not, and must be given in cash at the time of litigation both in cases of rape and of seduction.[35] Even where the standard fine is not payable, the indemnities must be paid. This applies to rape or seduction of a widow or divorcee — the cases treated by Philo — the gentile, slave, or captive,[36] the girl who has attained her majority,[37] and the girl below three years of age.[38]

To whom are these fines and indemnities paid? The Bible does not contemplate the independence of an unmarried girl from her father, therefore orders the payment always to be made to the father. In rabbinic law the girl attains independence from her father in several ways, either by attaining legal majority or by marriage or by her father's death, even if that

[33] The tannaitic tendency is to count the physical-mental anguish as a unit; the amoraim seem to emphasize the physical. Ket. 39a–b. The standard of measure here suggested is given by Maimonides, Yad, Na'arah Betulah, 2,6.

[34] M. Ket. 3,4.

[35] Ket. 39b.

[36] This is a conjectural statement on our part which has no evident ruling in the Talmud, but which finds support in *Tur*, E. H. 177, *Bet Yoseph* thereto and commentators. They set these cases not in the special category of rape and seduction but in the general category of torts. Maimonides, Yad, Na'arah Betulah, 2, 10–11, seems to oppose this ruling. However, it looks as if he admits the theory but sees no practical application in it, for to him a non-virgin has lost nothing in the experience of rape or seduction, neither depreciation nor pain nor shame. See *Kesef Mishneh* ad Yad, ibid.

[37] This is admitted even by Maimonides, Yad, Na'arah Betulah, 2,11.

[38] Maimonides might disagree also with this ruling, for since virginity returns if the girl was attacked at an age below three, then nothing was lost.

has occurred while she is an unmarried minor. She attains a state of semi-independence by betrothal until she enters her nuptials. In all cases of complete independence, all fines and indemnities are paid to the girl herself, and this is true even if at the time of the attack she was not yet independent but attained her independence before the court pronounced sentence.[39] There are opposing tannaitic traditions as to whether the girl or her father is entitled to the payments if she possessed only semi-independence at the time of the attack, that is, if she was betrothed but not yet wedded.[40] The halakah decides in her favor in that case also.[41] It is doubtful, however, whether this is true where the girl attained her semi-independent state after the attack but prior to the adjudication of the court.[42] Finally, according to some teachers, the item of indemnities paid for physical and mental anguish always goes to the girl herself, even if she is legally completely dependent upon her father; but this view does not prevail in the halakah.[43]

So long as under certain conditions the payments are made to the girl herself, a new angle in rabbinic law arises to distinguish the treatment of rape from that of seduction. So long as the payments went to the father, the girl's frame of mind at the time of the attack was of little consequence, because she had no right to waive her father's claim. But when with independence or semi-independence she herself became the litigant, her consent to the act had great bearing on the payments due. Rabbinic law, therefore, teaches that in rape all fines and indemnities are payable even if the girl had attained legal independence, because the act was an act of violence; but in seduction, if the girl enjoys independence or semi-independence, no payments are due at all, because hav-

[39] Ket. 41b.

[40] Ket. 38a reports one view in the name of R. Akiba in the Mishnah and its opposite in his name in the Beraita. See also Ket. 40a.

[41] Maimonides rules in favor of the girl only in respect to the standard fine, the father getting the indemnities, but Asheri rules that the girl gets everything. *Ṭur,* E. H. 177.

[42] Ket. 39a. Of course, Maimonides who denies the betrothed maiden the right to her indemnities, rules in this case that the indemnities go to the father.

[43] RABD cited in *Ṭur,* E. H. 177.

ing consented to the act she has waived all claims on the man, fines as well as indemnities.[44] The talmudic ruling seems to include in this law even the minor girl with an independent status, apparently assuming that some minors are intelligent enough to give consent to a sexual act and to waive legal monetary claims.[45] But it stands to reason that a minor girl below that age of intelligence is not capable of waiving legal claims; therefore the young minor girl in that status collects all fines and indemnities for seduction even if she has legal independence.[46]

c) Compulsory marriage and restricted divorce. Rabbinic law, as stated above, requires compulsory marriage only in the case of rape but not in that of seduction. This requirement, like the standard fine of fifty shekels, is intended for rape of a minor virgin only. Philo is specific in teaching that for rape of a widow or divorcee the law does not require the ravisher to marry his victim. Rabbinic law, either in the Talmud or in post-talmudic sources, has no definite ruling on the question of compulsory marriage for the woman who is either definitely non-virgin or definitely non-minor, but the student has the feeling that it is assumed that no compulsory marriage is required for the rape of a widow or divorcee or a girl who has attained legal majority. We would be less certain as to the rabbinic ruling in cases of statutory non-virgins, but the general logic of rabbinic law would lead us to believe that while moral persuasion may be used to make the offender marry the girl, no legal compulsion would be employed.[47]

Compulsory marriage, according to the Bible, is subject to

[44] Ket. 32a; 42a; Yad, Na'arah Betulah, 2,11.

[45] See Ket. ibid. and 36a. The Talmud itself does not definitely distinguish between *na'arah* and *ḳeṭanah* in respect to her waiving of fines and indemnities, although that interpretation in the above texts is not impossible.

[46] See Tosafot Ket. 42a on top. It should be noticed that the case of the insane girl is different. Although the insane cannot waive any claim, there is no fine or indemnity in her case. The reason is that as for the fine she has the status of a non-virgin, and as for depreciation and humiliation an insane person has neither of these losses (see Rashi Ket. 32a, s. v. *be-shoṭah*); as for pain we have said above that the seduced girl has no claim for pain.

[47] Some slight suggestion of this view is implied in Responsa of Kolon, 129; Responsa of RDBZ, I, 19; *Pitḥe Teshubah*, E. H. 177, note 6.

the consent of the girl's father. Philo gives the girl herself the right to reject the marriage, if she is orphaned of her father.[48] This is wholly in keeping with rabbinic law, which declares the minor orphan girl independent and therefore in authority to reject marriage to her ravisher. But later rabbinic law went further. It tended to give the minor girl more voice in her own affairs even while her father was alive. In that spirit the law teaches that the girl herself can object to the marriage even if the father consents.[49] Sometimes the law itself, so to speak, objects to the marriage and thus nullifies the requirement of compulsory marriage after rape. If the marriage should be an incestuous one, or in violation of any biblical marriage prohibition, it cannot take place.[50] Maimonides adds that even a rabbinical marriage prohibition nullifies the biblical requirement of compulsory marriage.[51]

Compulsory marriage in the case of rape has its biblical sequel in the injunction that "he may not put her away." The Bible says nothing about the possibility that the wife who had been raped and married to the culprit might some day desire to free herself from him. Apparently divorce proceedings initiated by the wife were beyond the social experience of the biblical author. In rabbinic times the wife had already attained the right of demanding a divorce, and the amoraim took it for granted that her right was not limited by the biblical injunction that "he may not put her away." They offer no biblical exegesis in support of this teaching, but treat it as a self-evident principle.[52] Josephus teaches that if the wife commits adultery the husband is permitted to divorce her despite the biblical restriction.[53] This agrees in spirit

[48] *De special. leg.* III, 71, ed. Cohn, vol. II, p. 204.

[49] Ket. 39b. The interpretation that RN gives this passage (ad Alfasi Ket. ibid.) is that if the girl rejects the ravisher, the compulsion ceases to apply, but still the father has a right to give her to him, if he so chooses.

[50] M. Ket. 3,4; Ket. 40a.

[51] Yad, Na'arah Betulah, 3,5. Commentators do not know the source of Maimonides' view. Possibly his decision rests on the general principle that a rabbinic prohibition supersedes a biblical law, if the infringement is only in a passive, not an active manner, or technically, *be-sheb ve-'al ta'aseh*. Yeb. 90b.

[52] Ket. 39b at the bottom.

[53] Josephus, *Antiq.* IV, 8, 23.

with the New Testament, which makes divorce in all cases a violation of law and yet permits it where the wife is unfaithful.[54] It agrees also in letter with rabbinic law, which teaches that the restriction against divorce in the case of rape is lifted if the wife is unfaithful.[55]

Restriction of divorce, being the counterpart of the law of compulsory marriage, should naturally be taken to apply only in such cases where compulsory marriage is required. One would judge, therefore, that where marriage is not required, if the culprit has married the girl he attacked, he may thereafter put her away at will. That would eliminate the restriction against divorce in the case of rape of a widow or a divorcee, a statutory non-virgin, a girl who has attained legal majority, or a girl whose marriage would constitute a violation of biblical law. We have no direct instruction on this point from talmudic sources, but the logic is conclusive. It remains doubtful, however, whether the view of Maimonides, that a rabbinical marriage prohibition nullifies the biblical requirement of compulsory marriage, is to be taken to mean also that if marriage has taken place the prohibition against divorce is nullified.[56]

III. POST-TALMUDIC LAW

It will be evident from the foregoing that the average case of rape or seduction could not be treated by the talmudic teachers on the basis of the strict technicalities of the law, as formulated by the rabbis in accordance with their biblical derivations. There were too many exceptions which constituted loop-holes to free the criminal from punishment. The non-virgin, the statutory non-virgin, the girl beyond the age of twelve and a half years, were apparently open to attack by men with but insignificant penalties. In addition, fines could

[54] Mat. 5:32.

[55] M. Ket. 3,4.

[56] See note 51. There is logic to say that if there is no compulsory marriage there is no prohibition against divorce. On the other hand, if Maimonides' view rests on the fact that the rabbinical law operates only passively, then it does not apply to the question of divorce where it would be a case of *ḳum va-'aseh*.

not be enforced by the court outside of Palestine, and we learn that even the indemnities were not enforceable in the diaspora.[57] Evidently, the rabbis were not limited in their treatment of rape and seduction to the technical rules here presented. They held the man guilty, in addition to the specific wrong done to the girl, of violation of standards of public morality and decency, and dealt with him on that score with a mighty disciplinary rod.

That was the spirit that dominated the treatment of rape and seduction by post-talmudic authorities. Under the head of public morality they would chastise the offender by flagellation, ban, and various devices of humiliation. Even where the case was not proven, if a man's conduct was such as to endanger the chastity of Jewish daughters, these penalties were imposed upon him.[58] The rectification of the wrong done to the girl was accomplished generally on the arbitration basis. The offender was pressed to make restitution to the girl and her family of all monetary losses sustained, to the point of providing full satisfaction for the wrong done to them. If the girl or her family were unreasonable in their demands, the court would set down a certain amount of indemnification as settlement in full for all charges.[59] If the man denied the attack altogether, the burden of proof was on the girl.[60] If she charged him with rape and he claimed it was seduction, the burden of proof was on the man.[61] If she claimed that she yielded to cohabitation on the promise of marriage made by the man, she was considered entitled either to marriage or to indemnities. In that case the court would use persuasion to get him to marry her, but not compulsion.[62] In general com-

[57] B. Ḳ. 84b. Depreciation and humiliation are also mentioned among the items that cannot be collected by authority of non-Palestinian courts, because the damage does not represent an actual financial loss.

[58] Responsa, *Shebut Ya'aḳob,* III, 138; *Ḥatam Sofer,* E. H. II, 105, et passim.

[59] *Ṭur,* E. H. 177, cited as a geonic practice.

[60] Responsa, RIBS, 41. Maimonides, however, believes there is ground in the girl's charge for imposing a rabbinical oath upon the man in support of his statement. See Yad, Na'arah Betulah, 2,12.

[61] Shebuot 36b; Yad, Na'arah Betulah, 2,13, and RABD thereto.

[62] *Bet Ḥadash, Ṭur,* Ḥoshen Mishpaṭ, 87; *Ḥatam Sofer,* E. H. II, 105; II, 160; I, 125. R. Joseph Kolon, Responsa, 129, exempts the man from any payment.

pulsory marriage was not favored by post-talmudic law, and was employed only in the exact specific biblical case, where the girl was a minor and a virgin, and even there with great hesitation.[63]

[63] Responsa RDBZ, 19.

CHAPTER IX

ADULTERY

THE sense of moral depravity which adultery conveys to the modern person does not apply to the primitive Semites. Amid the practices of lending and exchanging wives and of periodic sex orgies in which married men and married women were involved, there can hardly be a sense of defilement about a stealthy approach to another man's wife. They considered adultery an outrage of a person's private and exclusive right to the woman, a thievery of something he owned and guarded with fierce jealousy. The ancient Hebrews, who did not conduct orgies or practice lending and exchanging wives, were therefore more amenable to the biblical conception of adultery as defilement in a moral sense. But more primitively and basically they shared the idea of their neighbors that adultery was a violation of the husband's property rights. From this premise follow two conclusions, one which the law incorporated and another which the law sought to eliminate.

The first is that adultery is possible only on the side of the wife, because she is the property of her husband, but not on the part of the husband. The male can commit adultery only when he cohabits with the wife of another man. In other words, the wife owes faithfulness to her own marriage; the husband owes faithfulness to another man's marriage. The permission of polygamy and the prohibition of polyandry stem from the same root. Insofar as the marriage bond is concerned, the husband has his freedom with other women to marry them or to live with them without marriage; the wife can have no other men because she is owned by her husband. This conclusion, with slight modifications by talmudic and post-talmudic law, has been accepted by Judaism down to the present day.

The second conclusion is that in adultery there is an injured party, the husband. He and his kindred and sympathizers all felt outraged at the crime and sought revenge upon the culprit. What the law might do was a matter of public morals, but for the moment, the husband was not interested; he had been injured and sought redress according to the promptings of his jealousy and the rules of the primitive feud. First he turned his vengeance against his wife. Her guilt deserved the death penalty, and he could kill her unceremoniously and without public trial. But generally he would dramatize his passion and stage an act. He would strip her naked and send her out in disgrace before the mob,[1] or first humiliate her in her own household, tear down her veil and her ornaments, uncover, dishevel, or cut off her hair,[2] rip down her garments so as to expose her "shame," and then send her out to the mob to be sported with. The mob consisted of neighbors and tribesmen, men and women, young and old.[3] Insults and attacks were heaped upon the guilty victim; her nose and ears were cut off as a mark of disgrace.[4] When rage and outrage rose to the highest pitch, the mob pierced her with swords and hurled stones at her and thus made an end to her life.[5] The house of sin was set on fire and her children, if exposed by the father, were slain.[6] A kindlier husband might forgive her altogether,[7] or he might be satisfied to humiliate her, to show her nakedness to the mob, to cut her hair, her nose, and her ears, or to reduce her to servitude, but at least spare her life.

His account with the adulterer was another matter. He and his tribesmen pursued him relentlessly until they killed him. By the unwritten law of the day, which was not abandoned even in Philo's time,[8] the husband had full right to put the adulterer to death if circumstances gave him the opportunity.

[1] Hosea 2:5, 12; Ezek. 16:37; 23:27; Jer. 13:26; Nahum 3:5.
[2] See Büchler, Das Schneiden des Haares, WZKM, 19, pp. 91 f.
[3] Ezek. 16:41.
[4] Ezek. 23:25.
[5] Ezek. 16:39–40; 23:10; 25:26, 47.
[6] Ezek. 16:41; 23:25, 47.
[7] Ezek. 16:63.
[8] Philo, *de Josepho*, 44, ed. Cohn, I, p. 167.

The overhanging doom of the adulterer being pursued by the husband is not an unfamiliar picture in the Bible and the Apocrypha.[9] According to the rule of the day, the adulterer might save himself by offering ransom for his life to the injured husband, but the ransom demanded was probably more than he could pay, and more often the outraged husband would refuse to accept any amount in lieu of the adulterer's blood.[10]

It is the purpose of law to supersede primitive tribal usages and to regulate human affairs by standards of equity rather than of passion. The law, to be sure, incorporates some of the primitive usages, but it also rejects others. The law is selective and its selective process is progressively toward dispassionate judgment of right and wrong, for the purpose of maintaining order and decency in human affairs. The more highly developed the law the more readily it sheds the features of primitive tribal concepts.

I. PRE-BIBLICAL AND BIBLICAL LAW

The pre-biblical legislation of the Babylonians, Assyrians, and Hittites retains much of the primitive concept of adultery. They all declare adultery a capital crime,[11] and the court is the dispenser of justice. But it acts only in protection of the husband's property rights. Therefore the husband, if he finds his wife and her co-respondent in the act of adultery, may kill them himself without trial.[12] Furthermore, the wife is left to be dealt with by the husband himself, the court only waiting to be called in.[13] The husband may forgive his wife entirely, if he wishes. If he forgives her, he has renounced his property grievance and has no case against the adulterer, who then goes free.[14] Again, if the husband has left the city and provided no food for his wife during his absence, he loses

[9] Prov. 5:22; 6:29; Sirach 23:19–21.

[10] Prov. 5:9–12; 6:35. According to Frankenberg (ZAW, 25, p. 121) ransom is also recorded in Gen. 20:16. See Büchler, Die Strafe der Ehebrecher in die nach-exilischen Zeit, MGWJ, 55, pp. 196 f.

[11] C. H. 129; Assyr. Code, I, 13; Hittite Code, 197, 198.

[12] Assyr. Code, I, 15; Hittite Code, 197.

[13] C. H. 129; Assyr. Code, I, 14, 15, 16; Hittite Code, 198.

[14] Ibid.

ownership of his wife for that duration and has no claim on her for fidelity.[15]

The penalty for adultery provided in these early codes is death. In most cases the manner of execution is not given, but in a few instances drowning is recommended.[16] Where the husband agrees to a lesser penalty, the codes recommend cutting off the wife's nose or ears and turning the man into a eunuch in addition to disfiguring his whole face.[17] There is no mention of ransom to the husband in the case of adultery.

By adultery these ancient codes had in mind first, cohabitation with a married woman, and second, rape of a virgin bride betrothed to another man.[18] It has been conventionally accepted that ancient law considered betrothal equal to marriage and therefore violation of either was adultery. That is not quite true. We learn that even after betrothal, the girl's father may give her to another suitor, involving himself only in civil litigation.[19] Likewise, it is possible for another man to elope with a betrothed maiden and suffer no death penalty.[20] Furthermore, the groom's father suffers no capital penalty if he lies with the betrothed bride of his son, provided the son had not yet cohabited with her.[21] These laws indicate that the betrothed bride was not fully recognized as the wife of her betrothed husband. She was only the property he had purchased and which he owned not by possession but by contract. Any interference with delivery of the purchase, either by his father-in-law, his own father, or another suitor, has only civil but no criminal implication. However, violation of the betrothed bride by one who is not competing for her hand, who does not offer her *mohar,* who does not in any way interfere with the delivery of the girl to her purchaser, but commits an act of violence against him, constitutes a capital crime of the nature of adultery.

[15] C. H. 134.
[16] C. H. 129, 133.
[17] Assyr. Code, I, 15.
[18] C. H. 130.
[19] C. H. 160, 161; Hittite Code, 29.
[20] Hittite Code, 28.
[21] C. H. 155, 156.

Whether cohabitation with another man's concubine was considered adultery by pre-biblical codes cannot be said for certain. There are some indications, by no means conclusive, that it was considered adultery of a kind; perhaps of the severity of a capital crime, perhaps of lesser severity. However, secondary wives of lower rank, such as the slave-wife or the captive wife, were apparently treated merely as property of the master but not as wives in respect to adultery.[22]

The adulterer can escape capital punishment if he can prove on oath that he did not know the woman was married,[23] or can substantiate his claim that the woman made approaches to him.[24] The woman can escape punishment if she can prove that she was forced,[25] or if the circumstances were such that it might be assumed she did not commit the crime voluntarily. Generally the assumption is, as is natural, that the act took place by common consent,[26] but if it happened on a highway and there is evidence that the woman was struggling,[27] of if she was tricked by a procuress, claiming unawareness of the danger, the woman is exonerated.[28] On the other hand, certain circumstances strengthen the assumption that she is guilty, such as her going into a man's house,[29] receiving a man in her own home,[30] undertaking a journey

[22] Epstein, *Marriage Laws*, pp. 45, 48.

[23] Assyr. Code, I, 14, 22.

[24] Assyr. Code, I, 16. This law can be explained on one of two assumptions, either that when the woman approaches the man, he is not supposed to inquire whether she be married or not, since the situation is that of normal harlotry, or, even if he knows she is married, he is not expected to be so saintly as to turn down an offer, the guilt being entirely on the woman.

[25] C. H. 130; Assyr. Code, I, 12.

[26] C. H. 129; Assyr. Code, I, 14, 15, 23. Dr. Tchernowitz, *Toledot ha-Halakah*, III, pp. 203–4, sees a distinction between a betrothed and a married wife; the former is assumed to be involuntary unless proven to the contrary, the latter is assumed to be voluntary unless she can prove otherwise. The suggestion is very interesting, but based merely on the insufficient clarity of the wording of the law, which is inherent in the very nature of ancient legal writing and can really prove nothing.

[27] Assyr. Code, I, 12; Hittite Code, 197.

[28] Assyr. Code, I, 23.

[29] Assyr. Code, I, 13.

[30] Hittite Code, 197.

with a strange man,[31] or concealing the truth about the adulterous contact.[32]

The biblical law of adultery has gone beyond these more ancient laws in making adultery a moral crime rather than an injury to the husband. Hence, the crime and the penalty remain the same whether the husband prosecutes or not, whether the violation entailed violence on the part of the man or solicitation by the woman. The husband cannot forgive his wife, and his forgiveness has no bearing on the crime of the adulterer. The husband moreover cannot take the law into his own hand, but must submit the case to the properly constituted administrators of the law to deal with in accordance with proper legal procedure, inquiry, testimony, investigation, and judgment. There is no ransom for adultery; the culprit does not deal with the husband but with the law.[33]

As in the earlier codes, so in the Bible, adultery is a capital crime — "the adulterer and the adulteress shall surely die." [34] The death sentence is pronounced by the court; the witnesses in the case are the first to throw the stones, the rest is done by the people.[35] Stoning the victim was the more common form of execution both in biblical times and in the early post-biblical era; [36] sometimes slaying with the sword was employed; [37] in early days, however, the victim was burned to death.[38] As a rule, though, execution for adultery was rare in biblical times, even as in the rabbinic period, so that not a single actual case is reported in the Bible.

Vengeance upon the children and burning down the house of sin came to an end under the influence of the law. Cutting off the woman's nose or ears was not practiced among the ancient Hebrews under legislative authority. But the law did yield to the older practice of heaping shame upon the

[31] Assyr. Code, I, 22.

[32] Assyr. Code, I, 23.

[33] It goes without saying that the Bible has records of the more primitive practices among the early Hebrews, but these were not accepted as standards by the law.

[34] Lev. 20:10. See also Ex. 20:14; Lev. 18:20, Deut. 5:17.

[35] Deut. 19:15–18; John 8:1–2.

[36] Deut. 22:24; Ezek. 16:40; John 8:5.

[37] Ezek. 23:10, 25, 47.

[38] Gen. 38:24; Lev. 21:9; Jubilees 20:4. See Benzinger, *Archäologie,* p. 277.

woman. It ordered the woman to be stripped naked before execution, and that practice continued probably to the end of the Second Commonwealth, with the slight modification later of tying a girdle around her loins.[39] It ordered her hair to be uncovered and disheveled as a token of public disgrace, in place of the older usage of cutting off her hair.[40] Disfigurement of the culprit's face was not known to the Jews.

The Bible includes in adultery also cohabitation with a maiden betrothed to another, and specifies the death penalty for both by stoning.[41] One may suspect that, as in pre-biblical codes, the Bible too did not consider betrothal equal to marriage in respect to adultery, even though it speaks of the betrothed maiden as "his neighbor's wife"; therefore, even after betrothal breach of contract or elopement with another groom is possible without involving a capital offense. That suspicion would find support in the fact that Laban could give to Jacob the older sister Leah instead of the younger Rachel who had been betrothed to him,[42] or that Saul could give Merab to another man after she had been betrothed to David. However, the evidence for such suspicion is destroyed by the fact that these marriages and their corresponding betrothals are of the metronymic type, where the girl's father has the power of divorcing his son-in-law by taking the girl away from him. These instances may, then, represent the process of divorce in the metronymic marriage. This alone can explain the action of Saul in taking Michal from David and giving her to another man after she had been fully married to David.[43]

[39] See Mat. 27:27, 35; M. San. 6,3. The view of an anonymous teacher in the Mishnah that a woman victim is not stripped represents the later law. In the case of *soṭah,* the chest was bared — Soṭah 7a — but Sifre Numb. ed. Friedmann, p. 5a speaks of a linen sheet held up by the priest to hide the woman from view, which seems to indicate that more than her chest was exposed. Coinciding with the view of the anonymous teacher, Maimonides states — Yad, Sanhedrin, 15,1 — that the adulterous woman at the time of execution wears a one piece robe.

[40] See Büchler's monograph in WZKM, 19.

[41] Deut. 22:24.

[42] Gen. 29:20–26.

[43] I Sam. 18:19; 25:44. Tos. Soṭah 11,17 and San. 19b attempt to explain that neither the betrothal of Merab to David nor the marriage of Michal to him had legal validity. Gen. R. 32,1 explains the irregularity by the fact that Saul outlawed David and that thereby the latter lost the right of possession of his wife. See Ginzberg, *Legends of the Jews,* VI, p. 238, note 80.

We remain uncertain, therefore, how the Bible conceived of betrothal where elopement or breach of contract was involved. It is certain, however, that an attack upon the betrothed maiden, even where she yielded voluntarily, constituted a capital crime in biblical law. The concubine too was considered another man's wife in respect to adultery, but a secondary wife of a lower rank was not. Illicit contact with the former was a capital crime; with the latter only an act of immorality that must be atoned for by a sacrifice upon the altar.[44]

The Bible nowhere offers the adulterer any escape from the death penalty. Whether the woman consented to the crime or even if she solicited his approaches, he is guilty in the same degree. There is no suggestion in the Bible that he might claim he did not know the woman was married, and we are left to guess whether he would be exonerated, as was the case with Abimelech,[45] or that the law would expect him to make an investigation before he risked a criminal offense. The woman can have one defense, that she was violated and is therefore not guilty of voluntary adultery. The Bible provides for that defense in the case of a betrothed maiden, but it probably applies also to a married woman. In the city the claim of violence cannot be accepted, because the woman should have called for help; in the field it is valid.[46]

II. IN RABBINIC LAW

The general conception and treatment of adultery in rabbinic law follows closely the pattern set down by the Bible. The feud method of revenge upon the adulterer by the husband's tribesmen was long out of existence and thoroughly forgotten. The husband as an injured party was entirely ignored; he had no right to pardon his wife nor to affect the penalty of the adulterer. Mutilation or disfigurement of the woman was not permitted, but she was subjected to public disgrace. Her hair was not cut but disheveled and bared; she was not exposed naked but her chest was uncovered, and

[44] See Epstein, *Marriage Laws*, pp. 50–52, 59.
[45] Gen. 20:5, 9; see Gen. 12:18, 19.
[46] Deut. 22:24–27.

at the execution her clothes were removed and a one-piece robe was thrown over her for the sake of decency.[47]

The manner of execution and the technicalities connected with it occupy the greater part of the rabbinic law of adultery. The rabbis found three forms of execution in the Bible applied to adultery. Burning is prescribed for the priest's daughter.[48] Stoning is ordered for adultery of the betrothed virgin.[49] For adultery with a married woman the Bible demands that both shall be put to death,[50] but does not specify the manner of execution; the rabbis feel, therefore, that this means neither burning nor stoning but a more natural death, strangulation. These forms of execution were adopted by the rabbis for the various categories of adultery, but in rabbinic times they were no longer the same as in biblical days. Burning was carried out not by placing the victim on a burning heap, but by choking him to force his mouth open and then pouring down molten lead.[51] Stoning was carried out by throwing the criminal down a high precipice; actual casting of stones was not resorted to unless he survived the fall.[52] Strangulation, as said, is not known in the Bible, but is supposed to belong to the oral traditions of rabbinic law.[53] The Bible knows of hanging as a mode of execution,[54] which is in reality a form of strangulation. To the rabbis strangulation meant tying a noose around the culprit's throat and pulling both ends until he was choked.[55] This manner was considered most humane by the rabbis, because least disfiguring and closest in appearance to natural death. Therefore they prescribe strangulation in all death penalties of the Bible where a specific mode of execution is not stated.

The rabbis find in the Bible four categories of adultery, each one dealt with in a separate verse or group of verses.

[47] See note 39 above.

[48] Lev. 21:9.

[49] Deut. 22:24.

[50] Lev. 20:10; Deut. 22:22.

[51] M. San. 7, 2.

[52] M. San. 6, 4.

[53] The source of that tradition is not known to the amoraim — San. 53a on top — but see Yad, Sanhedrin, 14, 1.

[54] Numb. 25:4; II Sam. 21:9.

[55] M. San. 7,3.

They are: (1) Adultery with a married woman; (2) Adultery with a married woman who is a priest's daughter; (3) Adultery with a betrothed virgin; (4) Adultery with a betrothed virgin, discovered by the husband at his first approach to her. It is evident that the first and the second belong together, as adultery of a married woman; likewise the third and the fourth belong together, representing adultery of a virgin bride. But each group has special legal characteristics, and it will not be without benefit to follow the rabbis in their technical definitions of each of these categories.

(1) Adultery with a married woman. This is to the rabbis the standard type referred to in the Ten Commandments and repeatedly denounced by the prophets. The Bible condemns both man and woman to death, but does not say how; therefore the rabbis teach that both must die by strangulation.[56]

(2) Adultery with a married woman who is a priest's daughter. The levitical law states: "And the daughter of any priest, if she profane herself by playing the harlot . . . shall be burnt with fire."[57] This statement can also be rendered: "And the daughter of any priest, if she commit *adultery* . . . shall be burnt with fire." The original Hebrew permits either interpretation. The first is probably meant by the biblical author. Harlotry in defiance of parental authority in the case of a priest's daughter is treated with especial severity, as mentioned in a previous connection,[58] because it profanes priesthood and because the priests, in their conservatism, perpetuated in their penal code the older form of capital punishment, death by burning. But the rabbis knew of no capital punishment for harlotry under any circumstances whatever. They were forced, therefore, to adopt the second interpretation of the biblical statement, that *adultery* of a priest's daughter, not harlotry, was penalized by burning.[59]

If a special exception was made for the priest's daughter, with burning as her penalty, that rule was narrowed down by

[56] Sifra, Lev. 20:10; Sifre, Deut. 22:22; M. San. 10,1; San. 52b.
[57] Lev. 21:9.
[58] See pp. 164–5 above.
[59] Sifra, Lev. 21:9; San. 50b–51a.

the rabbis to the utmost. In the first place, it applies only to adultery of a married daughter, not of one who is only betrothed. In respect to adultery of a betrothed maiden, priest's daughter and Israelite's daughter are treated alike.[60] In the second place, it applies only to the priest's daughter herself, not to the man who committed the adultery with her. His penalty is strangulation, as in all cases of adultery with a married woman. Finally, whether her husband be a priest or not, whether her lover be a priest or not, makes no difference; the only thing that matters is that her father is a priest.[61]

(3) Adultery of a betrothed virgin. If committed voluntarily by both, the maiden and her lover, they are both put to death, and the Bible specifies stoning as the mode of execution.[62] The rabbis consider stoning the severest form of death sentence,[63] and the stringency of the penalty can be well understood, for the adulterer has not only lived with another man's wife, but put himself ahead of the husband.

The rabbis take the position that any ordinary case of adultery should be penalized by strangulation, the easiest death; that any severer penalty represents an exception to the rule. Hence, the exception must be defined as narrowly as possible. The Bible speaks of "a virgin maiden betrothed to a man" in connection with execution by stoning. She must be a maiden (*na'arah*), neither child nor woman, i.e., above the age of three and below the age of twelve and a half.[64] If she is below three, the act has no sexual status and there is no death penalty at all; [65] if she is above twelve and a half, strangulation and not stoning is the penalty.[66] She must be

[60] San. ibid. This is the view of Rabbanan. Other views are offered which the halakah rejects. See Sifra, ed. Weiss, p. 94c and Targum Jonathan, Lev. 21:9.

[61] San. 51a.

[62] Deut. 22:24.

[63] M. San. 7,1; San. 49b–50b.

[64] Sifre, Deut. 22:23; San. 66b. According to R. Me'ir, she must be above the age of puberty, while the prevailing view includes the maiden who is above the age of three.

[65] Nid. 44b.

[66] San. 66b. Between the ages of three and twelve the case is a standard one of adultery with a betrothed virgin. The man is stoned to death. But the girl, as a minor, cannot be penalized. Execution of both by stoning is possible only if the girl is between the ages of twelve and twelve and a half.

betrothed and not wedded. That means that she is still in her father's house and has not been delivered to her husband. Once she has been given over to the husband's representatives to be taken to his home, even though she has not yet reached his home, she is accounted as already wedded, and the penalty is strangulation, not stoning.[67] Again, she must be virgin; otherwise the death penalty is strangulation even though she be "a betrothed maiden." [68] Finally, she must be born a Jewess; if she is a convert, though "a betrothed virgin," the penalty is strangulation.[69]

The Bible states specifically, in the case of adultery with a betrothed virgin, that "ye shall bring them both out unto the gate of that city and ye shall stone them." The rabbis say a public execution at the gate of the city applies only to persons who are alone responsible for their acts, those who have legal independence. But we are dealing with adultery of a "virgin maiden who is betrothed to a man," who is still a minor and under parental authority. Her execution must take place at the door of her father's house, because the responsibility for the crime falls partly on the parents who did not guard her properly.[70] Public execution at the gate of the city applies only to the man, who always enjoys complete independence of parental authority in Jewish law. It applies also to the girl, if the crime was committed while she was a minor, but the execution takes place when she has attained majority.[71] Likewise, public execution of the maiden takes

[67] Ket. 48b. This rests on the legal principle that once the girl is put under the husband's authority, she is treated as wedded, not as betrothed. Second, here the rabbis borrow from the case of *moẓi' shem ra'*, where the girl is condemned "because she hath wrought a wanton deed in Israel to play the harlot in her father's house," to infer that being under parental authority is essential toward constituting a case for the penalty of stoning.

[68] San. 66b. We have no clear rule in the Talmud as to the statutory non-virgin. Probably she is accounted non-virgin in the law and the penalty is strangulation.

[69] Ket. 44a–b. Here too the rabbis borrowed from the case of *moẓi' shem ra'*, where the Bible describes the crime as "folly in Israel" and indicates that if her origin is not of Israel the crime is of a different quality.

[70] Ket. 45a. Again the rabbis borrowed from the case of *moẓi' shem ra'*.

[71] Ket. ibid. Yad, I. B. 3,10. If the crime was committed when the girl was betrothed but the trial did not come up until she was wedded, she is stoned at her father's house.

place if she has no father or the father has no house or if her parents are proselytes.[72]

(4) Adultery with a betrothed girl, discovered by the husband on his first approach to her. Deuteronomic law speaks of a man bringing charges against his newly-wedded wife, saying: "I took this woman and when I came nigh to her I found not in her the token of virginity." The law then rules that if the charge is proven false the husband is administered some kind of corporal punishment and is fined a hundred shekels and, furthermore, he can never thereafter put her away. But if the charge is found to be true, then the wife is to be stoned at the door of her parental home.[73] The intention of this biblical law is apparently not to legislate on charges of adultery, for lack of virginity may prove immoral conduct on the part of the girl at some time but not necessarily adultery after betrothal. The law has in mind not adultery but "harlotry in her father's house," as has been previously suggested.[74] It goes back to the original conception of parental authority. The girl who commits harlotry while under her father's authority and apparently without her father's knowledge is a rebellious daughter deserving the death penalty prescribed in the deuteronomic code for the "rebellious son." [75] In rabbinic times, however, harlotry was no longer a capital offense, even if committed in defiance of parental authority, for the father's right of life and death over his children had long been forgotten. The rabbis therefore could conceive of no charge against a woman "in her father's house" except adultery while betrothed to a man. Of necessity they had to force a new interpretation into the biblical text.

[72] M. Ket. 4,3; Ket. 44b–45b. The case here treated is of a girl conceived before the conversion and born after the conversion of her parents. If born gentile, there is no stoning; if conceived as a Jewess, she is treated as a daughter of Israel.

[73] Deut. 22:13–21.

[74] See pp. 164–5 above.

[75] Deut. 21:18 f. Dr. Tchernowitz, *Toledot ha-Halakah,* III, pp. 365–6, insists that not harlotry but adultery is the original intention of the Bible, and fully supports the rabbinic interpretation. Josephus, *Antiq.* IV, 8, 23, apparently takes our position, that the charge meant by the Bible is not adultery, for he says: "Let her be stoned because she did not preserve her virginity till she were lawfully married."

They conceived this biblical law to deal with the following case. A husband charges his young bride with adultery at the time of her betrothal and prior to her marriage, and presents the testimony of witnesses to prove his charge. So far, this would be a case belonging to the former category, adultery of a betrothed virgin. But it becomes a special case through his charge that as a result of the adultery he took to bed a non-virgin, he was defrauded of the fifty shekels paid as the price of virginity (*mohar*), and he wants to be refunded that amount. Furthermore, he wants to get rid of his wife and uses this slanderous charge to carry out his designs.

If his charges prove true, we have a case of adultery committed by a betrothed virgin; the penalty is stoning at the door of her father's house, exactly as in our former category, provided it has all the characteristics of that category. She must be born a Jewess, she must be above three and below majority in age,[76] she must be virgin, she must be, as of the time of the commission of the crime, betrothed and not wedded.[77] The execution at the door of her parental home in this case, as in the category treated before, turns into an execution at the public gate if at the time of the execution she has already attained her majority, if she has no father, if the father has no house, and if her parents are proselytes, even though she was born a Jewess.[78]

On the other hand, if his charges are false, the case turns against him. He has committed three offenses — slandered a Jewish daughter, attempted to defraud her of her *mohar*, and schemed to put her away on false accusations. The case against the husband is technically designated by the rabbis as *moẓi shem ra'*, slander, although not infrequently the rabbis apply this name to the situation as a whole, including the charges and counter-charges. For the three offenses involved, he is penalized threefold. For slander he is adminis-

[76] However, up to the age of puberty there is no death penalty for her because she is still a minor and below the level of responsibility.

[77] Sifre, Deut. ed. Friedmann, pp. 117a–118a; Ket. 44b–46b; Yad, Na'arah Betulah, 3; I. B. 3, 4–11.

[78] Provided she was conceived before her parents' conversion. See note 72 above.

tered flagellation; for theft of the *mohar* he is made to pay double; for the attempt to put her away on fraudulent charges, he is restricted against divorcing her all his life.

The payment of double the *mohar* amounts to one hundred shekels, the sum specified in the Bible,[79] and it is no novel thing in biblical legislation to fine the thief twice the value of the thing stolen. The rabbis speak of this payment as a fine, and consider it equal in nature to the fine of fifty shekels imposed on the offender in cases of rape and seduction. The logic is correct; both are theft of virginity, but here the fine is higher because fraud and slander are involved. The rules, therefore, that apply to payment of a fine in rape or seduction apply also to the payment of the hundred shekels in this case. There is no fine then for the girl below three or above twelve and a half, nor for one who has a reputation for moral laxity, nor certainly for one who is no virgin or even a statutory non-virgin.[80] The fine is not exacted if it is not a typical case of *moẓi shem ra'*, which means that, in addition to complying fully with the general rules of fines in rabbinic law for theft of virginity, as has been here stated, the girl must be born Jewish and "conceived in holiness"; the charge must be brought by the husband after his first contact with her and as a result of his discovery of her lack of virginity; and the charge must be that she committed adultery during the time she was betrothed to him.[81] Any of these characteristics lacking, the court may have on its hands the case of a capital charge against the woman, involving either stoning or strangulation, as the case may be, but no fine and no flagellation for the husband.

[79] Ket. 45a–46a. Josephus l. c. records a fine of fifty shekels, probably because he takes the other fifty shekels to be represented in the obligation assumed by the husband in the ketubah. He agrees therefore in part with the view of R. Jose — Ket. 39b at the bottom — that even where divorce is restricted the wife gets the standard ketubah.

[80] Yad, Na'arah Betulah, 1,8–10; 3,8. See pp. 184–6 above. It should be noted also that where the man is freed from the fine he is also freed from the penalty of flagellation. Various traditions are given in the Talmud as to the fine where the girl is an *eilonit,* deaf-mute, or insane. See Ket. 36a; Yad, Na'arah Betulah, 1,9, note of RABD and *Kesef Mishneh* thereto.

[81] Ket. 45a–46a. As to the specification that the husband have contact with her before he brings charges, the view of R. Elazar b. Jacob prevails in the halakah.

The restriction against divorce in the case of *moẓi shem ra'* has its modification in rabbinic law similar to those of rape, where, also, divorce is prohibited. If the marriage is discovered to be biblically or rabbinically forbidden or if the wife at any later time commits adultery, the restriction is lifted. It also seems to be accepted as a rule by the rabbis that where the case is not in every detail typical of *moẓi shem ra'*, or in other words, where the fine and flagellation are not imposed on the husband, the prohibition against divorce does not apply. Furthermore, the wife herself can sue for divorce, and if the grounds are recognized by the court the husband will be ordered to divorce her. The restriction against divorce, in the eyes of rabbinic law, is meant to penalize the husband, not the wife. Should he divorce her in defiance of the prohibition, he will be compelled to remarry her. However, if he is a priest who may not marry a divorcee, the divorce is final, but he suffers the penalty of flagellation for overstepping the restrictions against divorce.[82]

Having concluded our analysis of these various types of adultery and their respective death penalties, we go back to a further examination of the general treatment of adultery in rabbinic law. Three principles come to the surface. First, there is no adultery unless the marriage is fully valid beyond the shadow of a doubt. Second, there is no death penalty unless the crime was committed with full free volition. Third, capital punishment for adultery was meant by the rabbis to be and remain a theoretical teaching, but was not favored as a practical penal guide for the courts.

It is self-evident that there can be no violation of a marriage if there is no valid marriage. In Jewish law a marriage can be wholly invalid, or it may be defective, or it may have doubtful validity. A marriage is totally invalid if it is an intermarriage between Jew and gentile, if it is incestuous, if the groom is below legal responsibility for his act, such as a minor or an insane person, or if the essential legal formalities are not carried out. A defective marriage is one that has rabbinical sanction but no biblical validity, such as the marriage of a minor orphan girl, or the marriage of a deaf-mute man or

[82] See pp. 189–91 above; Yad, Na'arah Betulah, 3,4.

woman. A doubtful marriage is one where either of the persons is of doubtful sex, such as a hermaphrodite, or where there is doubt as to whether the essential formalities of marriage were carried out in the proper legal form.[83] In all these cases there is no capital punishment for adultery.

The principle that there is no capital punishment for adultery if it is not committed with free will and intent is specifically stated in the Bible in connection with adultery of a betrothed virgin.[84] The rabbis apply this rule to every form of adultery, as in fact to every kind of crime. But they expand the rule to exclude four kinds of adultery from capital punishment. The primary instance is adultery committed under irresistible physical compulsion. In such a case there is no penalty at all, even if the victim admits that the experience proved not unpleasant.[85] According to some teachers, that kind of exemption applies to the woman only; the male is incapable of compulsory intercourse.[86] Then there may be adultery under the threat of death. Here Jewish law maintains that morally it does not constitute compulsion, for the person should accept martyrdom rather than violate a cardinal prohibition such as adultery,[87] but legally it is compulsion and there is no penalty.[88] A third form of involuntary adultery is that committed under misapprehension, as where the woman mistook another man for her husband or where the man did not know that the woman was married. The carelessness is in itself a sin that calls for atonement, but does not call for capital punishment.[89] Finally, the law considers a girl under twelve and a boy under thirteen not responsible for his or her deeds. No matter, then, what the

[83] Yad, Ishut 4,7–12; I. B. 3,1.

[84] Deut. 22:26.

[85] Sifre, Deut. 22:26; Ket. 51b.

[86] This observation is made by Raba, Yeb. 53b, and is accepted by the halakah, Yad, I. B. 1,9. Yet certain unusual forms of compulsion are believed to be possible also for the male. See Yeb. 54a; Tosafot Yeb. 53b, s. v. *en;* Tosafot Yoma 82a, s. v. *mah; She'eltot,* Wa-Era', 42; RABD and *Maggid* ad Yad, ibid.

[87] San. 74a; Yoma 82a. Rashi, s. v. *af* and Tosafot, s. v. *mah* (Yoma 82a) maintain that martyrdom is not required of a woman in the case of compulsory adultery because hers is a passive part in the commission of the sin.

[88] Yad, Yesode ha-Torah, 5,4.

[89] Kerit. 2a.

crime is, there is no capital punishment for the minor. The co-respondent in this case, of course, is punished according to the guilt of his or her act, except that if the boy involved is below nine or the girl in the case is below three the act has no sexual significance, and then the co-respondent is also freed.[90]

It is common knowledge that the rabbis were averse to capital punishment for any crime.[91] In fact for two thousand years Jewish courts have not exercised the power of capital punishment even under their limited self-rule.[92] The whole matter was dealt with on the level of theoretical study of law rather than that of practical court action. Even on the theoretical level, the rabbis put difficulties in the way of declaring any crime, including adultery, a capital offense. The most potent of these is the requirement that the criminal be properly warned in the presence of witnesses of the severity of his crime before committing it, which the rabbis call *hatra'ah*. The witnesses, or other persons in the presence of witnesses, must warn the criminal at the time he is about to commit the crime that the act contemplated is criminal and will be punished by death. If the criminal is silent or acknowledges the warning by nodding his head, or says contemptuously "I know" and goes on with his act the law considers the warning as of no legal effect. He must say "I know and I do not care; I will take the consequences," to make it a legally valid warning.[93] Evidently this requirement puts an end to capital punishment for adultery, as for any other crime, unless the crime is staged in front of witnesses and is spiced by a bit of hasty dialogue between them and the criminal.

With the elimination of capital punishment, other penalties were employed. Flagellation was generally substituted for the death penalty. Where legal technicalities did not permit even flagellation on the basis of law, it was administered to the adulterer by the local courts in the interest of discipline

90 Nid. 44b–45a; Yad, I. B. 1,13.
91 M. Mak. 1,10.
92 M. Mak. ibid.; Yad, Sanhedrin, 14,11–14.
93 San. 40b–41a; Yad, Sanhedrin, 12,1–2.

and public morality, a right which local courts exercised freely wherever and whenever Jews enjoyed a measure of self-government.[94] The courts were not loath to borrow forms of punishment from non-Jewish sources.[95] From the Arabs they adopted the practice of shaving off the hair of the adulterous pair and leading them bareheaded through the marketplace.[96] A teacher of the fifteenth century in North Africa describes the following treatment of an adulterous couple. The heads of both were shaved, they were led bareheaded through the marketplace, the shaven hair was carried on a pole ahead of them, both were given the full measure of disciplinary flagellation, a ban was pronounced on both for thirty days, the woman was forcibly divorced from her husband, and her ketubah was torn up.[97] In superstitious communities, a plague or a drought was often ascribed to the hidden sin of adultery. The community got busy tracking down the criminals. If they were found, they were punished and humiliated and driven out of the city. If they were not apprehended, the community felt collectively responsible and tried to clear itself by praying and fasting and visiting the graves of the righteous to beg for their intercession with the Almighty for forgiveness.

III. DEFILEMENT

While capital punishment was merely a theoretical matter in rabbinic law, the question of "defilement" was of real and severe practical importance. In the earliest biblical days, adultery carried with it a sense of defilement, so that a woman who had known contact with another man, even if by force,

[94] Yad, I. B. 1,8, 10, 11, 15, and *Maggid* to 1,8.

[95] Cutting off the nose, a penalty referred to above (p. 173) may have come originally from the Egyptians as reported by Uhlmann, *Aegyptische Alterthum,* II, 25, 65, and found also among other races, Westermarck, *History of Human Marriage,* I, p. 314.

[96] See *Toratan shel Rishonim,* I, p. 29; Pirḳ. de R. E. ch. 14; Solomon Stern in Geiger's *Wissenschaftliche Zeitschrift,* 1837, p. 354; Büchler, Das Schneiden des Haares, WZKM, 19. Prof. Saul Lieberman argues, against Büchler, that cutting a woman's hair as punishment for adultery and parading her through the street was also an original Jewish custom. See *Jubilee Volume* in honor of Prof. Louis Ginzberg, Hebrew section, p. 267.

[97] Responsa Samson b. Ẓemah (TSBẒ), 191; *Orḥot Ḥayyim,* II, 109,9.

was considered no longer fit to be visited by her husband.[98] The deuteronomic code teaches that a woman who is divorced by her husband and thereafter marries another man, likewise cannot return to her former husband.[99] This does not run counter to the previous law, but adds the principle that not only adultery, but even a legitimate marriage, renders her unfit to be taken up by her first husband. The prophet Jeremiah speaks of adultery and second marriage as belonging to the same category, causing "pollution of the land" if the woman should return to her spouse.[100] The rabbis are therefore in full accord with the ancient tradition, when they rule that a woman who has committed adultery is "defiled" and cannot remain the wife of her husband, but must be divorced.[101] In respect to priestly marriages, they accepted the old law in full, ruling that even involuntary adultery of a priest's wife makes her unfit to remain with her husband, but in respect to Israelites they modified the old law to permit the wife's return to her Israelitish husband if her act was involuntary.[102]

In some respects this law of defilement follows the law of capital punishment, at least in that the marriage must be a valid one and the contact must be of sexual significance, neither the co-respondent below the age of nine nor the wife below the age of three.[103] In many other respects the law of defilement is severer. Any male contact makes divorce compulsory, whether by Jew or gentile, potent or impotent,[104] natural or unnatural,[105] or even simulated intercourse with a eunuch.[106] Furthermore, while in respect to capital punish-

98 Gen. 49:4; II Sam. 20:3; 11:11. See Jubilees 33:6–9; Epstein, *Marriage Laws*, p. 51. The Karaites retain the original law — Revel, *Karaite Halakah*, p. 34.

99 Deut. 24:1–4.

100 Jer. 3:1.

101 Sifre, Deut. 270, p. 122b. Cf. Sifre, Numb. ed. Friedmann, 7, p. 4a and 19, p. 66.

102 M. Ket. 4,8; Sifre, Numb. 7, p. 4a.

103 Nid. 44b. The expression *ḥuẓ min ha-ḳaṭan* in M. Soṭah 4,4, is taken by Maimonides and accepted by the halakah to mean one below the age of nine. See *Mishnah Commentary*, Soṭah 4,4 and Yad, Soṭah, 1,4.

104 Soṭah 26b.

105 Yeb. 55a–b.

106 Sifre, Numb. 13, p. 5b.

ment the fact of adultery, the validity of the marriage, and the woman's free consent to the crime must be established beyond doubt, in respect to defilement the law operates even where there is only a reasonable certainty.[107] Thus, where the husband has good ground for his charges but cannot prove them,[108] where the marriage is of doubtful validity,[109] where the wife is a minor above the age of three but below the age of legal responsibility,[110] or where she has committed adultery under misapprehension,[111] the law of defilement is applicable and divorce is compulsory.[112]

The severity of the law of defilement proved unduly harsh upon Jewish families under the hazardous conditions they had to endure. They were ceaselessly plagued by wars, seizures, piracies, pillage, and forcible conversion to Islam or Christianity. The law assumed in all these instances that the women were dishonored, and facts apparently justified that assumption. The woman therefore who was captured in war or seized as hostage or held for ransom by pirates or abducted by missionaries to be converted to another faith or caught in a city overrun by enemy troops, was assumed by the law to have been raped, unless she could prove to the contrary. The question was only, had the woman submitted voluntarily or had she been forced. If the former she could never again return to her husband. But how could the law establish a line of demarcation between voluntary and involuntary submission, or what circumstances would prove the one or the other? According to one amora, there is always a suspicion of voluntary submission unless witnesses testify that the woman was fighting her attacker from beginning to end.[113] Other teachers believe that any woman is ready to offer her-

[107] Sifre, Numb. 7, p. 4a and 19, p. 6b.

[108] Ket. 9a; Yer. Ket. 25a.

[109] Soṭah 27a; Sifre, Numb. 20, p. 6b; Yad, Soṭah, 2,2.

[110] This is the view of Maimonides whose talmudic sources are discussed by all his commentators. See Yad, I. B. 3,2, RABD and *Maggid* thereto, and Yad, Soṭah, 2,4. But Yer. Soṭah 17d states definitely that a minor girl having no will in the legal sense is not defiled by adultery and may remain with her husband, which is contrary to the ruling of Maimonides.

[111] Yeb. 87b.

[112] See Epstein, *Marriage Laws*, pp. 324–5.

[113] Ket. 51b.

self voluntarily to her attacker if she feels that otherwise her life is imperiled.[114] But the law had to accept the more lenient view of another amora, who teaches that any case of rape is assumed to be involuntary, even if the woman thereafter confesses that the experience was not unwelcome.[115]

This ruling of the law proved satisfactory in the case of the wives of Israelites, where involuntary adultery is no bar to their returning to their husbands. But the case is otherwise with the wives of priests, who cannot return to their husbands even where the adulterous contact has been definitely involuntary on their part, because that contact makes her a *zonah* by rabbinic definition.[116] Therefore, once the law assumes that under captivity, seizure, pillage, or conversion the women are dishonored, the wives of priests caught therein may never go back to their husbands. A woman's only escape from this doom is to find witnesses to testify that she remained untouched.

Hard and practical necessity forced the law to seek leniencies on behalf of the unfortunate woman. Of course, the law could not accept the mere statement of the woman herself or her husband,[117] but admitted any other testimony, such as the statement of a single witness, even a gentile or slave or minor, or even a witness in the name of another witness, which the law otherwise would not accept.[118] In the case of pillage, the law teaches that a single chance for hiding or escape breaks down the assumption of her being dishonored and that then she can testify in her own behalf.[119] Likewise in the case of forced conversion, teachers of the post-talmudic time declared that the woman could testify for herself and that her testimony was valid.[120]

114 Tosafot Ket. 26b in interpretation of the Mishnah. See E. H. Ishut, 7,11 and note of Isserles thereto. Maimonides in his *Commentary* to this Mishnah and in Yad, I. B. 1,9 and Ishut, 24, 19–20 opposes this view.

115 Ket. 51b; Yer. Soṭah 19d.

116 Yeb. 86a–b. See Epstein, *Marriage Laws*, pp. 325–8.

117 Ket. 21a; 27a–b; Tos. Ket. 3,2.

118 Ket. 27a. See note of Isserles, E. H. 7,2.

119 Ket. ibid.

120 Note of Isserles, E. H. 7,11, based on a liberal ruling of Asheri (*Responsa*, 32,8). However, this ruling is challenged.

CHAPTER X

COMMAND OF JEALOUSY

WHILE the law is inclined to be on the woman's side in cases of doubtful defilement arising out of external conditions, it seems to support the husband whenever the question of the wife's faithfulness arises from the husband's suspicions and jealousy. This legal attitude may be accounted for in a number of ways. More anciently the woman was generally held suspect as to her sex conduct; therefore the slightest suspicion of a husband was given credence by the court. Furthermore, the husband was her master and her moral guardian. The court had to support his authority. Lastly, by social standards, the woman's movements were pretty narrowly restricted. The husband had a right to add further restrictions as a matter of discipline. A woman submitting to these could not possibly arouse a husband's jealousy; she must have violated good taste in conduct and thereby given cause for suspicion. The jealousy of a husband, therefore, constituted an assumption of guilt against the wife, and upon her was the burden of proof of innocence.

I. PRE-BIBLICAL AND BIBLICAL LAW

The Code of Hammurabi conceives two possible situations of a jealous husband charging his wife with infidelity without legally valid evidence to support his charge. Both are assured the serious attention of the court, and in both cases the burden of proof rests on the defendant wife. The Babylonian legislator teaches, "If a man accuse his wife and she have not been taken in lying with another man, she shall take an oath in the name of God and she shall return to her house." [1] This represents an accusation based on no evidence at all, but prompted mainly by the jealousy of the husband, and the

[1] C. H. 131.

counter-evidence the wife is required to offer in defense is to swear she is innocent. In the next section the legislator declares, "If the finger have been pointed at the wife of a man because of another man and she have not been taken in lying with another man, for her husband's sake she shall throw herself into the sacred river." [2] Here we deal with suspicion arising from the woman's misconduct and bad repute, while there is no legal evidence to condemn her, and the testimony the woman must offer in her defense is the ordeal of sacred water. If she sinks she is guilty; if she escapes drowning she is innocent.

The similarity between these sections of the Code of Hammurabi and the Mosaic legislation in the matter of undetected adultery as given in the Book of Numbers has long been recognized. The ordeal of sacred water in both codes has been especially noted; other details have not escaped attention. But further search reveals one important detail, hitherto unnoticed, in which the Code of Hammurabi and the Bible agree. The Bible, like the Babylonian law, recognized two kinds of situations out of which the charges against the wife might arise. Accusations rise either out of the improper conduct and consequent bad repute of the wife, which Hammurabi designates "a finger have been pointed at the wife," or for no reason except the suspicions of a jealous husband. The first case is presented in the following verses: "If any man's wife go aside and act unfaithfully against him and a man lie with her carnally and it be hid from the eyes of her husband, she being defiled secretly, and there be no witness against her neither she be taken in the act. . . ." [3] In the next verse the second is given: "Or (and) [4] if the spirit of

[2] C. H. 132.

[3] Numb. 5:12–13; corresponds to C. H. 132.

[4] The traditional rendering of the conjunctive in this sentence is "and" and naturally gives the impression that only one situation is contemplated by the legislator. I render the conjunctive by "or" which is equally possible for the Hebrew "*waw*" and my support for this rendering is found in Numb. 5:29–30, where in summary of the law, the two verses say: "This is the law of jealousy when a wife being under her husband goeth aside and is defiled; *or* when the spirit of jealousy cometh upon a man and he be jealous over his wife . . ." The Hebrew for "or" in this case cannot be rendered by "and." My interpretation, furthermore, makes the text much clearer and simpler than has been done by the traditional interpretation.

jealousy come upon him and he be jealous of his wife and she be defiled, or if the spirit of jealousy come on him and he be jealous of his wife and she be not defiled . . ."[5] Here, then, as in the Code of Hammurabi, the husband may charge his wife with unfaithfulness merely on the basis of his jealousy without the slightest ground, and the law imposes upon her the duty of proving herself innocent. But while Hammurabi, in such a case, is satisfied with the woman's oath, the Bible prescribes, as in the other case, the ordeal of bitter water.

This ordeal is described in imposing detail. The husband brings an offering of barley-meal which is designated as a meal-offering of jealousy, and presents this and his wife before the priest at the altar. The priest places the woman "before the Lord," uncovers her head, and places in her hand the meal-offering of jealousy. He then takes some holy water in an earthen vessel, adds some earth from the ground of the sanctuary, and, holding the vessel in his hand and facing the woman, he pronounces the following oath: "If no man lay with thee and if thou didst not turn away in defilement, being under thy husband, be thou free from this bitter water that causeth the curse. But if thou didst turn away, being under thy husband, and didst become defiled and any man other than thy husband did lie with thee . . . then the Lord make thee a curse and an oath in the midst of thy people in that the Lord make thy thigh to fall and thy belly to swell; and this water that causeth the curse shall go into thy bowels for the swelling of the belly and for the falling of the thigh." To this pronouncement the woman answers, Amen, Amen! The curse is then written down on parchment and rubbed off into the bitter water; the meal-offering of jealousy is thereafter offered up on the altar; the woman then drinks down the bitter water and the ordeal is concluded. If she is guilty, the curse comes true, her thigh falls and her belly swells and she is accursed in the midst of her people, but if she is innocent, she emerges from the ordeal in good health and spirit, vindicated and triumphant and in due time begetting children.[6]

[5] Numb. 5:14; corresponds to C. H. 131.
[6] Numb. 5:11–31.

II. POST-BIBLICAL MODIFICATIONS

In the few centuries from the close of the biblical period to the end of the Second Commonwealth the ordeal of the bitter water was considerably modified and finally abrogated. The literature of that period is scant, practically silent, on the subject. But the Talmud has preserved abundant records both as to court action and Temple ritual in connection with the ordeal, and has dedicated a whole treatise to the subject under the name Soṭah. In these rabbinic records we find an account of the development of the ordeal together with its surrounding circumstances since its biblical origin.

In general, progress has been in the following directions. (1) The jealousy of the husband was deemed insufficient justification for charges of adultery against the wife. The law required a basis for the charges. (2) The ordeal, originally a Temple rite under the administration of the priesthood, became a function of the court, subject to court procedure and technique. (3) The ordeal and its attending ceremonials became more elaborate in form and richer in significance. (4) Ultimately the effectiveness of the ordeal wore off, its merits as a means of detecting hidden sin were questioned, and finally it had to be abrogated. (5) But even after abrogation, the soṭah situation, that is, wherein the wife is suspected of adultery, whose conduct warrants the suspicion though she has not been detected in the crime, continued to be a problem before the law and engaged the attention of generations of teachers after the collapse of the Jewish State.

The first progressive step in development of the law of soṭah, as indicated, was to allow no ordeal unless the husband presented valid grounds for his charges. This step was probably taken in the earliest period of rabbinic legislation. The rabbis understood the biblical command, not as we have here given it on its literal basis, to mean that when the woman acts suspiciously *and as a result* the husband is aroused to jealousy, he may test her guilt or innocence by the ordeal of the bitter water. It is not *either* bad repute of the wife *or* jealousy of the husband, but the bad repute of the wife *resulting in* the jealousy of the husband, that constitutes the basis for the ordeal. They were led to this conclusion not so much by the verbal indications of the biblical text as by their sense of fairness to the woman. The position of woman was higher in their day, her sense of honor more generally acknowledged, her freedom of motion more readily granted, and a husband's tyranny less tolerated. They could not see how on the mere basis of a husband's jealousy the wife could be subjected to the humiliations of the bitter water ordeal.[7] Therefore, the biblical law must be understood to mean that the jealousy of the husband is ground for the ordeal only if it have a basis in charges that can stand the investigation of the court, and that if found to be true would make her guilt probable in the eyes of the court.

A. The soṭah situation is thus given the following technical portrayal. The husband is jealous of his wife because she is fond of another man and is seen too often in his company. He commands her not to see this co-respondent privately any longer. This command is justifiable and the wife must obey it as a matter of law; it is designated technically as a "command of jealousy," in Hebrew, *kinnui*. But the wife violates the command and is found in the company of the co-respondent unchaperoned. She may be guilty of adultery or she may not, but at least she has justly brought that suspicion on herself by secret meetings with another man, technically designated as *setirah,* in defiance of her husband's command of jealousy. Under these circumstances the husband has a right to charge her with adultery, even though he has no proof, and the ordeal of bitter water is administered to prove her guilty or innocent.[8] The law is strictly technical about the soṭah situation leading to the ordeal. Compromising conduct on the part of the wife may cause the husband to doubt her faithfulness. He is entitled to complain to the court, he may demand a trial of the wife to establish her guilt or innocence, but that does not lead to the ordeal of bitter water, because it is not strictly a soṭah situation. The naming of a co-respondent by the husband and the presentation

[7] Tos. Soṭah 1, 1; see also Soṭah 2b: *Im ken en ledabar sof.*

[8] M. Soṭah 1, 2.

of testimony that the wife and the co-respondent have had secret and suspicious meetings together may constitute an indictment against the wife's conduct, but again, if there has been no command of jealousy, this does not constitute a soṭah situation and does not lead to administration of the ordeal. *Ḳinnui* and *setirah* are two legal technicalities necessary to establish a soṭah situation.[9]

Ḳinnui, or the command of jealousy, must be delivered by the husband to the wife in the presence of two witnesses,[10] and the co-respondent or co-respondents must be named in the command. The co-respondent may be a Jew or a gentile,[11] a minor of sexual potency[12] or a mature person of sexual debility;[13] the wife's own father or brother may be named as co-respondent;[14] and the command of jealousy may name one person or more than one.[15] The command should not be given in general terms, demanding that she give up social contacts with the co-respondent, but must be specific, prohibiting her to meet the co-respondent in privacy.[16] The husband should issue the command in a firm, earnest, calm tone, neither in jest, nor in a casual, conversational manner, nor in the heat of a quarrel.[17] Until the wife has violated the command of jealousy, the husband has a right to withdraw it; thereafter he is powerless.[18] In certain instances, the court itself will issue the command of jealousy in the name of the

[9] Ket. 9a.

[10] M. Soṭah 1, 1; Tos. Soṭah 1, 1.

[11] Soṭah 26b.

[12] Soṭah 24a. Sifre Numb. p. 3b and Soṭah 26b seem to rule that a minor cannot be named as co-respondent, but Maimonides (Yad, Soṭah 1, 6) interprets it to refer to a minor below the age of nine.

[13] Sifre Numb. p. 5b, #13; Soṭah 26b.

[14] Soṭah 24a; Yer. Soṭah 16b–c.

[15] M. Kerit. 2, 3; Yer. Soṭah 16c. Maimonides (Yad, Soṭah 1, 3) interprets this law to mean that the husband can give the wife not only a command of jealousy, concerning any one of a number of men by one command, but he can even command her not to be found in the company of these men together. He is supported in this interpretation by the Yerushalmi text. But see Yad, Soṭah 4, 16.

[16] M. Soṭah 1, 2; Soṭah 5b.

[17] Yer. Soṭah 16b. While the Palestinian amoraim seem to feel that a command given in jest does not count, Maimonides rules that it does constitute *ḳinnui-bedi'abad*-Yad, Soṭah 4, 18.

[18] Soṭah 25a.

husband, if the wife's conduct becomes so offensive as to reach the attention of the court. This is done in the interest of public morality and in defense of the husband's rights, but the court does not exercise this function except in the husband's absence, as when the husband is away on a long journey or confined in prison for a long period, or when he has become mentally unbalanced. Such a command of jealousy by the court, however, can have the effect only of discipline and penalties, so that, if she violates it, she is forcibly divorced and forfeits her ketubah, but it cannot lead to the ordeal of bitter water.[19]

The issuance of the command, according to some tannaitic authorities, is mandatory upon the husband when he begins to doubt his wife's fidelity. If her conduct is suspicious as it is unbecoming, he has no choice from a moral point of view but to restrict her loose ways by a command of jealousy. Other tannaim maintain that there is no moral obligation on the husband to issue it, that it is entirely optional with him.[20] The two points of view were carried over into the teachings of the amoraim, among whom there were even those who maintained that the husband committed a moral wrong in issuing the command of jealousy to his wife, for at best his command was based on mere suspicion.[21] In the interest of the purity of home life, the final rabbinic verdict is that the command of jealousy is mandatory upon the husband. A man should be indulgent with his wife if she has spilt his wine or poured out his oil; but let him arise like a man of might, if she is indiscreet in her conduct.[22] What constitutes misconduct to justify the man's jealousy? A hard and fast rule cannot be laid down, but Rabbi Me'ir gives the answer in the form of a parable. Some people have personal peculiarities in matters of food, others in their sex relations. Some one, if a fly falls into his cup of wine, will throw away the fly and drink the wine; similarly, a man seeing his wife conversing with her relatives and neighbors will make nothing of it but

[19] Soṭah 24a, 27a.
[20] Sifre Numb. p. 4a, #7; Soṭah 3a; Yer. Soṭah 16b.
[21] Soṭah 2a, 3a.
[22] Numb. R. 9, 2; see Yad, Soṭah 4, 18.

will continue his marital associations. Another finding a fly in his cup will pour out the wine, and likewise a man may object to the innocent freedom his wife enjoys and will lock her up when he is away from home. Yet another person finding a fly in his cup squeezes out the wine absorbed in the fly and drinks his cup. Like unto him is the husband who sees his wife going about with uncovered head and shoulders, weaving in the marketplace, and bathing together with men, and keeps quiet about it. . . . "He who is favored by God will find escape from her, for God will cause him to have a spirit of jealousy, and he will issue to his wife the command of jealousy." [23]

Violation of the command of jealousy, *setirah,* the secret and suspicious meeting with the co-respondent, which is the second essential in establishing a soṭah situation, must be proven by the testimony of witnesses. The earlier law, it seems, recognized the testimony of one witness or of the husband himself to prove *setirah,*[24] but the later law demanded two witnesses,[25] both having seen her together — not each one separately[26] — in secret companionship with the co-respondent in such a manner and for such a duration of time as to make carnal contact possible.[27] The *setirah* testimony does not and must not establish evidence of adultery; it must establish only the fact that the command of jealousy was violated and that adultery was possible. The question of adultery must remain doubtful in order to have a soṭah situation. If the witnesses, therefore, have caught her in the act, even if one witness only testifies to definite adultery, even a woman, a slave, a gentile, a relative,[28] her case becomes one of adultery charges, but is no longer a case of soṭah, and the ordeal is impossible. Likewise her own confession of adultery destroys the soṭah situation.[29]

[23] Tos. Soṭah 5, 9; Giṭ. 90a; Numb. R. 9, 8.

[24] The view of R. Eliezer, M. Soṭah, 1, 1.

[25] The view of R. Joshua, ibid. It is acknowledged, however, that the husband is justified in his jealousy and is consequently morally bound to divorce her even on the evidence of gossip. See M. Soṭah 6, 1.

[26] Yer. Soṭah 16c.

[27] Soṭah 4a; Yer. Soṭah ibid.

[28] Soṭah 31a.

[29] M. Soṭah 1, 5.

B. The second step in the law of soṭah, as can be seen from the foregoing and from what is to follow, is to put the court in control of the situation so as to insure proper deliberation and procedure and fairness of treatment. In respect to the husband's jealousy as in respect to the general authority of the husband in the household, the task of rabbinic law was to subject the husband to the higher authority of the court. The soṭah situation, according to rabbinic teaching, therefore, calls first of all for a proper court trial. It is first tried by the local *bet-din,* who clarify the issues involved, hear the testimony of witnesses both as to *ḳinnui* and *setirah,* take up the woman for cross-examination, and render a decision whether this is or is not a case of soṭah for the administration of the ordeal of the bitter water. If it is not a regular case of soṭah and the bitter water ordeal is eliminated, then they consider the other questions involved. If only improper conduct is involved and, at any rate, no capital charge of adultery can be established, they rule on the question of compulsory divorce and forfeiture of the ketubah. If a capital charge develops, it is referred to the lower sanhedrin of twenty-three judges, unless the local court is itself constituted of that number of judges and is empowered to deal with cases involving capital crimes. But, if the local court finds the case to be a true soṭah, it has to send husband and wife under the guard of two deputy judges to the high court of seventy-one judges in Jerusalem for administration of the ordeal.[30]

She is admitted into the court room alone, her husband remaining outside. The presiding judge addresses her in an awesome manner to impress upon her the seriousness of the ordeal, saying, "Daughter, much mischief comes from wine, levity, childishness, or bad company. Do not cause the great Name which is written in purity and holiness to be erased in the water. It is human to err, even as Judah erred concerning his daughter-in-law, Tamar, or as Reuben erred in lying with Bilhah, his father's concubine, or as Absalom in a similar sin, or as Amnon in violating his sister. If thou art defiled, confess! But if thou art innocent, stand firm by thy position, for this water is like dry poison on the human skin;

[30] M. Soṭah 1, 3–4.

put on a healthy skin there is no harm, but put on an open wound it penetrates and eats into it." [31] If she persists in her plea of innocence, she is led about from place to place in the Temple chambers in order to give her further chance to confess and to break down her resistance,[32] and finally she is brought out and placed at the eastern entrance to the Temple, outside the gate of Nicanor, where a large gathering of men and women are assembled to witness the ordeal.[33] Now the ordeal is to begin; it is to be administered by a priest under authority of the high court, and the priest is chosen by lot.[34]

Under rabbinic influence the law sought by every means to avoid the ordeal and therefore set up any number of restrictions to prevent its taking place. We have already seen how narrowly and strictly the rabbis defined the terms *ḳinnui* and *setirah,* and ruled that no case that did not fully meet these definitions could be tested by the biblical ordeal. We have also seen that they did not permit the ordeal to take place where there was some testimony as to the woman's defilement or a confession of guilt on the woman's part. They further ruled that a woman could be subjected to the ordeal more than once, either by different husbands or in respect to different co-respondents, but the same husband could not subject his wife to the ordeal more than once on account of the same co-respondent.[35] They also gave the husband the right not only to rescind his command of jealousy, as seen above, but to drop the case and to stop the ordeal even after the lower court had found her guilty of *setirah.*[36] The wife, too, was given the privilege, until the scroll of the curse was rubbed down into the sacred water, to refuse to go through the ordeal, even though persisting in her plea of innocence; [37]

[31] M. Soṭah ibid.; Tos. Soṭah 1, 6; Soṭah 7b; Numb. R. 9, 42.

[32] Soṭah 8a.

[33] M. Soṭah 1, 5–6.

[34] Tos. Soṭah 1, 7.

[35] Soṭah 18b–19a.

[36] Soṭah 24a. In that case divorce is compulsory, but the husband has to pay her the ketubah. The rabbis, however, do not tell us until which point in the ordeal process the husband can drop the case against his wife. Possibly this privilege is denied him once she enters the chambers of the high court and he remains behind.

[37] Soṭah 20a, 24a.

the privilege of confession to her guilt was given her till the last moment.

The husband must be alive at the time of the ordeal, else it does not take place. It must also be established that the husband has had contact with his wife prior to the suspected adultery with the co-respondent and that he has not had contact with her after the suspected defilement; else there is no ordeal. A betrothed bride, the wife of a minor, of a hermaphrodite, of a blind, lame, mute, or deaf husband, or a wife who is herself a minor, blind, lame, mute, or deaf, is exempt from the ordeal. Nor can the ordeal be imposed on the wife if her marriage to her husband is biblically or rabbinically prohibited, because then she cannot return to her husband even if proven innocent. On that account a wife proven to be sterile, if her husband has no other wife or children by another wife, cannot go through the ordeal, because the husband would not be allowed to keep her on account of her sterility.[38] All these restrictions, of course, did not completely abrogate the ordeal, but they certainly rendered it, as the rabbinic teachers conceived and desired it, a very rare occurrence.

C. The elaboration and interpretation of the ceremonial of the ordeal is the third rabbinic contribution to the law of soṭah. The woman is clothed in black or in ragged garments. Her ornaments and jewelry are removed; her head covering is taken off and put under her feet; her hair is disheveled; a rope is tied around her above her breast; the upper part of her blouse is torn open so as to bare her chest. The meal-offering is placed in her hand and the priest holds the vessel of bitter water. She is made to stand throughout the entire ordeal. The priest faces her and states the charges on which account the ordeal is administered to her. Then he recites the oath and curse as given above and adds by way of interpretation that this oath is pronounced not only to accurse her for the adultery, if true, with which she is now charged, but also for any adulterous act committed by her ever since betrothal to her husband or any adultery she might commit in

[38] Soṭah 23b–24a; 25b–26a; 27a–b; Yeb. 38b; Yer. Soṭah 19c–d. See Yad, Soṭah 2, 2, 3, 5, 7, 9, 10.

the future. To all this the woman answers: Amen, Amen. Thereafter, the priest writes down this oath in Hebrew upon a parchment and allows it to dry. When it is completely dry, he rubs it off into the bitter water until none of the writing remains on the parchment, then he causes her to drink the water. The priest then offers up the meal-offering of jealousy and with this the ordeal is concluded. The next few moments are moments of suspense; the effect of the ordeal is now becoming evident. If she is innocent, she emerges uninjured and in good spirits and goes back triumphantly to her husband and her home. If she is guilty, her face becomes yellow, her eyes bulge, her veins distend all over her body, her belly swells, her thigh falls, and she is quickly removed from the Temple court to die outside so as not to defile the sanctuary.[39]

The halakah further elaborates this ceremony by a code of regulations. The ordeal can be carried out any day, but never at night.[40] Only one woman at a time is given it.[41] The scroll of the oath must be written by a priest who is of age, neither a layman nor a minor. It must be written like a Torah, with ink on parchment and in the traditional Hebrew script.[42] Tradition has it that a gold tablet was set in the wall of the Temple with the oath of the soṭah inscribed upon it from which the priest copied as he wrote the scroll. This tablet was contributed by Queen Helena and was also useful as a sun dial to signal sunrise.[43] The bitter water is made up of half a *log* of water obtained from the laver in the Temple and drawn into a new earthen vessel, into which are also put a few handfuls of earth and some wormwood or bitter herbs, in order to give a bitter taste to the mixture. The earth must come from the ground of the Temple, and for that purpose one of the marble slabs of the floor in the Temple was left loose, to be lifted by the priest in order to dig the earth from underneath it.[44] The meal-offering consists of barley flour,

[39] M. Soṭah 1, 5–6; 2, 1–6; 3, 1–4; Sifre Numb. p. 5a, #11; Tos. Soṭah 1, 7–2, 6; Soṭah 20b; Tosafot Soṭah 14a, s. v. *mebi'*, and Yad, Soṭah, chapter 3, and *Mishneh Lemelek* thereto.

[40] Megil. 20b.

[41] Soṭah 8a.

[42] M. Soṭah 2, 4; Sifre Numb. 6a, #16; Soṭah 17b–18a; Yad, Soṭah 4, 7–11.

[43] M. Yoma 3, 10; Tos. Soṭah 2, 1–2; Yer. Soṭah 18a.

[44] M. Soṭah 2, 2; Soṭah 20a.

which is first put into a rush basket and when ready for the sacrifice is placed into a regular Temple vessel. The meal-offering is held by the woman during the entire ordeal. At the end of the ordeal, the priest places his hands under those of the woman; they lift it up together; then he takes it away from her and offers it up on the altar in accordance with standard sacrificial requirements. There is a difference of opinion among the teachers whether the drinking of the bitter water comes before the meal-offering or after it, but the law decides that the ceremony is properly executed either way.[45]

The Agadah put its masterful stroke upon the soṭah ordeal to give it moral interpretation and significance. It accounts, in the first place, for the very name of bitter waters, in Hebrew, *hame'orarim,* whose numerical value, 496, equals the 248 anatomical members in the man's body and the like number in the woman's body.[46] The water comes from the laver in the Temple, because the laver of the Tabernacle in the wilderness was made out of the mirrors of the righteous Jewish women who in Egypt under oppression kept themselves pure. By this water, the symbol of purity is presented to the woman in order to emphasize the contrast between her and the ideal Jewish woman, pointing out that this daughter of Israel under no compulsion or oppression but by the impulse of her wickedness has broken faith with the tradition of her ancestral mothers.[47] The black and ragged clothes she wears, the basket of meal-offering she holds up in her hand, the uncovering of her hair and the baring of her chest are, of course, meant to humiliate her, to fatigue her, to shame her, as a just retribution for her shameful conduct.[48] In fact the rule of justice, "measure for measure," explains one detail after another in the ordeal. Respectable Jewish women have their hair covered; this one uncovered it in flirtation to show her charms to her lover; therefore let her be humiliated by uncovering her hair.[49] Because she braided her hair to beautify herself for her lover, therefore, also, let her hair be disheveled.

[45] M. Soṭah 2, 1; 3. 1–2.
[46] Yer. Soṭah 20a; Numb. R. 9, 13 end.
[47] Numb. R. 9, 12.
[48] Numb. R. 9, 43; M. Soṭah 2, 1.
[49] Numb. R. 9, 13.

As she stood up in full height to receive her lover so let her stand up throughout the whole ordeal. She ornamented herself with a belt for illicit love; let a rope be tied around her over her breast. She served her lover wine to drink; she herself now drinks bitter water. The sacrifice of barley meal, the food of cattle, is meant to remind her that she acted like a beast when she was feeding her lover the delicacies in the house.[50] She showed him her nakedness, therefore her nakedness is now exposed; she painted her face, therefore her face now turns yellow; she penciled her eyes, therefore now her eyes bulge; she made her thigh approachable, therefore her thigh falls; she received her lover on her belly, therefore her belly swells.[51]

III. OBSOLESCENCE OF THE ORDEAL

The rabbinic mind penetrates further into the complex soṭah situation and, this time with a little halakic and with a good deal of agadic equipment, brings the fourth contribution to its development. It tries to evaluate the effect of the ordeal. The biblical assurance that if the woman be guilty she will die and if innocent will gain in health and fertility, was not and could not be questioned by men of the deep faith of the rabbinic teachers. These things must happen if every detail of the ceremony and every circumstance connected with the people involved run to form. The rabbis proved more lavish in their assurances than was the Bible. They promised if the wife were guilty she would not only die — that was not miraculous enough — but would sicken abnormally and die unnaturally. Her fair skin would turn black, her ruddy complexion yellow, her mouth would extend, her neck swell, her flesh decay, her joints fall apart, and she would perish from sheer decomposition.[52] Similar to the fate of the guilty woman would be that of her corespondent; when she died he would die too.[53] Escape from the effect of the bitter water is impossible. Of one adulterous woman it is told that to escape the effects she substituted her

[50] Philo *de spec. leg.* III, 57, ed. Cohn, II, p. 200; M. Soṭah 1, 7; Tos. Soṭah 3, 2–5; Numb. R. 9, 23; Soṭah 8b–9a.

[51] Numb. R. ibid.

[52] Numb. R. 9, 20.

[53] M. Soṭah 5, 1; Sifre Numb. 5b, #15; Numb. R. 9, 18; Yad, Soṭah 3, 17.

identical twin sister to take the drink in her place. On the return of the sister from the ordeal, however, the guilty sister met her with embraces and kisses. It was through these kisses that the guilty wife inhaled the odor of the bitter water and died immediately.[54] An innocent woman is not hurt by it if she is completely innocent. If she has any kind of guilt upon her conscience it will reveal itself in the harmful workings of the bitter water at some time or other.[55] Even having had harmless meetings with a man contrary to the husband's command of jealousy is guilt for which the bitter water will take its toll,[56] so that the woman proven free of the charge of adultery by the test will some day pay her penalty by a painful death, as a result of the workings of the bitter water.[57]

Yet, the immediate effect of the bitter water upon the innocent woman, according to biblical promise, is better health and greater fertility. The promise was taken literally in Temple days, so that within ten months after the ordeal a birth was expected.[58] It was thought a good and sensible threat to be offered by the sterile woman to God. In prayerful and reverential manner, though firm and defiant, she would address the Almighty thus: "Thou, O good God, better give me children, else I will act so as to arouse my husband's suspicion against me. He will issue a command of jealousy; I will disobey it. He will impose upon me the ordeal of bitter water; I will drink it. Then according to Thine own word, being innocent, I will bear children." [59] With perfect faith in the biblical promise, the rabbis ventured into promises of even larger blessing. The humiliation of bitter water, if the wife be innocent, would add to her health if she was sickly, and give her beauty if she was homely. Not only would she become more prolific, but she would have easy labor. She would give birth to boys now instead of girls; she would have twins instead of single births; and the chil-

54 Numb. R. 9, 5.
55 Yer. Soṭah 18d.
56 Tos. Soṭah 2, 3; Sifre Numb. 7a, #21.
57 Yer. Soṭah 19a.
58 Josephus, *Antiq*. III, 11, 6.
59 Ber. 31b; Yalḳut Shime'oni, I Samuel, #78.

dren she bore would be fair of complexion instead of dark, tall instead of short.[60]

But faith is sometimes hard tried by the realities of life. And the circle is a vicious one; the greater the challenge of reality, the weaker the faith, and the weaker the faith, the stronger the mastery of reality. No doubt at one time the ordeal of the bitter water actually exposed the guilty person. But in the course of time moral discipline weakened; there was too much occasion for the ordeal and, as is natural, the frequent exercise of the test rendered it ineffective.[61] The biblical and rabbinical promises were not fulfilled. How did the rabbis meet this challenge of reality? They offered a few explanations. In the first place, the death of the adulterous woman, if it did not occur on the spot, was merely a postponement of retribution. Her penalty would overtake her some day, perhaps within six months, perhaps after a year or two or three. The postponement was due to some merit of personal piety which the woman possessed, even though it was not known in the mortal world.[62] Second, the ordeal establishes the guilt of the wife in contrast to the guiltlessness of the husband, for the Bible says, "The man shall be free from sin." But if the husband's conduct is not without reproach, the ordeal is ineffective upon his wife.[63] Hence, blame the ineffectiveness on the hidden guilt of the husband. In the third place, the ordeal is intended to prove a doubtful case but not to execute punishment on a certain case of adultery. That is the business of the courts. Is it not possible that the woman's adulterous acts were long known to the husband? Of course, the ordeal would not work, so long as the husband had certain knowledge of adultery. There is a fourth excuse, an extension of the third. Whenever moral standards are so broken down that one may commit adultery without making a secret of it the ordeal becomes ineffective, for it seeks out only secret sin.[64] All these were

60 Tos. Soṭah 2, 3; Sifre Numb. 6b, #19; Soṭah 26a; Numb. R. 9, 50; Yad, Soṭah 3, 22.

61 Tos. Soṭah 14, 2, 9; Soṭah 47a; Yer. Soṭah 23b.

62 M. Soṭah 3, 4–5; Sifre Numb. 4b, #8, and 6b, #19; Soṭah 20b–21a; Numb. R. 9, 39.

63 Sifre Numb. 7a, #21; Soṭah 28a, 47b.

64 Sifre Numb. 3b, #7; Tos. Soṭah 14, 2.

intelligent and plausible excuses, but the institution could not subsist on excuses very long. Its ineffectiveness was too evident in the last days of the Jewish State, and the religious leader of the day, R. Johanan b. Zakkai, was courageous enough to abrogate it completely.[65]

IV. DEFILEMENT

The final contribution of the rabbis to the law of soṭah was to clarify the legal effects of the soṭah situation where the ordeal was not or could not be administered. The question had considerable importance both during the time when the ordeal was in vogue and after it was abrogated. The soṭah situation, it will be understood, is one in which adultery is justifiably suspected. Adultery, we have seen in the previous chapter, causes "defilement," that is, the husband may no longer keep her as his wife. This defilement, as a matter of fact, applies equally in respect to the co-respondent, so that after she is divorced or widowed she may not be taken in marriage by her lover.[66] The ordeal clears up the matter completely. Either she dies and the problem is at an end, or she remains alive and is free to go back to her husband or, when divorced or widowed, she may marry the co-respondent.[67] Even with the admission of the rabbis that sometimes the bitter water takes no effect until years later, she is innocent in the eyes of the law and free from any prohibitions until her belly swells and her thigh falls, showing evidence of the effects of the bitter water.[68]

While the ordeal was still in use, the "defilement" rested upon the woman from the time she violated the command of jealousy to the moment she drank the bitter water.[69] If there

[65] M. Soṭah 9, 9. Olitzki, *Flavius Josephus und die Halacha,* p. 22, note 27, believes that the ordeal was abrogated before the days of R. Johanan b. Zakkai. Wahrmann, *Untersuchungen über die Stellung der Frau in Judenthum,* p. xii, note 20, refutes Olitzki's proofs. Olitzki's mistake lies in the fact that the "court in Jerusalem" — M. Soṭah 1, 4 — does not exclude *"Ḥanut"* referred to in San. 41a and 'Ab. Zar. 8b. See 'Aruk of R. Nathan s. v. *Ḥanut.*

[66] M. Soṭah 5, 1.

[67] Sifre Numb. 6b, #19; M. Soṭah 4, 4.

[68] Soṭah 26a; Yad, Soṭah 3, 21.

[69] M. Soṭah 1, 2.

was testimony that she had committed adultery or if she confessed to adultery or if she refused to stand the ordeal or if by statute she could not be put through it, as, for instance, if she or her husband was deaf or lame or the like — in all such cases, as said, the ordeal could not be administered to her — the husband must divorce her and she forfeited the ketubah.[70] If, however, she was willing to go through the ordeal and the husband was unwilling, divorce was compulsory because she was "defiled," but he had to pay her the ketubah.[71] The same is true if there was no testimony to *setirah,* that is to her violation of the command of jealousy, but the husband himself was convinced of trespass, either by his own knowledge or by his giving credence to the persistent rumors; he must, in obedience to the law, divorce her, but must pay her the ketubah.[72] In such a case, however, so long as there was no testimony for *setirah,* the prohibition against her marrying the co-respondent was only rabbinical in nature.[73] Leniency in such a case consists in the fact that if, in defiance of the law, the woman marries her lover and has children by him, he will not be compelled to divorce her, simply for the sake of protecting the children's name.[74]

With abrogation of the ordeal, the possibility of proving the woman innocent came to an end. If she could not be proven innocent, she stood condemned in the eyes of the law. Lenient as the rabbis were toward doubtful adultery arising out of external conditions, so severe were they toward doubtful adultery arising out of a woman's indiscreet conduct. They had especial reason for their severity in a soṭah situation where the woman had received a command of jealousy from her husband and violated it. If she could not prove her innocence, the law condemned her as guilty. The rabbis, therefore, warned husbands to say nothing to their wives sounding like a formal command of jealousy, even if witnesses were not present, for by such a command they might invite legal difficulties which would compel them to divorce

70 M. Soṭah 4, 1–3; Yad, Soṭah 2, 2.
71 M. Soṭah 4, 2; Yad, Soṭah 1, 2.
72 M. Soṭah 6, 1; Sifre Numb. 6b, #19; Yeb. 24b.
73 See Epstein, *Jewish Marriage Contract,* pp. 110–12.
74 Yad, Soṭah 2, 12–15; *Kesef Mishneh* thereto.

their wives, since the ordeal was no longer administered.[75]

In all cases, therefore, where a true soṭah situation arises, divorce is compulsory and the woman forfeits the ketubah. Where there is no testimony as to *setirah,* but the husband is convinced thereof by his own observation or through persistent rumor, the law still holds good that he is bound to divorce her and pay the ketubaḥ. Even if there has been no soṭah situation at all, that is, if no command of jealousy has been given by the husband and no specific co-respondent named, the husband must divorce his wife if she is found in a compromising position with another man. The talmudic instances of that situation are a man coming out of her room while she is donning her undergarments; the woman in company of a man in a hiding place; kissing or hugging a man or sitting on his lap. Divorce may be enforced by the court or may be only a religious duty, but the loss of the ketubah by the woman is a definite court penalty, not so much for adultery, not proven, as for misconduct.[76] Of course, legally valid testimony to her adultery, where there has been no soṭah situation, renders divorce legally compulsory with total loss of the ketubah to the wife.[77]

In all cases of charges of adultery, even where substantiated by the woman's confession or by the testimony of witnesses, there is no effect upon the children she has borne to her husband. They are protected by the law, and ascribed, beyond doubt, to the husband.[78] Even if the woman herself testifies the children are not her husband's, her testimony is not recognized.[79] Later teachers, however, believed this to be the case only in normal family life, where an act of adultery is rare and exceptional; but where the wife is acknowledged to be persistently unfaithful to her husband, the legitimacy of the children may be doubted.[80]

[75] Soṭah 2b; Yad, Soṭah 4, 19.

[76] Epstein, *Jewish Marriage Contract,* ibid.

[77] See previous chapter, pp. 213 f. and Ket. 101a–b.

[78] Soṭah 27a; Yer. Soṭah 17a.

[79] E. H. 4, 29. See note 39 of *Ba'er Heṭeb* thereto.

[80] E. H. 4, 15. On the subject of Soṭah a monograph has been published by Dr. Nahum Wahrmann under the title *Untersuchungen über die Stellung der Frau im Judenthum in Zeitalter der Tannaiten,* Breslau, 1933, which may be consulted with benefit.

BIBLIOGRAPHY

A. SOURCES

I. PAGAN

The Code of Hammurabi, translated by D D. Luckenbill, in *The Origin and History of Hebrew Law* by J. M. P. Smith, Chicago, 1931.

The Assyrian Code, translated by D. D. Luckenbill, ibid.

The Hittite Code, translated by Arnold Walther, ibid.

Herodotus, *History,* translated by George Rawlinson, N. Y., 1932.

II. JEWISH

a. Biblical Literature

The Old Testament, standard Masoretic text; English translation of the Jewish Publication Society, Philadelphia, 1917.

The Septuagint, Greek text and English translation, published by James Prott and Company (n.d.), N. Y.

Targum Onkelos of Pentateuch, ed. A. Berliner, Berlin, 1884; Targum Jonathan, Pentateuch, ed. M. Ginsburger, Berlin, 1903; Targum of Prophets and Megillot, in *Mikra'ot Gedolot,* Warsau, 1902; Targum Yerushalmi, ibid.; Samaritan Targum, ed. A. Brüll, Frankfort a. M., 1875.

b. Hellenistic Literature

Apocrypha and Pseudepigrapha of the Old Testament, ed. R. H. Charles, London, 1913.

Philo Judeus, Works, German translation under editorship of Leopold Cohn, Breslau, 1909–29; supplemented by the English translation of C. D. Yonge, London, 1854–5.

Josephus, Works, translated by W. Whiston, (n.d.), N. Y.

c. Talmudic Literature

Mishnah, standard texts in Babylonian and Palestinian Talmuds, cited by treatise, chapter and section.

Tosephta, ed. M. Z. Zuckermandel, Pasewalk, 1881.

Abot de R. Nathan, ed. S. Schechter, London, 1887.

Mekilta, ed. M. Friedmann, Vienna, 1870.

Sifra, ed. I. H. Weiss, Vienna, 1862.

Sifre Numbers, ed. H. S. Horovitz, Leipzig, 1917.

Sifre Deuteronomy, ed. M. Friedmann, Vienna, 1864.

Babylonian Talmud, standard edition, cited by treatise, folio and side.

Palestinian Talmud, Venice, 1523, cited by treatise, folio and column.

Minor Treatises, standard edition of Babylonian Talmud; the following cited according to the editions of M. Higger: — Derek Ereẓ, N. Y., 1935; Semaḥot, N. Y., 1931; Kallah, N. Y., 1936; Soferim, N. Y., 1937.

Midrash Tannaim, ed. D. Hoffmann, Berlin, 1908–9.

Midrash Rabbah, Pentateuch and Megillot, Warsau, 1924.

Pesiḳta Rabbati, ed. M. Friedmann, Vienna, 1885.

Pesiḳta de R. Kahana, ed. S. Buber, Lyck, 1868.

Tanḥuma, ed. S. Buber, Wilno, 1913.

Yalḳut Shime'oni, Warsau, 1876.

Seder Eliyahu Rabba, ed. M. Friedmann, Vienna, 1904.

Pirḳe de R. Eliezer, Warsau, 1879.

Pirḳe de Rabbenu ha-Ḳadosh, in *Oẓar Midrashim,* ed. J. D. Eisenstein, N. Y., 1915.

Midrash Bereshit, ed. L. Ginzberg, in *Ginze Schechter,* N. Y., 1928.

Oẓar Midrashim, ed. J. D. Eisenstein, N. Y., 1915.

d. Post-talmudic Sources

Abraham b. David (RABD), notes on Yad, standard edition of *Yad ha-Ḥazaḳah.*

——— Sefer Ba'ale ha-Nefesh, Venice, 1850.

Abrahams, Israel, Ethical Wills, Philadelphia, 1926.

Adret, see Solomn b. Adret.

Alfasi, see Isaac Alfasi.

'Anan, founder of Karaism, Sefer ha-Mizwot, ed. Harkavy, *Studien und Mittheilungen,* VIII, St. Petersburg, 1903.
'Amude Shlomo, see Solomon Luria.
'Amude Yerushalayim, Israel Eisenstein, notes on Yerushalmi, in edition of Wilno, 1922.
'Aruk, Nathan b. Yeḥiel of Rome, talmudic dictionary, Yusefob, 1869.
'Aruk ha-Shulḥan, Yeḥiel Michal Epstein, code, Wilno, 1924.
Asher b. Yeḥiel (Asheri), abstract of talmudic law (Halakot), in standard edition of Babylonian Talmud.
——— Responsa, Venice, 1606.
Ba'al ha-Ṭurim, see Jacob b. Asher.
Ba'er Heṭeb, glosses to *Shulḥan 'Aruk,* Judah Ashkenazi, in standard edition of *Shulḥan 'Aruk.*
Baḥya b. Asher, Kad ha-Ḳemaḥ, homilies, Warsau, 1872.
Baḥya b. Paḳuda, Ḥobot ha-Lebabot, Lemberg, 1837.
Be'er ha-Golah, marginal notes to *Shulḥan 'Aruk,* Moses b. Naphtali Hirsh Ribkas, standard edition of *Shulḥan 'Aruk.*
Be'er Sheba', responsa and novellae, Issachar Baer Eillenberg, Warsau, 1890.
Besamim Rosh, Isaac de Molina, responsa ascribed to Asheri, Cracow, 1880.
Bet Ḥadash, Joel Sirkes, glosses to *Ṭur,* in standard edition of *Ṭur.*
Bet Shemuel, Samuel b. Uri Shraga Phoebus, notes on *Shulḥan 'Aruk Eben ha-'Ezer* (E. H.), in standard edition of E. H.
Bet Yoseph, see Joseph Karo.
Binyamin Ze'eb, responsa, Venice, 1538.
David Corfu, responsa, Saloniki, 1803.
David Kimḥi, Bible commentary, in *Miḳra'ot Gedolot.*
David Luria, commentary on Pirḳe de R. Eliezer, Warsau, 1852.
David b. Zimra (RDBZ), responsa, I and II, Venice, 1773; III, Fürth, 1781; IV, Livorno, 1652; V, Livorno, 1818.
Derashot, Judah Katzenellenbogen, homilies, Venice, 1594.
Eben ha-'Ezer (E. H.), refers to *Shulḥan 'Aruk Eben ha-'Ezer,* see Joseph Karo.

Eben Sapir, Jacob Sapir, travels, Lyck, 1866.
'Ein Mishpaṭ, see Joshua Boaz Baruch.
Eliezer b. Joel Halevi (REBJH), legal treatise under the name of REBJH, ed. V. Aptowitzer, Berlin, 1912–36.
Elijah Mizraḥi, responsa, Jerusalem, 1938.
Emunot we-De'ot, Saadya Gaon, Constantinople, 1562.
Ethical Wills, see Abrahams, Israel.
Ginze Ḳedem, B. M. Lewin, Vol. V, Jerusalem, 1934.
Ginze Schechter, ed. L. Ginzberg, New York, 1928.
Halakot Gedolot, ed. J. Hildesheimer, Berlin, 1890.
Ha-Manhig, Ibn Yarḥi, ritual guide, Berlin, 1855.
Ḥatam Sofer, Moses Sopher, responsa, Vienna, 1880.
Ḥavvot, Ya'ir, Ḥayyim Yair Bachrach, responsa, Frankfurt a. M., 1699.
Hegyon ha-Nefesh, Abraham bar Ḥiyya ha-Nasi, Leipzig, 1860.
Ḥelḳat Meḥoḳeḳ, Moses Lima, notes on *Shulhan 'Aruk Eben ha-'Ezer* in standard edition of E. H.
Ḥiluf Minhagim, Joel Miller, Vienna, 1798.
Ḥobot ha-Lebabot, see Baḥya b. Paḳuda.
Ḥoshen Mishpaṭ (H. M.) refers to *Shulḥan 'Aruk Ḥoshen Mishpaṭ;* see Joseph Karo.
Ḥuppat Hatanim, Raphael Meldola, Lublin, 1872.
Ibn Ezra, Abraham Ibn Ezra, Bible commentary, in *Miḳra'ot Gedolot.*
Isaac Alfasi, digest of talmudic law (Halakot), in standard edition of Babylonian Talmud.
Isaac Halevi, responsa, Neuwit, 1736.
Isaac b. Sheshet (RIBS) responsa, Constantinople, 1547.
Isserles, see Moses Isserles.
Issure Bi'ah (I.B.) section in Maimonides' *Yad.*
Jacob b. Asher, Ṭur, code, standard edition.
——— Ba'al ha-Ṭurim, commentary on Pentateuch, in *Miḳra'ot Gedolot.*
Jacob Mann, Texts and Studies, Cincinnati, 1931.
Jacob Molin, (MAHRIL), Minhagim, Warsau, 1874.
Joseph Karo, Shulḥan 'Aruk, code, containing Oraḥ Ḥayyim (O.H.), Yoreh De'ah (Y.D.), Eben ha-'Ezer (E.H.), Ḥoshen Mishpaṭ (H.M.), standard edition.

——— Bet Yoseph, notes on *Ṭur*.

——— Kesef Mishneh, notes on *Yad*.

Joseph Kolon, responsa, Venice, 1519.

Joseph b. Leb, responsa, Amsterdam, 1726.

Joshua Boaz Baruch, 'Ein Mishpaṭ, marginal notes on Talmud, in standard edition of Babylonian Talmud.

——— Shilṭe ha-Gibborim, marginal notes on Alfasi, in standard edition of Babylonian Talmud.

Judah b. Asher, responsa under the name of Zikron Yehudah, Berlin, 1846.

Judah he-Ḥasid, Sefer Ḥasidim, ed. J. Wistinetzki, Frankfurt a. M., 1924.

Judah Halevi, Kuzari, Pressburg, 1860.

Kad ha-Ḳemaḥ, see Baḥya b. Asher.

Keneset ha-Gedolah, notes on *Ṭur* and *Bet Yoseph,* Ḥayyim b. Israel Benveniste, O. H., Livorno, 1792; Y. D., Constantinople, 1711–16; E. H., Ismir, 1731; H. M., Ismir, 1660–1734.

Kesef Mishneh, see Joseph Karo.

Keter Torah, Aaron b. Elijah of Nicomedia, karaitic commentary on Pentateuch, Gozlowa, 1866.

Ḳimḥi, see David Ḳimḥi.

Ḳobeẓ 'al Yad, IV, Berlin, 1887; XII, Jerusalem, 1936.

Kol Bo, code, Venice, 1547.

Kuzari, see Judah Halevi.

Lebush, Mordecai Yoffe, code, Prague, 1709–10.

Magen Abraham, Abraham Abele Gombiner, glosses to *Shulḥan 'Aruk Oraḥ Ḥayyim,* in standard edition of O. H.

Maggid Mishneh (*Maggid*), Vidal of Tolosa, commentary on *Yad,* in standard edition of *Yad.*

Mahril, see Jacob Molin.

Maimonides, see Moses b. Maimon.

Malmad ha-Talmidim, Jacob Anatoli, Lyck, 1866.

Masa' Ḳrim, Ephraim Dainard, travels, Warsau, 1878.

Mayim Rabbim, responsa, Raphael Meldola, Amsterdam, 1737.

Me'il Ẓedaḳah, responsa, Jonah Landsofer, Prague, 1757.

Me'iri, commentary on Babylonian Talmud by Menaḥem b. Solomon Me'iri.

Melamed le-Ho'il, responsa, David Hoffmann, Frankfurt a. M., 1926–32.

Menorat ha-Ma'or, ed. H. G. Enelow, New York, 1932.

Miḳra ki-Peshuṭo, Bible commentary, A. Ehrlich, Berlin, 1899.

Mishneh le-Melek, glosses on *Yad,* Judah Rosanes, in standard edition of *Yad.*

Mordecai, abstract of talmudic law (Halakot) by Mordecai b. Hillel Ashkenazi, in standard edition of Babylonian Talmud.

Moreh Nebukim, see Moses b. Maimon.

Moses Alshakar, responsa, Sidlikov, 1834.

Moses Isserles (RMA), glosses on *Shulḥan 'Aruk,* in standard edition.

Moses b. Maimon (RMBM), Mishnah Commentary, in standard edition of Babylonian Talmud.

——— Yad ha-Ḥazaḳah (Yad), code, standard edition.

——— Moreh Nebukim, Wilno, 1914.

——— Sefer ha-Miẓwot, Lemberg, 1860.

——— Responsa, ed. Freimann, Jerusalem, 1934.

——— Shemonah Peraḳim, introduction to Mishnah Commentary Abot.

——— Sha'are ha-Musar, ethical monograph, attributed to Maimonides, edited by Abrahams in his *Ethical Wills.*

Moses de Trani (MABIT), responsa, Lemberg, 1861.

Moses b. Naḥman (RMBN), Bible Commentary, in *Miḳra'ot Gedolot.*

——— Iggeret Hakodesh, Basel, 1607.

——— Commentary on Maimonides' *Sefer ha-Miẓwot,* in the edition of the latter, Warsau, 1870.

Naḥalat Abot, Meshulam Solomon Kohn, Fürth, 1811.

Naḥmanides, see Moses b. Naḥman.

Nehar Miẓrayim, Raphael Aaron b. Simeon, Alexandria, 1906.

Netibot ha-Shalom, notes on *Shulḥan 'Aruk,* Moses Nehemiah Feiwish, Koenigsberg, 1861.

Neveh Shalom, Elijah Hazan, Jerusalem, 1930.

Ohale Tam, responsa, Tam b. Yaḥya, included in *Tumat Yesharim,* Venice, 1622.

Oraḥ Ḥayyim (O.H.), see Joseph Karo.
Orḥot Ḥayyim, code, Aaron ha-Kohen of Lunel, Florence, 1750 — Berlin, 1899.
Orḥot Ẓaddiḳim, ethical treatise, anonymous, Zalkowa, 1838.
Oẓar ha-Ge'onim, B. M. Lewin, Jerusalem, 1928–42.
Oẓar Kol Minhage Yeshurun, A. Hirschowitz, Lemberg, 1930.
Panim Me'irot, responsa, Me'ir b. Isaac Eistenstadt, Lemberg, 1889.
Peraḥ Maṭeh Aharon, responsa, Aaron b. Ḥayyim Peraḥia, Amsterdam, 1703.
Peri Ḥadash, Hezekiah de Sola, Notes on *Shulḥan 'Aruk,* in standard edition of *Shulḥan 'Aruk.*
Perishah, notes on *Ṭur,* Joshua Falk, in standard edition of *Ṭur.*
Pinḳas Medinat Liṭa, S. Dubnow, Berlin, 1925.
Pitḥe Teshubah, notes on E. H., Abraham Hirsh Eisenstadt, in standard edition of E. H.
RABD, see Abraham b. David.
Rashi, see Solomon Yiẓḥaḳi.
RDBZ, see David b. Zimra.
REBJH, see Eliezer b. Joel Halevi.
Reshumot, periodical, Vol. IV, Jerusalem, 1926.
Reshit Ḥokmah, ethical treatise, Elijah Vidas, Warsau, 1868.
RIBS, see Isaac b. Sheshet.
RMA, see Moses Isserles.
RMBM, see Moses b. Maimon.
RMBN, see Moses b. Naḥman.
RSBA, see Solomon b. Adret.
Samson b. Ẓemaḥ (RSBZ), responsa, Amsterdam, 1738.
Sede Ḥemed, collection of responsa, Ḥayyim Hezekiah Medina, Warsau, 1891–1907.
Sefer Ba'ale ha-Nefesh, see Abraham b. David.
Sefer ha-Agudah, code, Alexander Süslin, Cracow, 1571.
Sefer ha-Masa'ot, travels, Joseph Tcharney, St. Petersburg, 1884.
Sefer ha-Miẓwot, see Moses b. Maimon.
Sefer ha-Miẓwot, see 'Anan.
Sefer Ḥaredim, code, Eliezer Azkari, Zalkowa, 1807.

Sefer Ḥasidim, see Judah he-Ḥasid.
Sefer ha-Pardes, see Solomon Yiẓḥaḳi.
Sefer ha-Taḳḳanot, Jacob Saul Eliashar, Jerusalem, 1883.
Sefer ha-Yashar, Jacob (Rabbenu) Tam, Koenigsberg, 1847.
Sefer Miẓwot Gadol (SMG), code, Moses of Coucy, Muncacs, 1905.
Sefer Taḳḳanot Kandia, Artom and Cassuto, Jerusalem, 1943.
Sefer TSBZ, ritual code, Samson b. Ẓadok, Warsau, 1902.
Sefer Yere'im, code, Eleazar b. Samuel of Metz, Zalkowa, 1804.
Sha'are ha-Musar, see Moses b. Maimon.
Sha'are Ẓedeḳ, geonic responsa, ed. Joseph Ardit, Saloniki, 1792.
Shebut Ya'akob, responsa, Jacob Risa, Lemberg, 1861.
She'elot Ya'abeẓ, responsa, Jacob Emden, Lemberg, 1884.
She'eltot, geonic code, Warsau, 1874.
Shemonah Peraḳim, see Moses b. Maimon.
Shene Luḥot ha-Berit (SLH), Isaaiah Horowitz, Ostraha, 1806.
Shilṭe ha-Gibborim, see Joshua Boaz Baruch.
Shulḥan 'Aruk, see Joseph Karo.
Shulḥan 'Aruk, ritual guide, Leon de Modena, translated and edited by Solomon Robin, Vienna, 1867.
Sifte Kohen (SK), glosses on *Shulḥan 'Aruk* (Y.D. and H.M.), Sabbatai b. Me'ir, in standard edition of *Shulḥan 'Aruk.*
SLH, see Shene Luḥot ha-Berit.
SMG, see Sefer Miẓwot Gadol.
Solomon b. Adret (RSBA), Novellae, Warsau, 1922.
——— responsa, I, Bologna, 1539; II, Livorno, 1657; III, Livorno, 1778; IV, Petrokov, 1883; V, Livorno, 1825; VI–VII, Warsau, 1868; VIII (ascribed to Naḥmanides), Warsau, 1883.
Solomon Luria, 'Amude Shlomo, running commentary on SMG, Basel, 1600.
——— Yam shel Shlomo, talmudic commentary on various treatises of the Babylonian Talmud, various dates and places of publication.

Solomon Yiẓḥaḳi (Rashi), Bible commentary, standard edition of Bible.

——— commentary to Babylonian Talmud, standard edition.

——— Sefer ha-Pardes, code, compiled by disciples of Rashi, ed. H. L. Ehrenreich, Budapest, 1924.

Taḳḳanot ha-Ḳehillot di-Ḳahal Ashkenazim, communal enactments, Amsterdam, 1737.

Teshubot ha-Ge'onim, ed. Asaf, Jesusalem, 1929.

Teshubot ha-Ge'onim, ed. Harkavey, Berlin, 1887.

Teshubot ha-RMBM, ed. A. Freimann, Jerusalem, 1934.

Toratan shel Rishonim, geonic responsa, ed. Horowitz, Frankfurt a. M., 1881.

Tosafot, glosses to Babylonian Talmud, standard edition of Talmud.

Travels of Petaḥia, ed. Grünhut, Frankfurt a. M., 1905.

TSBZ, same as RSBZ, see Samson b. Ẓemaḥ.

TSBZ, see Sefer TSBZ.

Tumat Yesharim, collection of comments and responsa, Benjamin b. Abraham Mutal, Venice, 1622.

Ṭure Zahab (TZ), glosses on *Shulḥan 'Aruk,* David b. Samuel Segal, in standard edition of *Shulḥan 'Aruk.*

Ya'arot Debash, homilies, Jonathan Eybeschutz, Warsau, 1889.

Yad Ephrayim, notes on Y.D., Ephraim Solomon Margolies, in standard edition of Y. D.

Yad ha-Ḥazaḳah, see Moses b. Maimon.

Yad ha-Ḳeṭanah, novellae on Maimonides' code, anonymous, Koenigsberg, 1855–59.

Yad ha-Levi, novellae on *Sefer ha-Miẓwot,* J. B. Hurwitz, Jerusalem, 1925.

Yam shel Shlomo, see Solomon Luria.

Yoreh De'ah (Y.D.), see Joseph Karo.

Yosef Omeẓ, ritual code, Joseph Hahn Nordlingen, 1725.

Ẓemah Ẓedeḳ, M. Schneerson, responsa, Wilno, 1871–84.

Zikron Yehudah, see Judah b. Asher.

Zikron Yosef, responsa, Joseph b. Menaḥem Steinhart, Fürth, 1763.

Zohar, Wilno, 1911.

Ẓofnat Pa'aneaḥ, Joseph Rosen, responsa, Warsau, 1935.

III. CHRISTIAN

New Testament, revised version, standard edition.
Justin, Hist. Philippicae, ed. Watson, 1855.
Tertullian, de corona, ed. Dodson, Oxford, 1842.
——— de virgibus velandis, in Ante-Nicean Christian Library, Vol. XVIII, Edinburgh, 1870.

IV. MOHAMMEDAN

Koran, translated by Maulvi Muhammad Ali, second edition, London, 1920.

B. LITERATURE

Abrahams, I., Jewish Life in the Middle Ages, Philadelphia, 1896.
Albeck, C., Das Buch der Jubiläen und die Halacha, Berlin, 1930.
Asaf, S., Le-Ḥayye ha-Mishpaḥah shel Yehude Bizanẓ, in *Jubilee Volume* of S. Krauss, Jerusalem, 1936.
Benzinger, I., Hebräische Archäologie, Tubingen, 1907.
Bettan, I., Studies in Jewish Preaching, Cincinnati, 1939.
Bernfeld, S., Dor Tahapuḥot, Warsau, 1897.
Büchler, A., Die Schneiden des Haares als Straffe der Ehebrecher, *Wiener Zeitschrift für Kunde des Morgenlandes* (WZKM), XIX.
——— Die Straffe der Ehebrecher in die nach-exilischen Zeit, *Monatschrift für Geschichte und Wissenschaft des Judenthums,* LV.
Cohen, Boaz, Responsum of Maimonides Concerning Music, in *The Jewish Music Journal,* II, 2, N. Y., 1935.
Ellis, Havelock, Studies in the Psychology of Sex, Philadelphia, 1906–12.
Epstein, L. M., The Jewish Marriage Contract, New York, 1927.
——— Marriage Laws in the Bible and the Talmud, Cambridge, 1942.
Ewald, H., Die Alterthümer des Volkes Israel, Göttingen, 1866.

Federbush, S., Lifnim mi-Shurat ha-Miẓwah, in *ha-Do'ar,* New York, 1943.
Finklestein, L., Jewish Self-Government in the Middle Ages, N. Y., 1924.
Ginzberg, L., Cabala, in the *Jewish Encyclopedia,* N. Y., 1902.
——— Legends of the Jews, Philadelphia, 1909–39.
——— Beitrage zur Lexicographie des Aramäischen, in *Festschrift Adolph Schwartz,* Berlin, 1917.
Grayzel, S., The Church and the Jews, Philadelphia, 1933.
Güdemann, M., Geschichte des Erziehungswesen, Vienna, 1880–88.
——— Quellenschriften zur Geschichte des Unterrichts, Berlin, 1891.
Halevy, I., Dorot ha-Rishonim, Frankfurt a. M., 1901—Berlin, 1920.
Heinemann, I., Philons griechische und jüdische Bildung, Breslau, 1932.
Hershberg, A. S., Ha-Halbashah ha-'Ibrit ha-Ḳedumah, Warsau, 1911.
Hofmann, D., Bemerkungen z. Geschichte d. Synedrion, *Jahrbuch der jüdischen literar. Gesellschaft,* V (1907).
Jewish Encyclopedia, New York, 1902.
Kayserling, M., Die jüdische Frau, Leipzig, 1879.
Kohler, K., Essenes, in *Jewish Encyclopedia.*
Lagarde, P., Materialien, Leipzig, 1867.
Lauterbach, Z., The Ceremony of Breaking a Glass at Weddings, *Hebrew Union College Annual,* Vol. II, Cincinnati, 1925.
Lieberman, S., Al Haṭa'im ve-'Onsham, in *Ginzberg Jubilee Volume,* Hebrew section, New York, 1945.
Löw, L., Der synagogale Ritus, in *Monatschrift für Geschichte und Wissenschaft des Judenthums,* 1884.
——— Die Lebensalter, Szegedin, 1875.
Moore, G. F., Judaism in the First Century of the Christian Era, Cambridge, 1932.
Neuman, A. A., The Jews in Spain, Philadelphia, 1942.
Nowack W., Lehrbuch der hebräischen Archäologie, Leipzig, 1894.
Olitzki, M., Flavius Josephus und die Halacha, Berlin, 1885.

Peters, J. P., Religion of the Hebrews, Boston and London, 1914.
Revel, B., Karaite Halachah, Philadelphia, 1913.
Ritter, B., Philon und die Halacha, Leipzig, 1879.
Schechter, S., Some Aspects of Rabbinic Theology, New York, 1910.
Slouschz, N., Travels in North Africa, Philadelphia, 1927.
Smith, W. R., Kinship and Marriage in Early Arabia, London, 1903.
Stern, S., Das Abschneiden des Haupthaares in *Wissenschaftliche Zeitschrift für jüdische Theologie,* 1837.
——— Das sorgsame Bedecken des Haupthaares, in *Zeitschrift für jüdische Theologie,* 1837.
Tchernowitz, C., Toledot ha-Halakah, New York, 1943–5.
Uhlemann, M. A., Aegyptische Alterthum, Leipzig, 1857–8.
Wahrmann, J., Untersuchungen über die Stellung der Frau in Judenthum, Breslau, 1933.
Weiss, I. H., Dor Dor ve-Dorshav, Wilno, 1919.
Wellhausen, J., Die Ehe bei die Arabern, Göttingen, 1893.
——— Arabische Heidenthum, Berlin, 1887.
Westermarck, E., History of Human Marriage, New York, 1922.
——— Marriage Ceremonies in Morocco, London, 1914.
Wolfson, H. A., The Philosophy of Spinoza, Cambridge, 1934.
Zeitlin, S., First Canonization of Hebrew Liturgy, *Jewish Quarterly Review,* Vol. XXXVIII.
Zukunft, Die, periodical, #38, New York, 1933.

INDEX

Abrahams, I., 46n, *et passim*
Active Intellect, 19
Adultery, 194f; primitive treatment of, 195; Akkadian law of, 196–9; biblical law of, 199–201; rabbinic law of, 201f; four categories of, in rabbinic law, 201–9; legal essentials of, in rabbinic law, 209–10; treatment of, in rabbinic law, 201–2, 210–12; penalties for, in rabbinic law, 211–2; capital punishment for, discouraged, 211; involuntary, 210; of betrothed, 200, 204–5; of priest's daughter, 203–4; *moẓi shem ra'*, 206–9; law of "defilement" in, 212–5; leniencies in law of "defilement," 215
Affectionate relations between the sexes, 108–10. *See* Flirtation
Albeck, C., 164n
Asaf, S., 128n
Asceticism, attitude to, post-exilic, 8; Christian, 10; rabbinic, 14; of post-talmudic halakists, 17; of moralists, 17–9; of philosophers, 19–22; of cabalists, 22
Attack by woman on male genitals, 3

Bar-miẓwah, 91–2
Barren woman, marrying a, 142, 144–5
Bath house, mingling of sexes in, 29–30; improper for certain persons of the same sex, 33
Benzinger, I., 37n
Bernfeld, S., 162n
Betrothed, relations between, 106–8, 126–31. *See* Chaperonage
Bettan, I., 18n, 78n
Bitter water, ordeal of. *See Soṭah*
Bostonai, 176
Bride, veiling of, 38–9, 50; gazing at, 118–9; cutting hair of, 55, 58–9
Büchler, A., 37n, *et passim*
Buggery, 3, 132–4
Burial, attending the dead of opposite sex at, 34

Cabalists, on sex morality, 22–3; on asceticism, 22
Capital punishment. *See* Adultery
Castration, 138–40
Celibacy, 10, 14–5, 141–3; Essenes on, 9; Christianity on, 10
Chaperonage, 11, 16, 119f; history of, 120; between close relatives, 120–1; between divorced couple, 125; between betrothed, 126–8; between son-in-law and mother-in-law, 124; qualifications for, 121–2; derivatives of the law of, 123; communal enactments regarding, 128–31; special precautions, 123f
Chorus, mixed, 98–100. *See* Music
Christian, attitude to celibacy, 10; edicts on contact between Jew and gentile, 172; on segregation in church, 80; on covered head, 40–1
Church Fathers, on nakedness, 29
City life, dangerous to morality, 6, 12
Coeducation, 89
Cohen, Boaz, 94n, 97n
Command of Jealousy (*ḳinnui*). *See Soṭah*
Communal enactments, 17, 63, 78, 88, 89, 101, 102, 127–31, 141, 144, 162, 173
Compulsory marriage. *See* Rape
Concubinage, 69
Contraceptives, 145–6

Cosmetics. *See* Ornaments and cosmetics

Dancing, mixed, 93, 100–3; at weddings, 102–3; *ḥerem* against, 102; in Europe, 101–2
"Defilement." *See* Adultery, *Soṭah*
Defloration, 155–6
Deinard, E., 72n
Despoiling nature, 138f
Divorced, familiarity between, 125–6
Disguise. *See* Garments of opposite sex
Doctor, male, attending female patient, 112
Dress, modesty in, 18, 24f, 35–6. *See* Nakedness, Exposure, Veil, Garments of opposite sex
Dualism, 18–9

Education, types of, 83f; home instruction, for boys, 83–4; for girls, 84–6; through public assemblies, 85; formal schooling for boys, 86–7; for girls, 87–8; male teachers for females and vice versa, 87–9; coeducation, 89
Eliashar, J. S., 75n
Ellis, Havelock, 29n
Emancipation of woman, 15, 72–4, 220
Enelow, H. G., 75n
En Sof, 22
Epstein, L. M., 11n, *et passim*
Essenes, 9
Evaluation of woman, 8, 9, 13, 17, 72
Ewald, H., 37n
Exposure, 16, 31f; shameful, humiliating, indecent, 31; Noah's, 33; male, 33–4; female, 32, 34, 36; a cause for divorce, 34; in holy places, 31; in sight of close kin, 33; of hands, feet, face, 51. *See* Face, Hair, Head, *Shema'*

Face, covering of, 42f; not required in biblical and post-exilic time, 42; nor by rabbinic law, 43; but considered laudable, 44; practiced among Persians and Arabs, 44; also in Italy, Africa, Caucasus and entire Orient in Middle Ages, 45; not practiced in Babylonia, nor in Europe, 45–6
Familiarity, 112f. *See* Gazing at a woman, Greeting a woman, Speaking with a woman, Play and Merriment, Walking behind a woman, Wine drinking
Fines, 184–6. *See* Rape and seduction
Finkelstein, L., 63n, 129n
Flirtation and love making, 104f. *See* Kissing, Affectionate relations, Touching a woman
Fornication, 167f; leniency of law toward, 167–8; rabbinic law on, 167–70; prevalence of, among males, 169–70; in modern times, 70. *See* Prostitution, non-professional
Freimann, A. H., 96n
Funerals, segregation at, 89f

Garments of opposite sex, 3, 64f; motive of prohibition, 64; extensions under rabbinic law, 65–6; enforcement, 66–7; exceptions, 67
Gazing at a woman, 11, 16, 39, 117f
Geiger, A., 39n
Gentile woman, relations with, 170–3; Church edicts, 172; penalties, 171
Ginzberg, L., 22n, *et passim*
Golden mean, 21
Grayzel, S., 172n, 178n
Greeting a woman, 16, 116
Güdemann, M., 89n

Hair, covering of, 46f; originally not required, 46–7; motive of, 47, 49; amoraic law, 47; reciting *Shema'*, 47–8; no exception for virgins, 48–51; exception made in post-talmudic time, 50–2, 55; reasons for exception, 49–50; no exception in Orient, 51
Hair, cutting of, 55f; origin of custom, 55, 58, 59; motive of, 56, 59; not known in Talmud, 57; not known in Orient, 58–9; first reference to, 58; developed in Eastern Europe, 58–60; legal considerations favoring, 59, 60; a token of modesty for married women,

59–60; as a marriage ceremonial, 55–6; not of Jewish origin, 58; as a sign of mourning, 58; as humiliation for slaves, 56; practiced in monastic orders, 56; required by nazirites, 56. *See* Peruque
Hair, dishevelment of, 56–7
Halakah and agadah, 16
Halakist, 16–17
Ḥalalah, 156
Halevy, I, 94n
Handshaking with a woman, 112
Harem, 69
Harlotry, 152f. *See* Prostitution
Head, covering of, male, 32; female, 32, 41, 47; motive of, 41–2. *See* Veil
Heinemann, I., 181n
Hellenic standards, 27
Ḥerem against mixed dancing, 102
Herschberg, A. S., 70n
Higger, M., 45n, *et passim*
Hilarity, 94
Hirschowitz, A., 38n
Hoffmann, D., 94n
Homosexuality, 3, 64–5; of males, 134–8; of females, 138

Incest, 3
Intermarriage, 10

Jus primae noctis, 155, 156, 157

Kawwanah, 22–3, 150
Kayseling, M., 88n
Ḳedeshah (m. *Ḳadesh*), 135–6, 153–4, 163, 165–8, 171; as temple votary, 153, as street votary, 154; as *Zonah,* 175
Ḳinnui, 220f. *See Soṭah*
Kissing and hugging, 105–10; without lustful intent, 109–10
Koest, 125
Kohler, K., 10n
Krauss, S., 29n, *et passim*

Lauterbach, Z., 38n, 175n
Legalism, post-exilic, 10–11; rabbinic, 15
Levity, 16, 113. *See* Hilarity, Play and merriment, Wine drinking
Lewin, B. M., 93n, *et passim*
Lex talionis, 180
Lieberman, S., 44n
Love-making, 104f; of engaged couples, 106–8. *See* Affectionate relations, Flirtation, Kissing
Löw, L., 80n, 82n, 99n
Lutzki, M., 144n
"Lynch law," 171

Maccabean revolt, 27
Mamzer, 127
Mann, J., 38n, 88n
Masturbation, 146–7
Men of the Great Synagogue, 11
Miller, J., 157n
Mingling of sexes, 5, 11, 18, 76; in First Commonwealth, 5, 69; in post-exilic time, 6–7, 70, 76; rabbinic attitude to, 13, 15, 16, 71, 72, 73, 76, 77, 78–83; moralists' attitude to, 18, 74, 77
"Minhag Romania," 128
Moore, G. F., 7n, 12n
Moralists' views, 17f; vs. philosophers', 22; on mingling of sexes, 18, 74, 77
Moẓi shem ra', 165, 206–9
Music, general prohibition against, 18, 94–7, 99; religious, 96–7; at weddings, 97–8; mixed chorus, 98f; not restricted in the Bible, 93; in the synagogue, 100

Nafḳa, 70, 161
Nakedness, 4, 25–30; of male, 26, 28, 30; of female, 26, 30, 31; shameful, humiliating, obscene, 26f; of father or mother, 3; in public, 28; indoors, 28; in holy places or at worship, 27; Church Fathers on, 29; Philo on, 27
Nazirism, 8f, 57
Neuman, A. A., 82n
Nowack, W., 70n
Nudity, 25f. *See* Nakedness
Nurse, attending patient of opposite sex, 34

Olitzki, N., 232
Onanism, 144
Ordeal of bitter water, 218, 225, 226–